The Intersectional Other

Critical Perspectives on Psychology of Sexuality, Gender, and Queer Studies

Series Editors: A.L. Jones (Alice Miller School), Damien Riggs (Flinders University), Rebecca Stringer (University of Otago)

Mission Statement

The series seeks to publish scholarship that engages critically with the social and political uses of psychological knowledge, and with transformative paradigms that address obstacles to change. The series is open to a wide range of approaches that may be classified as "psychological", including manuscript proposals that focus on well-being, subjectivities, clinical practice, discourse, and their intersections.

Advisory Board Members

Meg John Barker, Virginia Braun, Chris Brickell, Heather Brook, Victoria Clarke, Charlotte Patterson, Elizabeth Peel, Esther Rothblum, and Gareth Treharne

Books in Series

The Intersectional Other: Reimagining Power in the Margins, by Alex Rivera
Racism and Gay Men of Color: Living and Coping with Discrimination, by Sulaimon Giwa
Home and Away: Mothers and Babies in Institutional Spaces, by Kathleen Connellan, Clemence Due, Damien W. Riggs, and Clare Bartholomaeus
Assisted Reproduction: Conceptions, Controversies, and Community Sentiment, by Alexandra Sigillo and Monica Miller
The Reproductive Industry: Intimate Experiences and Global Processes, edited by Vera Mackie, Nicola J. Marks, and Sarah Ferber
The Psychic Life of Racism in Gay Men's Communities, edited by Damien Riggs

The Intersectional Other

Reimagining Power in the Margins

Alex Rivera

LEXINGTON BOOKS

Lanham • Boulder • New York • London

Published by Lexington Books
An imprint of The Rowman & Littlefield Publishing Group, Inc.
4501 Forbes Boulevard, Suite 200, Lanham, Maryland 20706
www.rowman.com

86-90 Paul Street, London EC2A 4NE

British Library Cataloguing in Publication Information Available

Library of Congress Cataloging-in-Publication Data Available

ISBN 9781793635044 (cloth) | ISBN 9781793635068 (paperback) |
ISBN 9781793635051 (ebook)

∞™ The paper used in this publication meets the minimum requirements of American National Standard for Information Sciences—Permanence of Paper for Printed Library Materials, ANSI/NISO Z39.48-1992.

Contents

Acknowledgments

I foolishly thought at the beginning of the COVID-19 pandemic that having access to greater lengths of time at home would be a remarkable help for this passion project of mine. In March 2020, when I signed the publishing contract, I remember thinking, "Wow, it's so scary that this is happening, but surely it will be over soon, and, in the meantime, I'll have more time to dedicate to my book while offices are closed." It's laughable now how wrong I was then—none of us, including the majority of the world's best scientists, foresaw the length of time we'd be stuck isolated, mostly depressed, Zoom-fatigued, and restless at home. And, as the parent of a young child fighting through school closures and surges, I inevitably had to put the project on hold many times. To be a better parent. A better partner. To give my all to myself and my family during a time of great duress. As near and dear as I held this book, my family came first.

That being said, in some darker moments during the COVID-19 pandemic, this book felt like an impossibility, and without the help of a few key people in my life, I sometimes wonder if it, and my aspirations of empowering the Othered, would have ever made it to print. It is with deep gratitude that I want to recognize and thank my partner, Joey, for his endless contributions to the continuation of this passion project. We rarely talk about the sacrifices partners make for each other as part of the co-parenting process. It's naturally *assumed* sacrifices will be made, and thus they become invisibilized as years go on. Joey, thank you (a million times over) for every lunch packed, every boo-boo tended, and every tear wiped while I put pen to paper. I promise I've noticed everyone, and, more importantly, see the love that comes with them.

To my friends and family—and especially Ollie, my three-year-old, barely two when this started—thank you for being my inspiration. For protesting injustices over the last two years. For encountering your own Othernesses and being thoughtful about the ways in which you interact with the world. For your vulnerabilities. I hope this book inspires you as well, to find power in those Othered parts of you.

To the amazing Intersectional Others who agreed to be a part of this project—Dawn, Dylan, Loa, Nora, Somya, and Stevie—wow, I am just blown away with your unique presences, and the words you contributed here. Thank you for creating change in this world, whether through education, research, policy work, health advocacy, or grassroots activism. I hope you see yourselves reflected in these pages and know I consider myself extremely lucky to have shared this space with you.

And lastly, to my editor, Kasey Beduhn, thank you so much for your patience and kindness through this strange time (and my first book)! You have been so thoughtful and helpful along the way. In so many ways, I couldn't have done this without you. You made a lifelong dream for me a reality. I'm truly grateful.

Introduction

Much like in Shonda Rhimes's *Bridgerton*, I imagine a world in which marginalized people are assumed natural powerholders in the United States and where Black,[1] Indigenous, and People of Color (BIPOC) and queer and transgender[2] people have access to immense wealth and social capital. Where it isn't radical to see Black upper- and middle-class people walking the streets. But, as many, including contributors at *Oprah Magazine*, have pointed out, *Bridgerton* is historically inaccurate (Jean Phillipe 2020), and this is part of the appeal of the show—the flip of it. The truth is, we live in a nation where queer and trans folks of color are Othered and subject to inequities systemically—less wealth, less social capital, more stigma, and more violence. However, much like the fantasy that is *Bridgerton*, I suggest that we can rewrite the narrative of marginalized lives, which have often been from the perspective of the ones doing the Othering. Instead, let us reclaim Otherness as something that has the capacity to both be powerful and to give us power.

This is an important moment in history. The year 2020, as difficult as it was for the United States and the world, laid bare and opened our eyes to the racial injustice and systemic oppression that undergird our society. One need only look to the defining moments of 2020 to witness the power that can result from enduring, confronting, and wielding Otherness. The nationwide Black Lives Matter protests. The intercommunity solidarity in the #StopAsianHate movement. In 1989, bell hooks, Black queer feminist author-activist, made a statement in her work *Choosing the Margin as a Space of Radical Openness* that would later inspire the formation of this book's premise. She said, "As a radical standpoint, perspective, position, 'the politics of location' necessarily calls those of us who would participate in the formation of counter-hegemonic cultural practice to identify the spaces where we begin the process of revision" (15). These words sunk

1

deep into my unconscious mind when I first read them as a college student and rose again when I reflected two years ago on my responsibilities as a queer psychologist of color, but also as a human being, in the face of historical trauma and systemic oppression, juxtaposed with the rising racial and sexual consciousnesses of those around me. We were ready to talk about change.

In late May 2020, while I was writing this book, George Floyd was murdered by a white[3] police officer, Derek Chauvin. As the jury deliberated, I found myself preparing for anger and exhaustion again, because so rarely do the Othered see justice done. Instead, we see countless examples of injustice—the anti-Asian Atlanta "spa shooting," the killing of young Daunte Wright, the reversal of anti-discrimination protections for queer and trans people in healthcare and the workplace—at the hands of white supremacy and queerphobia. And in our continued heartbreak, we look to our communities to share in our grief and anger. But it should not be on the shoulders of marginalized people to heal ourselves day after day without reprieve. The inability to rest is yet another effect of our communities' intergenerational and ever-present traumatization.

When George Floyd whispered "I can't breathe" before his death, it instantly became a symbol of the inescapable weight and cost of Otherness. It reminded those of us who are Othered that we, too, deserve safety, rest, and love. We, too, deserve personal, collective, and societal power. Rage erupted and, with it, I saw the power burst forth, along with solidarity, community, and a refusal to be breathless any longer. In the therapy room, I saw my queer and trans clients of color scream, cry, and organize with #BlackLivesMatter and #StopAsianHate. I listened and again shared in their grief, knowing I would hold it through the next five sessions that day. And then I screamed and cried and organized with my people, too. It reminded me of the bell hooks quote once again, that those of us who suffer and exist in the margins—yes, those of us who feel invisible—are the ones responsible for history and society's revisions (or is it revolutions?), not those in the mainstream.

Today, on April 20, 2021, the jury came back, and Chauvin was found guilty on all three charges—second-degree unintentional murder, third-degree murder, and second-degree manslaughter. Many rejoiced in the verdict, feeling justice was finally done. However, even as the verdict was delivered, news from Columbus, Ohio, announced yet another Black life was taken at the hands of police. Sixteen-year-old Ma'Khia Bryant would never see her graduation. She would never get to make the mistakes we all should get a chance to make as young adults—to party a little too hard, stay out too late, experience that first real heartbreak. All because her call to police, placed to protect her from harm, resulted in her death. It made the words of the Black Lives Matter movement earlier in the day feel all the more prescient:

330 days to confirm what we already knew. 330 days of reliving George's murder, fearing the system would let us down again, and mourning so many more that we lost. For a murder witnessed by millions. This isn't proof the system works. It's proof of how broken it is. Because it took this long, and this much attention. Until we have a world where our communities can thrive free from fear, there will be no justice. (Black Lives Matter, April 20, 2021)

Derek Chauvin's conviction doesn't mean police brutality has ended, nor does it mean the justice system is now equitable. If that were true, Ma'Khia Bryant would still be here today. We must continue to fight, as Marsha P. Johnson said, until there is liberation for all of us, else risk liberation for none of us.

Bell hooks went on to say in that same work that joy in life, and especially the joy that is created from difference, is able to be experienced expressly because one moves "out of one's place." In so moving, she said,

We confront the reality of choice and location. Within complex and ever shifting realms of power relations do we position ourselves on the side of colonising mentality? Or do we continue to stand in political resistance with the oppressed, ready to offer our ways of seeing and theorising, of making culture towards that revolutionary effort which seeks to create space where there is unlimited access to the pleasure and power of knowing, where transformation is possible? (15).

I knew if I wanted to stand in resistance as a person and psychologist, I needed to recognize that moving "out of place" or to be "Other" was what was needed to rise in this cultural moment and every moment after.

POWER FOR THE INTERSECTIONAL OTHER

This work will primarily focus on the use, manifestation, and evolution of power for the people I call "Intersectional Others," those of us who carry intersecting, historically Othered identities. It will also critically engage with the deficit model by which Medicine, Psychology, and other oppressive systems in the United States have viewed Intersectional Others, and specifically queer Black, Indigenous and People of Color (QBIPOC). Contextualized with real narratives from individuals with these identities, this book will focus on how they might establish true visibility and power. Part of recentering the narratives of those who have been invisible or marginalized is to make them the center of this narrative. However, because the construct of "power" societally has been so intertwined with whiteness and straightness, we must completely deconstruct and reframe the conversation on power for these communities and this intersection.

It can be tempting, to be sure, to use the same white queer icons of old, like Harvey Milk, or modern-day icons, like Ellen DeGeneres, who have been repeatedly hailed in media and by historians as major changemakers in the gay liberation movement, to steer the narrative of this book. Instead, I argue that QBIPOC have always existed, and while some of their stories—due to the nature of historical memory as a reflection of the oppressors' ideology rather than the oppressed—may have been forgotten, many can also be found. Writing the book in such a way as to highlight Intersectional Others as their own heroes and revolutionaries, with their own struggles for liberation and ways of getting there, subverts this oppressive history and takes a strong stance in doing so. White queer and trans stories, therefore, must be secondary, and present only to contextualize the narratives of those they previously eclipsed. This book exclaims that intersectional power is worthy of study and, more importantly, worthy in its own right.

The purpose of this book is not to describe all marginalized voices—doing so is impossible. Rather, it will analyze the specific intersections of Othered racial and sexual identities, while also including a broad range of experiences around this intersection. QBIPOC may also identify as trans. They may also identify as disabled, as neurodivergent, as working-class, and so on. Therefore, it is to the benefit of the reader and the broader conversation on intersectionality and Otherness to give life to these differences as much as we can, acknowledging there are constraints on doing so and that not all experiences can be encompassed in this book, nor can we describe each experience in its entirety. Indeed, historical memory, even with consistent fact-checking, is never complete. We can only try our best to recapture it and represent the resistances and voices of QBIPOC to the best of our abilities.

THE RECLAMATION OF LANGUAGE
AND ITS APPLICATION TO THIS BOOK

Language itself, and indeed the language of Intersectional Otherness, is shaped through the contradictions of oppression. A paradox often develops for those who hope to use it in the service of the societally oppressed, whereby it becomes hard to disentangle the voices of the oppressor from your own. However, for those that attempt this disentanglement, the use of language is an act of resistance, which may bring about meaningful change. Bell hooks (1989) wrote,

> Trapped as we often are in a cultural context that defines freedom solely in terms
> of learning the oppressor's language . . . it has been extremely difficult to move

beyond this shallow, empty version of what we can do, mere imitators of our oppressors, toward a liberatory vision—one that transforms our consciousness, our very being. The most important of our work—the work of liberation—demands of us that we make a new language, that we create the oppositional discourse, the liberatory voice. (29)

It is imperative to critically examine the ways in which white, straight dominance has impacted the stories of Intersectional Others, so that we may bring about a voice of liberation, rather than reinforce the voice of oppression once again.

Culture and societal language evolve rapidly, transforming as society itself transforms. Even while writing this book, for instance, the commonly used phrase "people of color" was superseded by "Black, Indigenous, and People of Color (BIPOC)." The term BIPOC was originally conceived in 2013 but gained widespread use in the wake of George Floyd's death and the protests that followed, around June 2020. Many believe it to have been co-opted by the Black Lives Matter movement, but the exact origin is unclear (Garcia 2020).

The BIPOC Project, cofounded by queer Black organizer Merle McGee and queer Asian American organizer Fiona Kanagasingam, states, according to its website, that it aims "to build authentic and lasting solidarity among Black, Indigenous, and People of Color (BIPOC), in order to undo Native invisibility, anti-Blackness, dismantle white supremacy and advance racial justice." The term "BIPOC" thus unapologetically brings Black and Indigenous identities and issues to the forefront among other conversations about the racially marginalized, as they have historically been two of the most Othered groups in the United States, with their lives and concerns made invisible societally. If this was the intention, it seems to have worked to a large extent, as even those who seemingly despise the acronym are still talking about it with fervor, contributing to the dialogue about racial oppression and equity, if only by shouting into the digital void. These despisers are part of the movement, too, as they push the newer term into the spotlight a little more with every disparaging word.

As our primary tool for expression and communication, language holds not just power, but our history as human beings, through its syntax and phonetics, as well as through its evolution over time (Shashkevich 2019). The language of identity and naming, in particular, is highly personal and interwoven with ancestral history, community, and personal affiliation or psychology. It can delineate our immigration history and position in the diaspora (e.g., identifying as Afro-Latinx). It can provide a sense of community (e.g., identifying as queer). It can transform and project our sense of self in the way we want the world to see it (e.g., changing our name). It can also harm our sense of self, through bullying, misgendering, and assaults on our personhood—it has the power to do that, too. For those wishing to align language more closely with their senses of self, it has the power to embody fullness, truth, humanity, and affirmation. But when language becomes oppressed and policed systemically, it can cause irreparable damage, not just to self-esteem, but also through the denial of life-affirming services, such as healthcare.

Language as Resistance

Language has evolved not only as a product of colonialism and global oppression but also as a product of resistance—a revolution of social norms and reclaiming of Otherness. This resistance is perhaps most obviously embodied in the concept of "abrogation." Abrogation is defined as the post-colonial rejection of the oppressor's language (e.g., "American English") as "correct" or "superior," and accompanying beliefs that other dialects are "incorrect" or "inferior." In validating and elevating previously marginalized language, the act of abrogation effectively resignifies the oppressor's language, subverting its inherent epistemic violence in order to serve the oppressed.

At Marie Claire's 2016 Power Trip Conference, Opal Tometi, cofounder of Black Lives Matter, gave a speech on the power of language to create social change. She discussed the ways in which three seemingly innocuous words, #BlackLivesMatter, became instrumental in galvanizing an anti-racist movement centered on Black justice, forcing a nation to reckon with its racist systems and beliefs. "It's not that we created a movement," Tometi said. "It was there. People were already inspired. We participated in a particular way and made an intervention that says, 'We have to acknowledge what it is'" (Evans 2016). As Tometi pointed out, language reclamation forces us to acknowledge not only the roots beneath our words but also the potential oppression lurking within. In the subversion of that oppression, it has the power to help but also the power to harm.

At the heart of linguistic reclamation is the right to self-definition, of forging and naming one's own existence. Because the self-definition we speak of here is originally formed not through the words of the oppressed but those of the oppressor, it depends upon pejoration for its very revolution. Reclaimed language is never without controversy. It will always be, in its very nature, polemical. Gerald Vizenor, mixed Anishinaabe (Chippewa)[4] American scholar and professor of American Studies at the University of New Mexico, wrote about the tension between speaking English and tribal languages as activism in his book *Manifest Manners* (1999):

> The English language has been the linear tongue of the colonial discoveries, racial cruelties, invented names, the simulation of tribal cultures, manifest

manners, and the unheard literature of dominance in tribal communities; at the same time, this mother tongue of para-colonialism has been a language of invincible imagination and liberation for many people of the postindian worlds. English . . . has carried some of the best stories of endurance, the shadows of tribal creative literature, and now that same language of dominance bears the creative literature of distinguished post-Indian authors in cities. . . . The shadows and language of tribal poets and novelists could be the new ghost dance literature, the shadow literature of liberation that enlivens tribal survivance. (105-6)

Indeed, while language negotiation holds within it our painful histories of oppression and colonization as a settler-colonial nation-state, those histories are still critical to understanding our own contemporary formation. As Vizenor (1994) pointed out, it is potentially problematic, in fact, to completely abandon the use of the oppressor's language—such as English, in the case of the United States—in the name of decolonizing experiences. This is because the traumatic history for the Othered and resistances to those traumas are embedded within it, and thus abandoning it may be a barrier to reclamation. It is only by holding the complexities of these linguistic histories that we can truly understand the evolution of communities and cultures over time.

Queering Language

The term "queer" itself was once used pejoratively by straight, cis people to denote strangeness and a sense of deviance from sexual or gender norms in mainstream society (Brontsema 2004). Queer as a community term gained traction in the 1980s, and is now widely adopted, particularly in younger generations in the United States. Even its most common predecessor, "LGBT" (i.e., lesbian, gay, bisexual, and transgender), excludes the identities of those whose letters are not included in the acronym—Two-Spirit, asexual, and polyamorous people, among so many other communities—who may not see themselves reflected in the larger categorization of LGBT. Therefore, "queer" becomes a radical term as it unites a multitude of Intersectional Others in a way few words can. Claiming queerness represents a choice to be a part of an historically Othered community, and embrace that community, history, and all.

The term "queer" is more than an umbrella term, however, and it certainly is more than a synonym for "gayness." Being part of the liberatory rhetoric shared by both grassroots activism and academia during the 1980s and early 1990s, the word "queer" has been fundamental to the agency of LGBTQIA2S+ communities (Rand 2014). In many ways, it is the embodiment of possibility, a crossing whereby many people's experiences may be seen, and many futures imagined, perhaps especially those of Intersectional

Others, who exist at multiple crossings simultaneously. As Cuban American queer theorist José Muñoz said in *Cruising Utopia* (2009), "Queerness is the idealist in us that hopes and reaches for the 'then and there,' beyond the 'here and now'" (29). It is a flexing of temporality and spaciality which allows us to dream of new possibilities for ourselves and our communities. Queer Cree Canadian writer Billy Ray-Belcourt (2016) said:

> Queer is a floating signifier, refusing to attach to any one body, history, biology, or world, always-already that which we cannot fully enflesh or completely imagine...For us, queer theory happens in the discursive and temporal openings created when questions are left unheard, in the archives of missing and murdered queer and trans Indigenous peoples that aren't yet compiled, and in the symposia where we meet with others like us forced to intellectualize in places that can't sustain us.

Queerness thus provides a unique pathway to transgress normative racial, sexual, and gender expectations (Anzaldua 1987; Kumashiro 2001).

"Queer," as expansive and transgressive as it can be, is not a term accepted by all, and understandably so. Even within the numerous LGBTQIA2S+ communities, there are criticisms of the word. For one, it may obscure painful hierarchies that exist racially or otherwise within or outside the broader queer umbrella, such as the oppression of women, BIPOC, trans, or working-class people (Blackwood and Wieringa 1999). In *Global Divas: Gay Filipino Men in the Diaspora*, gay Filipino American scholar and professor of American Studies at the University of Minnesota, Twin Cities, Martin Malanansan IV (2003) wrote about the complications of rainbow symbolism, saying,

> Seemingly separate brands of color are fused into a unitary amalgam and one single cultural emblem of queer togetherness and belonging. While these important symbols and meanings of unity provide a potent impetus for community efforts, they at once obscure the contradictory and uneven queer spaces. (4-5)

An intention of solidarity does not preclude division, and to imply all QBIPOC are oppressed equally does nothing to solve systemic inequities—to the contrary, it obscures them.

Finally, in 2021, public awareness of these issues is in such a place that larger institutions and governmental offices, like Northwestern University and the State Department, are adopting the use of the Progress Pride Flag, created in 2018 by digital designer Daniel Quasar. A recreation of the 1978 rainbow flag designed by artist Gilbert Baker, the Progress Pride Flag highlights intersectional experiences of QTBIPOC using black and brown stripes, as well as light blue, pink, and white stripes to represent trans experiences (Wareham

2020). Even now, however, there is resistance to these inclusion efforts. In an interview with *ABC News*, one trans Army veteran, Sachel Pemberton, implied that the State Department's use of the Progress Pride Flag in June 2021 was performative, for instance, and did little to address anti-LGBTQ-IA2S+ legislation sweeping the nation at the time (Cathey 2021). The use of "queer" as a self-identifier may also feel foreign or performative to some who adhere strongly to the more singular identities of "gay" or "lesbian," due to the fact that these particular terms were critical to personal identity formation in the context of the larger queer liberation struggle. We cannot condemn that adherence, just as we cannot condemn the reclamation of the word "queer," as these processes are all part of the negotiation and tension we have between our personal experiences and our communities through language.

VOCABULARY

I say all this to give context for the specific vocabulary I use in this book, as it was chosen carefully, with identities, social movements, and activism in mind. Accessibility is an important part of my work. Therefore, I will seek to define some key terms here, so that readers may refer back to this list if they encounter terms they are unfamiliar with. This is by no means a list of every keyword in the book, but it defines the ones used more frequently.

"Intersectionality" is a term coined by Kimberlé Crenshaw in 1989, originally as part of Black feminist discourse in legal work, which creates a theoretical framework to describe the ways in which people live at the intersections of various social, cultural, and political identities—such as race, class, gender, and sexuality—and experience overlapping systems of privilege and oppression as a result. The origin of the concept of intersectionality came much earlier, largely through the important works of Black and Brown queer feminists, such as Gloria Anzaldua (1978) and the Combahee River Collective (1977).

"Othering" can be defined as the intentional marginalizing of an individual, group, or community. It is often thought to be a product of oppression and sits opposite constructs like "empowerment" and "liberation."

"Intersectional Other" is a term coined in this work to define a person who carries multiple historically Othered identities, such as an Asian American disabled woman or Diné Two-Spirit person. It is an attempt to renown "multiple marginalization" using the framework of intersectionality. In this book, we specifically use the term "Intersectional Other" to mean QBIPOC.

"LGBTQIA2S+" stands for lesbian, gay, bisexual, transgender, queer (or questioning), intersex, asexual, Two-Spirit and other sexual and gender identities that are not straight or cis. Other variations that the reader may come across in this book include LGBT, LGBTQ, and LGBTQIA, which are often used in research. LGBTQIA2S+ was used here to recognize the important contributions of, and history of invisibilizing, Two-Spirit people.

"Queer" is an umbrella term, which is intentionally broad, that can encompass any identity beyond the binary of cisgenderism and heteronormativity. For the purposes of this book, we are using it mainly to describe non-heteronormative sexuality. It is often considered a community word, as it reclaims a previously pejorative term for collective identity purposes (Brontsema 2004).

"Trans(gender)" may be defined as a person whose gender identity differs from the sex they[5] were assigned at birth. "Trans" is often used as shorthand for transgender.

"Cis(gender)" may be defined as a person, or description of a person, whose gender identity is the same as the sex they were assigned at birth. "Cis" is often used as shorthand for cisgender.

The acronym "BIPOC" stands for Black, Indigenous, and People of Color. It is a term used to center the voices and issues of Black and Indigenous people, who have historically been marginalized in this country. People of Color (POC) is a common variation of this term.

The acronym "QBIPOC" stands for queer Black, Indigenous, and People of Color—that is, people who identify as both on the queer spectrum and as BIPOC. In some cases, this book may also use the term "QTBIPOC," which refers to a group of queer and transgender BIPOC, meant to approximately encompass those on the queer spectrum and those on the transgender spectrum who also identify as BIPOC.

AUTOETHNOGRAPHY AND
AUTHOR POSITIONALITIES

This book's purpose is to not only recenter and de-vilify marginalized voices but also to put bodies of literature on race and sexuality in conversation with one another. Its other, and perhaps even more important, purpose is to put the researcher and researched in conversation with one another by exposing the vulnerability of the researcher and subverting the social hierarchies researchers perpetuate through their intended "empiricism." One way I do this more broadly, as the author, is by writing via "autoethnography." Autoethnography, as a form of ethnography, well-known linguistic scholar Carolyn Ellis (2004) wrote, is "part *auto* or self and part *ethno* or culture" (31)—it is "something different from both . . . greater than its parts" (32).

Autoethnography is a modality of research which seeks to decolonize societally accepted narratives by merging experience, emotion, and storytelling with mainstream discourse. In embracing personal thoughts, feelings, stories, and observations as a way of understanding the social context they are studying, autoethnographers shed light on their interactions with their environment, making their emotions and thoughts visible to the reader. It is therefore a modality that plainly rejects the normative deep-rooted binaries in research and academia—that of the researcher and the researched, objectivity and subjectivity, and the personal and the political (Ellingson and Ellis 2008, 450–459). Scholars have also pointed out that it shares several conceptual similarities with queer theory, even going so far as to call it a "queer method." Both refuse to blindly accept orthodox methodologies of study and focus instead on fluidity, relationality, and groundedness in real-world experiences (Jones and Adams 2016). Autoethnography, for all these reasons, is a fitting modality for this book.

Intersectional Others deserve to talk about their own experiences, and thus lived experience must be at the heart of the book, even my own. The lived experiences I refer to here may take the form of self-report and discussions of my interactions with others as a queer hapa person, the experiences of the QBIPOC scholars and activists whose work I choose to shine light on, or the experiences of the QBIPOC changemakers I interview. The reader may have also already noticed that I freely use personal pronouns, rather than succumbing to third-person narration as per academic norms. Because mainstream history and social norms are inevitably defined by those who have colonized, oppressed, and silenced Others, styles of narration which value vulnerability and humanity become powerful examples of decolonial resistance.

As a hapa (i.e., mixed Asian) bi+/queer cis woman, I benefit greatly from racial and sexual privilege—this book cannot be written without me acknowledging that. I benefit not only from racial privileges associated with my whiteness but also from the privileges associated with being Chinese American in this country. Yes, East Asians are marginalized in certain respects—and in fact I was verbally assaulted while writing this very book one day at a community park during the COVID-19 pandemic—but we are not nearly as marginalized as some communities of color, including Brown Asian Americans and Pacific Islanders, whose experiences are often lumped with ours under a pan-Asian or Asian/Pacific Islander (API) umbrella. These invalidations often come from well-intentioned Asian Americans hoping to be more inclusive, but ultimately obscuring very distinct needs and histories.

My bisexuality and queerness also afford me privilege. My bi-ness enables me to chameleon myself if I feel unsafe—to pass as straight. This is particularly true as a bi+ femme with a young child, which may be coded differently, and even more positively, by straight society. In many ways, I consider both my racial and sexual identities queered. They take fluid form, and their levels of perceived "goodness" and marginalized status can differ dramatically depending on the perceiver. I can strategically use this queering in ways other

QBIPOC cannot, making me much less of a target overall and that in itself is an immense privilege. This privilege is one of the main reasons I chose to focus my writing on the race and sexuality intersection, rather than focusing more broadly on all QTBIPOC identities. It is a decision rooted in an ethos of cultural humility, a desire to provide trans and nonbinary authors the space to author their own works and claim their own histories, and a desire to author something within my own lived experience.

I also recognize that I hold privilege as a psychologist. My chosen profession has historically Othered many queer folks of color, and still does today. As a practicing therapist, I have a great deal of gatekeeping power—the power to diagnose, to write letters for life-affirming surgeries, to endorse disability accommodations. This is why it is of the utmost importance to approach this subject matter with as much humanity and humility as I can muster. In writing this book, I was forced to reckon with Psychology's dark history and my part in it. I critique it greatly in the following chapters, but my critiques can never really capture the dehumanization and cruelty that my profession has, at times knowingly, unleashed on queer people and BIPOC in this country, as well as the lasting damage it has had on the psyches and communities of marginalized people. We have much work to do to create real systemic change in healthcare, and if I have one hope for this work, it is that it will be a small means of transformation to this end.

NOTES

1. This book will capitalize all historically marginalized racial identities ("Black," "Indigenous," "Brown," etc.) in an effort to recenter these experiences, as well as to reflect a shared sense of identity and community. See rationale in: Martis, Eternity. 2016. A capital idea: Reflections on the politics of capitalization. *Ryerson Review of Journalism.*

2. This book will henceforth use "trans" rather than "transgender," and "cis" rather than "cisgender," as shorthand, but more importantly to acknowledge the historical stigmatization associated with the use of "transgender" and "transsexual," as well as to encourage gender self-determination. See rationale in: Zimman, Lal. 2019. Trans self-identification and the language of neoliberal selfhood: Agency, power, and the limits of monologic discourse. *International Journal of the Sociology of Language,* no. 256: 147–175.

3. This book will not capitalize "white" in an effort to recenter the voices and experiences of Black, Indigenous, and People of Color (BIPOC), who have been historically marginalized. See rationale in: Laws, Mike. 2020. Why we capitalize "Black" (and not "white"). *Columbia Journalism Review.*

4. To support language decolonization, this book will first list Indigenous identities in their respective languages, such as "Anishinaabe," and provide the reader with

the settler translation secondarily, such as "Chippewa" when either (1) describing precolonial interactions, or (2) in present-day descriptions when tribes or individuals are known to prefer these terms (e.g., using Diné, instead of Navajo).

5. This book uses a singular "they" pronoun, rather than "he or she" when discussing a person whose gender identity is unknown. This is done to allow for a wide spectrum of gender identities, rather than subscribing to cis-centered narratives on gender. See rationale in: Zimman, Lal. 2019. Trans self-identification and the language of neoliberal selfhood: Agency, power, and the limits of monologic discourse. *International Journal of the Sociology of Language*, no. 256: 147–175.

Chapter 1

Us Versus Them

The Historical Significance of Otherness and Power

Otherness is not a new concept; however, it is rarely written about in academic literature from the lens of the Othered. Historically, "Othering" has been referred to the intentional or unintentional marginalizing of an individual, group, or community and has often been set in binary opposition to the construct of "power," which psychologists have defined as the potential to influence, have authority over, or use tools to enact change in individuals, groups, society, or systems (Tedeschi and Bonoma 2017), as well as "liberation," which has been defined succinctly by some philosophers as the "utopian speculation" toward freedom (Marcuse 1969, 3). For our purposes, perhaps the best summary of the relationships between "Otherness," "power," and "liberation" is that drawn by Brazilian educator and revolutionary Paulo Freire, who in his well-known work *The Politics of Education: Culture, Power and Liberation* said that power was inherently dialectical (Freire 1985). At once, it is both negative and positive; at once, it is working on people and through people. What this means is that, on the one hand, power might repress and dominate, but, thankfully, never in totality. On the other hand, power will always be at the root of humanity's fight for liberation, for a better world. Power, liberation, and Otherness are thus forever linked.

The act of Othering varies in presentation, from overt violence to internalized oppression. We can see Othering as a behavioral product of oppression, as it involves "psychological and political components of victimization, agency, and resistance," whereas "power relations produce domination, subordination, and resistance" (Prilleltensky 2003, 195–201). To put it simply, making a person feel that they are Other is to make them feel as if they don't belong, that they are deviant or abnormal, and that they are inferior to their perpetrator(s). Othering can be perpetrated by a single person, but more often it is an action committed by a group of people or a system of thought, values, laws, and structures aimed at securing dominance.

The fact that marginalized people experience negative effects from Othering—that is, disproportionate rates of stigma, discrimination, and negative health outcomes—is well-established (Meyer 2003; Williams, Neighbors, and Jackson 2003), and contested by few scholars in Psychology or Medicine. The majority of research on psychological health and identity, however, focuses on the impact of carrying a singular identity (e.g., sexuality, ethnicity, ability), rather than the effect of stressors on multiple intersecting identities, such as those affecting queer Black, Indigenous, and People of Color (QBIPOC). This is a significant issue to consider, because, while white gay men, for instance, might encounter prejudice, their lived experiences are not the same as the lived experiences of gay men of color, who do not benefit from the privileges associated with being white in the United States (Ferguson 2018; Nadal et al. 2017). That is, power and inequality differentially impact individuals who are multiply marginalized.

THE SOCIAL AND COGNITIVE UNDERPINNINGS OF OTHERING

In many ways, Othering is inherently part of any social system. As human beings, we rely on social categories to define our senses of belonging and safety. It is often hypothesized that our brains evolved to make these rapid categorizations to avoid disease and danger, as our ancestors primarily lived in small social groups and needed to be vigilant at all times in the event conflict between groups occurred (Brewer and Caporael 2006, 161). Diving into the large body of social psychology literature dedicated to ingroup bias and stereotyping, we see that our brains go one step further than just categorizing other human beings we come in contact with, however; we are actually prone to making assumptions about those categories.

The "Blue Eyes, Brown Eyes" Exercise

If we define "ingroup bias" as acceptance and association, we can view Othering as the attempt to reject and vilify differences in other groups. In many ways, the rationale and assumptions behind Othering behavior is arbitrary, although it can feel extremely personal. After the assassination of Martin Luther King Jr. in 1968, Iowa schoolteacher Jane Elliott developed a classroom exercise called *Blue Eyes, Brown Eyes*, which famously exposed ingroup bias in young children (Elliott 2003). In the first half of the exercise, brown-eyed third graders were told they were superior to their blue-eyed peers, and praised as such throughout the day. Elliott was shocked to see how quickly her students turned to Othering. The blue-eyed children became frightened, timid, and uncertain, while the brown-eyed children excelled academically and became arrogant and domineering.

In the second half, Elliott reversed the order, making the blue-eyed children superior, with the same results. The initial exercise disturbingly demonstrated the ease with which ingroup bias occurs, despite how arbitrary the conditions may seem. Also evident in this experiment was the ease with which bias occurs in even the youngest of us, as the average age of the children in the experiment was only seven years old. Since this classic experiment, several other studies have replicated these results with varying types of groups, including those that have demonstrated a change in fMRI readings when being confronted with an outgroup member versus an ingroup member (Cikara et al. 2017; Gallup et al. 2017; Amodio and Devine 2006; Tajfel et al. 1971). The conclusion Elliott drew from her exercise was that racism is learned. Racism can be created, she said, and "as with anything, if you can create it, you can destroy it." Thus began Jane Elliott's anti-racist advocacy work (Erikson 2004, 145–157).

Ingroup Favoritism and Outgroup Derogation

Human social cognition is linked to prejudicial behavior, and two robust phenomena in particular may contribute to the ways in which we react to other people around us, "ingroup favoritism," and its opposite, "outgroup derogation." "Ingroup favoritism"—that is, responding positively toward those who seem most like us while rejecting those who seem dissimilar—may be a precursor to Othering and is an extension of ingroup bias (Tajfel et al. 1971). Prejudicial attitudes and behaviors easily emerge when we choose to define ingroup status identity, such as race or sexuality. These biases often lead to inaccurate social assumptions, such as the belief that members of the ingroup (e.g., white Americans) are more heterogeneous than the outgroup (e.g., Asian Americans). Without being checked, this type of assumption may develop into a racist belief, such as "all Asians are infected and spreading COVID-19," despite the fact that the majority of known cases are actually white Americans (Centers for Disease Control and Prevention [CDC] 2021).

It is not enough to stop there, as prejudicial perceptions and outgroup derogation can result in harmful behavior. Between March 16, 2020, and March 30, 2020, just 14 days, former president Donald Trump said and typed "Chinese virus" more than 20 times; his tweets correlated with a rise in anti-Asian hashtags on Twitter (Bostock 2021). The secretary of state at the time, Mike Pompeo, endorsed the language, calling COVID-19 the "Wuhan virus" and, in moments of cruel humor, the "Kung Flu." Members of the

Trump administration would go on to use this prejudicial nomenclature for the remainder of his presidential term. One study indicated that, by October 2020, Trump's prejudicial "Chinese virus" tweets, and their variations, were retweeted 1,213,700 times and liked 4,276,200 times in total. It concluded he was by far the greatest spreader of anti-Asian rhetoric related to the pandemic of all politicians during the period (Stop AAPI Hate 2020).

Other prejudicial behaviors surged during the same period. There is an accumulating body of evidence that former president Trump's rhetoric on the campaign trail, for instance, emboldened members of the U.S. public to more openly express and act on their existing prejudices—a phenomenon some scholars have labeled the "Trump effect" (Costello 2016; Newman et al., 2021). Illustrating this trend, a report by the Center for the Study of Hate and Extremism at California State University, San Bernardino (2021) found that anti-Asian hate crimes increased by nearly 150% in 2020, a striking contrast to the decrease of 7% in overall hate crimes seen nationally during that time. In January 2021, a surge of hate crimes against Asian Americans occurred in the San Francisco Bay Area, resulting in the violent death of a 84-year-old Thai American elder, who was shoved to the ground and killed in broad daylight early in January (Wiley 2021).

A report released by Stop AAPI Hate, a not-for-profit coalition which records hate crimes and incidents, found that there had been 9,081 reported anti-Asian incidents during the length of the pandemic, from March 2020 to June 2021 (Yellow Horse et al., 2021). In an interview with KQED, Russell Jeung, Stop AAPI Hate cofounder and professor of Asian American Studies at San Francisco State University (SFSU), said, "We saw how hate speech by using the term 'China virus' led to hate violence. And I think that has invited a climate where people can target Asian Americans" (Wiley 2021). While we cannot draw a causal relationship between the former president's prejudicial speech and these acts of hate, the statistics and anecdotal evidence from victims certainly demonstrate a disturbing association.

Threat Theory and Its Contribution to Othering

Perhaps Othering is more complicated than "we humans see ingroups this way and outgroups that way." We may also perceive threat, which then contributes to Othering behavior. It is important to understand here that we are talking about "perceived threat" and not validating bigotry by implying a group is inherently threatening and therefore deserves a prejudicial response. To the contrary—the whole point of this section is to delineate the ways in which perception can be easily manipulated to vilify an outgroup, regardless of the actual actions of that group.

"Integrated threat theory" (Stephan and Stephan 2000) and the association between perceived threat and prejudice has been well-established (Esses et al. 2001; LeVine and Campbell 1972; Sherif 1966). Literature on this topic (Stephan et al. 2005, 15–17) suggests that there are four types of threat which can consequently lead to prejudicial attitudes and behaviors: (1) realistic threat (e.g., warfare, competition for resources), (2) symbolic threat (e.g., threats to your worldview, morals, or values), (3) intergroup anxiety (e.g., worries about ridicule or rejection), and (4) negative stereotypes (e.g., negative expectations, such as "all queer people have HIV" or "black people are aggressive"). It is possible to perceive these four threats at the same time. For instance, in one study (Stephan et al. 2005) examining the causal effects of perceived threat on attitudes toward immigrants among American-born participants, researchers found that the highest level of prejudice occurred when participants viewed immigrants as both a realistic and symbolic threat. Intergroup anxiety and negative stereotypes also led to greater prejudice toward immigrants in the study.

Perceived threat can be exploited by authoritarian, nationalist governments for power. In *How Fascism Works* (2018), scholar Jason Stanley wrote about commonalities in contemporary fascist political movements, including resemblances to the former Trump administration. Those commonalities included the government's invocation of a mythic national past marked by cultural purity, which "needed to return" (e.g., Trump's "Make America Great Again" movement, Mussolini's "Myth of Rome"); an anti-intellectual assault on education, science, and expertise (e.g., Khmer Rouge killings of intelligentsia, undermining of scientists and health officials in COVID-19 response); an attack on the public's ability to perceive truth due to normalized lying behavior (e.g., Trump's "fake news," Hitler's "Lügenpresse"); and sexual anxiety about marginalized folk as a threat to traditional gender roles and "family values" (e.g., Trump administration's anti-trans military policy, Nazi Party internment and execution of queer individuals); and among others.

Fascism is not created in a vacuum. Indeed, it is actually, as scholar Jason Stanley (2018) wrote, "Stark economic inequality, when the benefits of liberal education, and the exposure to diverse cultures and norms are available only to the wealthy few" (156), conditions inherent to capitalism, which ultimately enable the emergence of fascist rhetoric and the vulnerability of the populace. Many social justice advocates and researchers (Abramowitz and McCoy 2019; Newman et al. 2021) have pointed out that former president Donald Trump "played on" racialized and sexualized fear when he attempted to justify a prejudicial response or legislative action. Similarly, right-wing leaders across history have used threat-based rhetoric to amplify the fear of their base, a base typically comprised of white, straight individuals who feel anxious and vulnerable about their circumstances or future (Lamont, Park, and Hurtado 2017). By aligning with threat-based rhetoric, research shows that those individuals are able to direct their anxiety toward what they perceive to be an impending racial and sexual apocalypse (Ott and Dickinson 2019; Sanchez 2018).

White, straight vulnerability was most evident when Trump took advantage of the white working class during his 2016 election campaign. One qualitative study, for example, analyzed 73 of Trump's campaign speeches and demonstrated patterns of rhetoric specifically targeting their concern of declining national socioeconomic standing. In doing so, he was able to then appeal to their personal narratives of "moral status," the notion that they were hard-working victims of globalization. He often paired this with criticism of the "rich elite," portraying the white working class as protectors of the "real America" and drew them in direct contrast to Muslims and immigrants (Lamont, Park, and Ayala-Hurtado 2017, 175–180), who became Others onto which to project their freshly induced fears.

THE CONSTRUCTION AND
POLITICIZATION OF OTHERNESS

Othering has been used strategically to shape, form, and continually reconstruct U.S. nationalism as it intersects with marginalized identities. Indeed, by its very nature, to be Othered is to be defined against those in power—the "them" in the "us versus them." To whom, how, and when these definitions occur changes depending on the needs of the groups in power. If we do a retrospective on the varying degrees of belonging and marginalization in U.S. society, we can plainly see that a group's sense of belonging is fluid, not static. They are positioned and hierarchized according to the needs of white, heteronormative society. The positioning of queer people and Black, Indigenous, and People of Color (BIPOC) from an early point in American history affords white, straight people immense power and privilege because they are functioning off the assumption that they are "normal."

Nature and nurture both play a part in constructing the concept of "Otherness" in the context of race and sexuality in the United States. While we may see "nature" as the part of our brain that is predisposed to categorizing and projecting assumptions onto groups with identities that we perceive as different than, or similar to, our own (i.e., ingroup bias; Mullen, Brown, and Smith 1992), "nurture" is the part of our brain that takes in environmental information, and then socially constructs which categories, values, and assumptions to assign to those groups.

Social construction is not a solo effort—we all jointly construct our understandings of history and meaning in the world based on shared assumptions we make about reality. To better understand the premise of social constructionism, it is helpful to conjure the words of philosopher Friedriche Nietzche from his writings in *The Will to Power*, who said, roughly translated: "Facts do not exist, only interpretations" (1967, 481). In other words, history may unfold and events may empirically occur, but what we take away from these events and what meaning we attribute to them is dependent on our social context and perspective. When we gaze at anything, we are not gazing at a reality free of history. Attributions of primitivity, for instance, may seek to strip people of their social context. However, those deemed "primitive," too, have their own histories. None of us function or exist outside of our historical context.

DEFINING WHITENESS AND STRAIGHTNESS AGAINST OTHERNESS

As Palestinian American scholar and "father of postcolonial studies" Edward Said once wrote, it is critical that all fields of study explore and analyze "how all representations are constructed, for what purpose, by whom, and with what components" (Said 1993, 314). This is because representations are never neutral but reflect the power dynamics inherent in stratified social systems. In these systems, representations are deployed for the purpose of creating and maintaining ideological definitions of "difference." Once created, representations have the power to then define cultural boundaries, outlining who does and does not "belong" to a nation or social group. "Identities" are not rooted in some shared history, static in time—they are in active construction. Rather than rigidly determined, "identities" as we know them are fluid and malleable.

These days, we commonly hear the phrase "race is socially constructed," but there was a time when this wasn't the case. During the 19th century, the prevailing sentiment in the United States and Northern Europe was that race was purely biological. Not only this, but it was thought that racialized attributes could be scientifically measured, such as in craniometry, the measurement of skulls, and anthropometry, the measurement of the human body (Jackson and Weidman 2004). These methods, along with the belief that some races were genetically superior to others, are now completely invalidated by science and considered part of the legacy of scientific racism (Collins 2004), but at one time were thought to be commonsensical. We know now that we are just as likely to have a similar genetic makeup to someone of another race as we are to someone of our own race (Rosenberg et al. 2002). This is because race is a concept that shifts over time depending on definitions by those in power, border politics, sociopolitical movements, and other matters of historical context.

The Creation of "Whiteness" in the United States

We can get an interesting retrospective on the socially constructed nature of race by investigating the treatment of those who were once considered Black, but are now considered white, in the United States. When the Founding Fathers signed the Constitution in 1787, they largely considered White Anglo-Saxon Protestants (WASPs) to be the bearers of guaranteed constitutional rights and citizenship. Today, WASPs still retain a substantial amount of national wealth and social capital, benefiting from the sociopolitical landscape and legacy they inherited over time (Baltzell 1987). Once immigration opened for newcomers who did not occupy this cultural designation, the government and U.S. citizenry were forced to reckon with their own racial hierarchy and boundaries between whiteness and non-whiteness. The definition of whiteness has expanded and restricted over the years based on these reckonings.

In his book *Whiteness of a Different Color* (1999), historian and professor of African American Studies at Yale University, Matthew Jacobson, drew a parallel to modern-day experiences of BIPOC by examining the movement of Italian immigrants from racialized Others to accepted white citizenry. Between 1880 and 1920, a surge of newcomers to the country—a wave mainly comprised of Italian, Jewish, and Slavic immigrants that was then termed the "New Immigration" wave—engendered a national panic and led the United States to adopt a more restrictive, politicized view of how whiteness was to be allocated. Journalists, politicians, social scientists, and immigration officials embraced the habit, separating ostensibly white Europeans into "races."

Upon entry to the United States, some of these groups were designated "whiter" than others—thus more worthy of citizenship—while others were seen as "too close" to Blackness to be socially redeemable. Today, we rarely contest the fact that Italianness and whiteness are intertwined, despite the fact that racialized power and labels shifted significantly over the next 50 years for Italian Americans. Eventually, they were designated by the same politicians and immigration officials as "whites in good standing." The legacy of racial oppression differs for Italian communities than it does for BIPOC today; however, their trajectory offers a window into the fluidity and social construction of racial hierarchies over time.

Critical Race Theory and the Expansion of Whiteness Studies

By the mid-1990s, several books centering whiteness studies were published (e.g., Allen 1994; Roediger 1995; Ignatiev 1995), illustrating its development as a burgeoning field of interest. It took off, and, in April 1997, the

University of California, Berkeley, decided to host a conference on the topic, although highly controversial at the time, entitled *The Making and Unmaking of Whiteness*; the contents of the conference were seen as so relevant that they eventually became a book published by Duke University Press, though not for a few years (Rasmussen et al. 2001). By 2003, *The Washington Post* reported that at least 30 institutions, including Princeton University and the University of California, Los Angeles, offered courses on whiteness (Fears 2003). It was clear that whiteness studies as a body of research had made its way into mainstream discourse and was expanding at a rapid rate.

However, while the critical study of whiteness and racial politicization has become increasingly popular as an educational tool in the last decade or so—informing anti-racist pedagogy, research, and public understanding—its emergence continues to be met with significant resistance on multiple fronts. In 2014, Notre Dame University made national headlines when it began offering a *White Privilege Seminar*, about which the right-wing *Tea Party News Network* issued a response article entitled *More Progressive Indoctrination: Notre Dame to Teach White Students That They Are Inherently Racist* (Haq 2014). Notre Dame was one of many universities to introduce courses on whiteness between 2010 and 2018—others that "caused a stir" included Harvard, Florida Gulf Coast University, and Boston University. In late 2020, the Trump administration issued a memo ordering federal funding to be diverted away from what he called "racial sensitivity training," because he found it to be "divisive" and "anti-American propaganda," specifically naming critical race theory and white privilege as such propaganda (Schwartz 2020). Whiteness has never been a neutral construct, nor teaching it a neutral endeavor.

White Supremacy's Hold on the United States

When we talk about the power of "whiteness," it is critical to define it in conjunction with white supremacy. There is a temptation to be gentle when discussing whiteness because, by design, whiteness and white people are not typically the subject of racialized conversation. But it does not serve the readers of this book to placate here, as white supremacy is critical to our understanding of racial and sexual formation in this country, and thus it is at the crux of this book. Much of our national understanding of racial Otherness has been defined against whiteness, and hierarchically so, with white people at the top and the Othered in varying positions below them. Founded on pillars of slavery, colonialism, and Orientalism (Smith 2016), white supremacy is importantly also, at its core, tied to the heteropatriarchy, making it critical for understanding the oppression of Intersectional Others.

White Supremacy and Police Brutality

The hierarchy of white supremacy has been painfully evident to QBIPOC, who are often on the receiving end of differential treatment and brutality. Countless studies, for instance, have shown racial bias in policing, and recent protests are bringing greater national awareness to the heavy toll it takes on Black and Brown lives intergenerationally (Baldwin 2018; Jean 2020; Lawson 2015). At the first police briefing to the public after the March 2021 Atlanta, Georgia, "spa shooting" of six Asian and Asian American women, the Cherokee County sheriff spokesperson Captain Jay Baker remarked that Robert Aaron Long, the white, straight shooter, was just "having a bad day," presumably in an attempt to sympathize (Chappell, Romo and Diaz 2021).

The outrageous justification of mass murder only confirmed what many QBIPOC already know through personal experience—when police see whiteness and straightness, they pause and humanize, and when they see Otherness, they suspect the worst and shoot to kill. Studies show that queer and trans BIPOC face higher odds of discrimination when encountering the police, compared to white queer and trans people (24% vs 11%; What We Know Project 2021). Police did not pause before killing Breonna Taylor, who was asleep in her bed; or Tamir Rice, playing with his toy gun; or Elijah McClain, who was walking home from his local convenience store. No, these Others were deemed suspicious by nature of living in a world where police are trained to shoot first and examine bias later, if at all.

On January 6, 2021, a confederate flag was brought into the Capitol building for the first time in U.S. history, carried in the arms of thousands of white supremacists and Trump supporters, who succeeded in invading one of the most secure buildings in the nation. For scale, this was a feat not even accomplished by rioters during the Civil War era (Brasher 2021). Even though Trump had rallied thousands to Washington, D.C., and despite the fact that his "Save America" rally was the starting line for the insurrection that day, he tweeted after the happenings that he would "never condone violence." Shortly after his tweet, a video appeared on his Twitter feed, where he appeared in an open, warm stance. In it, he said directly to the mob, "I love you. You're very special" (Caldwell 2021). The tone of this response bore an eerie resemblance to Captain Baker as he justified the actions of Robert Aaron Long, both peppered with sympathy, despite the heinous violence they witnessed.

Among the white supremacists who staged the coup was QAnon "shaman," Jake Angeli, who had, prior to the insurrection, spread conspiracy theories and far-right ideology, including the belief that satanic child abuse was rife in the Capitol (Forrest 2021). Other Trump supporters chanted "Hang Mike Pence," referencing the news that the former vice president refused to contest the integrity of the electoral voting process; they went so far as to construct a gallows in the Capitol (Beer 2021). And then there were the Three Percenters, a far-right militant group that believed only 3% of Americans, "the true patriots," helped overthrow the British in the American Revolution, and that they should continue that patriotic legacy (Bordonaro 2003).

Perhaps most disturbing of all were the photos that surfaced after. The nation watched as photographs surfaced of police officers taking selfies with rioters and congress members applauding the insurrection, from a safe distance with deniability, of course. Some even openly promoted it before and while it took place, such as Arizona GOP representatives Paul Gosar and Andy Biggs (Sollenberger 2021). Other representatives under investigation by the Federal Bureau of Investigation (FBI) were found to have ties to right-wing extremist groups, such as the Oath Keepers and the Proud Boys, including Mo Brooks (R- Alabama), Lauren Boebert (R-Colorado), and Marjorie Taylor Greene (R-Georgia) (Broadwater and Rosenberg 2021). Those with a more discriminating eye may have noticed a similarity to the plot of the 1978 novel by neo-Nazi William Luther Pierce *The Turner Diaries*, which depicted a violent overthrow of the Capitol, murder of congress members, and a symbolic win over democracy by white nationalist groups (MacAlear 2009, 192). In many ways, the insurrection accomplished the primary goal of the novel, which was to awaken the mainstream to an emerging sense that fringe bigotry was now normal.

But this is not the extent of white supremacy's hold on whiteness. To quote critical race theorist Francis Lee Ansley (1989):

By "white supremacy" I do not mean to allude only to the self-conscious racism of white supremacist hate groups. I refer instead to a political, economic and cultural system in which whites overwhelmingly control power and material resources, conscious and unconscious ideas of white superiority and entitlement are widespread, and relations of white dominance and non-white subordination are daily reenacted across a broad array of institutions and social settings. (74)

White supremacy cannot be reduced to hate crimes or conscious acts by those who perpetrate. Rather, it is an invisible, far-reaching web of power that lifts white-dominated systems, structures, and people up, while simultaneously keeping non-white systems, structures, and people down. The insidiousness of white supremacy can best be summed up in the quote by queer theorist Richard Dyer, "White power secures its dominance by seeming to not be anything in particular" (Dyer 1988, 44). As the unmarked category against which differences are constructed, whiteness never has to speak its name, and never has to acknowledge its role in political and social relations (Lipsitz 1995). Despite its pseudo-invisibility, whiteness and white supremacy certainly affect racial and sexual narratives in the United States. We may not be the producers of white ideology, but we are all consumers, and, therefore, we are all responsible for understanding the ways in which whiteness pervades our psyches, regardless of our race.

THE JUXTAPOSITION OF SEXUAL CONSTRUCTION WITH RACIAL CONSTRUCTION

Juxtaposed with racial construction is social and political sexual construction. At one time it was more common in the United States to believe in sexual essentialism, much like the scientific racism noted earlier. Gender theorist and psychologist Sandra Lipsitz Bem, known for her work on the "androgyny model," discussed the ways in which these constructions become both manufacturers of cultural oppression and power over time, despite the fact that they are, indeed, fabricated. She said,

> Although the concepts of homosexuality, hetereosexuality and bisexuality may be historically and culturally created fictions, like the concepts of masculinity and femininity and the concepts of black, Hispanic, Asian, Native American, and white, they are fictions that have come to psychological reality if they are institutionalized by the dominant culture. Accordingly, they can have extraordinary political power both for cultural oppression and for the resistance to cultural oppression. (Bem 1993, 175)

The hopeful part of this is that, although racial and sexual norms are social fictions that can be used to harm or oppress Intersectional Others, they can also be used for the opposite—for resistance and empowerment.

Sexual essentialism, the idea that sexuality is a static, intrinsic trait or characteristic based out of biological mechanisms which set its parameters, has been critiqued by several scholars, perhaps most famously by philosopher Michel Foucault in *The History of Sexuality* (1976), who found evidence that the concept of "homosexuality" was a socially constructed category, dependent on historical, cultural, and social context, even in Western society. While same-sex encounters, such as those found in mentor-mentee relationships, were discussed in ancient Greek texts, for instance, the moral discourse was vastly different than it was in post-19th-century Western society (Foucault 1976). Even in the Renaissance (14th–17th century), when European Catholic texts had clearly begun labeling same-sex encounters as "sinful," they did not focus on "homosexuality" as an identity, Foucault found. Neither the First, nor Second, Vatican Council, for instance, referenced homosexuality in their texts, but "homosexual acts" were referenced frequently, often called *crimen pessimum*, Latin for "worst crime" (World Heritage Encyclopedia 2021).

Catholic and Christian discourse on queerness was eventually brought to the United States by European settlers, leading to a similar construction into the 19th century. It was at this time that Foucault identified the proliferation of sexuality in Western society as a moral discursive topic, repudiating the tenets of sexual essentialism (Foucault 1976). In 1911, for instance, the Chicago Vice Commission detailed a "great increase of sex perversion," but did not use the word "homosexual" (Riemer and Brown 2019). By 1943, Psychiatry, an emerging medical field, had co-opted this idea, but with the new label of "sexual deviance." With the help of World War II and the military-industrial complex, "sexual deviance" did indeed become a medical, rather than criminal issue, coming closer to consideration as a trait for pathologization (Riemer and Brown 2019).

This medical endorsement of anti-queer discrimination enabled the military to send home approximately 9,000 sailors and soldiers who were suspected "sexual psychopaths," creating a new sexual construction based in identity, not simply behaviors, at last (Herek and Belkin 2006). In 1945, the *American Journal of Psychiatry* published a study by Lieutenant Colonel Lewis H. Loeser entitled *The Sexual Psychopath in the Military Service*, which analyzed the backgrounds of 270 so-called "sexual psychopaths." In it, Loeser made a careful distinction between what the military termed "true homosexuals" and those with "no disease." He ultimately concluded that "[t]he problem of sexual psychopathy in the military service is essentially that of homosexuality" (99). What Loeser failed to mention was the fact that sexual psychopathy was created and defined intentionally by the military to target queers, so his conclusion was self-reinforcing. Those who were suspected homosexuals received a "blue discharge," a mark which made reintegration into society challenging, to say the least (Riemer and Brown 2019). The construction of homosexuality as sexual psychopathy led to persistent diagnostic oppression, as well as queer and transphobic research and practices. "Homosexuality" and "Transsexualism," for instance, were institutionalized disorders in the Diagnostic and Statistical Manual of Mental Disorders (DSM) for years after the wave of blue discharges, details of which will be discussed later in the book.

Sexual Fluidity as a Challenge to Sexual Essentialism

Studies on sexual fluidity for queer women across the lifespan likewise have challenged sexual essentialism, revealing a "capacity for context-specific flexibility in erotic response" (Diamond 2008, 13). In other words, sexual identity is not fixed—the lifetime experiences of queer people encompass a myriad of identifications, and if a spectrum of queer identities and expressions exists now, logically we can assume they have also existed in the past. Literature on U.S. lesbian experiences alone has extensively examined the privileging of "butchness" (i.e., more masculine in appearance, preferences, or behavior) over "femmeness" (i.e., more feminine in appearance, preferences, or behavior) historically (Bennett 2000), although many intersectional scholars have critiqued this binary as it centers white queerness, assuming that all lesbian experience revolves around these identities and expressions (Hammonds 2004). The binary fails to accurately reflect the contemporary plurality of queer women of color's experiences and relying on these representations invalidates those who deviate from them (Maltry and Tucker 2003).

As we might suspect, even if we ascribe to such a binary, the meaning of masculinized versus feminized gender representation also varies depending on cultural context. Researchers have identified that, in urban areas of the United States, for instance, more masculinized womanhood is often associated with queerness, where, in some rural areas, it is viewed as heteronormative (Bennet 2000). When you factor in possible intersecting identities, such as being queer and BIPOC or being queer and disabled, that fluidity and multilevel expressionism are even more pronounced. Many Intersectional Others, and in particular QBIPOC feminists (e.g., Anzaldúa and Moraga 1981; Bambara 1970), have noted the ways in which gender, sexuality, and race all intersect to create unique positionalities, experiences, and oppressions. Although essentialism is a convenient historical narrative for those making generalizations about marginalized experiences, it remains an overly simplistic model for understanding the complexities of human experiences, particularly QBIPOC experiences.

The Weaponization of Sexual Essentialism and Constructionism

Interestingly, at various points in U.S. history, both sexual constructionism and sexual essentialism have been used to Other queer folk, with some anti-LGBTQIA2S+ groups weaponizing the national rhetoric of sexuality as "a choice," implying it could be changed and thus was invalid, and others weaponizing the national hysteria of the "gay gene," implying that one could use genetic screening to eliminate queerness from society altogether. And while there may be some genetic component to human sexual behavior, recent studies have definitively stated what many of us intuitively knew all along—that there is no gay gene and, moreover, that any genetic influence on sexuality is less than 25% of the picture (Ganna et al. 2019, 6). Insistence to the contrary is simply a willful denial of the science.

In addition to the social construction of race and sexuality over time, we can consider the ways in which U.S. racial and sexual hierarchies operate within the binary constructions of whiteness-Blackness and straightness-gayness. Within this normative context, mainstream society will always view intersectionality and non-gay queerness as threatening, as both cross, and indeed reject, the cultural boundaries that have been established hegemonically. The very existence of Intersectional Others thus becomes a revolutionary existence of sorts, defying racial and sexual constructions set by those intent on Othering them. In existing, we also defy reactionary measures employed by the mainstream, such as cultural erasure and invisibility, which attempt to reduce power and validity for historically marginalized groups.

THE ROLE OF EUGENICS IN CONSTRUCTING OTHERNESS

Contrary to popular belief, the eugenics movement was not a European phenomenon. It was in fact widely supported in the United States during the Progressive era, from the late 19th century into World War II, and is still supported today in certain circles (Kline 2010). Had you walked into the main hall of the U.S. Museum of Natural History on August 21, 1932, for instance, you might have spied large bison or giraffes showcased right alongside a Black family in loincloths, labeled "primitive humans" on the accompanying plaque. The contents were not thrown together haphazardly; they were meant to imply that those darker-skinned folk in the display had more in common with animals than other "advanced" humans.

Two rooms over, prominent scientists would have gathered that same day for the Museum's Third International Eugenics Congress—it was the biggest conference on eugenics in the world (Stillwell 2012). In its heyday, the American eugenics movement received monumental funding from institutions including the Carnegie Institute, the Rockefeller Foundation, and IBM, all economic powerhouses in their own right today. It was even endorsed by then-president Theodore Roosevelt as a movement for "social betterment" (Ordover 2003) and widely accepted by the academic community. By 1928, 376 different universities included eugenics as part of their curriculum. In fact, Adolf Hitler directly referenced the American eugenics movement as personal inspiration in *Mein Kampf* in 1924 (Edwin 2003).

The Birth of Cultural Relativism

A Jewish scientist born in Germany in 1858, Franz Boas—the "founding father" of U.S. anthropology—grew up with intimate knowledge of the eugenics movement and precursors to the holocaust perpetrated by the Third Reich (Whitfield 2010). He thought himself to be a devout follower of the scientific method and became a harsh critic of eugenics after visiting Baffin Island in the arctic, where he was able to speak and live with the Baffin Island Inuit community as an ethnographer (Prasad 2007, 590). Originally, he intended to study what he was told was a "primitive society" of Indigenous people by his European colleagues. Instead, he found himself to be the primitive one—inept in both his interactions with the Inuit people and his ability to survive the arctic climate (Whitfield 2010). Boas's utter ineptitude caused him to rethink his profession entirely, and he determined afterward that not only was scientific superiority relative and dependent on the sociocultural arena one was in but so followed the constructs of "culture" and "education" shortly behind. The idea of "cultural relativism" was thus born.

At the time, Boas's writings and, indeed, cultural relativism itself were quite radical. Western societies were heavily invested in the notion that some races were more suited to conquer the world, and some more suited for colonization and servitude. This would become the justification for Jim Crow, for instance, as well as the forced sterilization of immigrants, BIPOC, the impoverished, queer people, disabled people, and those with mental health issues throughout the 20th century. In fact, more than 20,000 people living in the United States would be sterilized by federally funded programs between 1909 and 1989 (Reilly 2015, 355–368). The implicit message behind these sterilizations was that their future generations were not only considered unassimilable but also unwanted and unworthy of support, by the state or nation. It was an idea that pervaded U.S. society—the idea that a white (wealthy, straight, cis, able-bodied) America was the only America worth having. This idea persists strongly today, although perhaps less publicly endorsed.

Franz Boas was not only radical for his ideas but also his mentoring practices, which were regarded as highly unusual in the 1920s and 1930s. During his tenure at Columbia University, he mentored women, not just men like his colleagues. More importantly, for our purposes anyway, though, was the fact that he mentored queer women of color, not just straight women or white women. Perhaps this could be seen as an effort to create his own cultural reality. If so, it was very effective, as some of his students—Margaret Mead and Ruth Benedict, both queer, and Zora Neale Hurston, a queer woman of color—to name a few, were prolific authors and scholars known for their revolutionary views on cultural relativism, gender, race, and sexuality (Prasad 2007, 590–596).

During her time with Boas, Zora Neale Hurston, Black queer creative and anthropologist, not only began her work on *Mules and Men* (1935) but also became a prominent figure of the Harlem Renaissance, when she helped redefine Blackness and queerness in the eyes of white, straight society through her collaboration with other creatives—such as Black gay scholars Alain Locke and Langston Hughes—as well as her development of the intersectional newsletter *Fire!!*, known at the time for its "radical" ideology, including topics such as sex work, colorism, queerness, and interracial relationships (Johnson and Johnson 1979). Many of Hurston's works were posthumously recognized for their brilliance and social consciousness.

Hurston's mentor, Boas, later went on to write several papers denouncing eugenics and questioning America's "inherent greatness." He questioned the arbitrary nature of craniometry and racial measurement, stating there was no way to measure these attributes without bias. I submit that he, in fact, questioned the very nature of American reality, which came to be because white, straight, able-bodied teachers taught cultural superiority to their white, straight, able-bodied students (Prasad 2007, 590–596). The idea of race being heritable was not, therefore, a scientific fact, but rather a particular view buttressed by racially and sexually motivated individuals and institutions calling themselves "scientists." When we create our own realities, we can always find evidence to support those realities. We can also find policies to continue the legacy of those realities. And on and on it goes.

Chapter 2

The Making of Intersectional Others

It is important for readers to understand, as this book embarks on the undertaking of reconstructing historical events and memory, that queer Black, Indigenous, and People of Color (QBIPOC) are in a unique position. They are not only subjected to the oppressions of white, straight society, but also subjected to the oppressions of Black, Indigenous, and People of Color (BIPOC) straight society as well as white queer society, a complex intersection and array of oppressions that has sometimes been called "double oppression" (Kumashiro 1999) or "double jeopardy" (Beale 1979). One way in which this is accomplished is through the erasure of QBIPOC voices—the complexity of their daily lives, the heroics of their actions, and their contributions to the greater cause of liberation for all oppressed people. That is, invisibility, compounded by these various cross sections of oppression, has been a critical component in the Othering of Intersectional Others over time.

A COMMENT ON ERASURE
AND HISTORICAL MEMORY

It is just a fact that the histories of QBIPOC activism in the United States have not been told as kindly, nor as completely, as those of the more "assimilable" white LGBTQIA+ movement. Indeed, many scholars who have sought to study intersectionality have pointed out the ways in which queer scholarship, as a body of work, has historically marginalized non-white queers through its general inattention to racial issues and operative hierarchies (Hammonds 2004). Asian American Studies, for instance, as an academic field, explicitly denied queer sexualities in the 1970s, causing the people—who pointedly did exist—at this intersection to have their experiences erased in scholarship

(Sueyoshi 2020, 130). Indeed, systemic inequities affect the very fabric of academia, skewing the visibility of marginalized experiences and knowledge, even in social justice circles where inclusion is ostensibly a primary goal of the scholarship (Chakravartty, Kuo, Grubbs, and McIlwain 2018).

In *Talking Back: Thinking Feminist, Thinking Black*, Black queer author and activist bell hooks (2014) wrote, "Our struggle is also a struggle of memory against forgetting" (4). In other words, we must not let hegemony cause forgetfulness—we must instead choose to remember and reimagine the experiences of those history might otherwise forget and erase. To prevent the pervasive erasure of non-hegemonic identities necessitates the intentional seeking out of community sources, and even what might be considered "non-traditional," "collateral," or "hearsay" evidence by mainstream historians. Of this, queer historian John Howard, Emeritus professor of Arts and Humanities at King's College, said,

> This hearsay evidence—inadmissible in court, unacceptable to some historians—is essential to the recuperation of queer histories. The age-old squelching of our words and desires can be replicated when we adhere to ill-suited and unbending standards of historical methodology. (Howard 1997, 5)

This especially applies to intersectional histories, which are even more "squelched" and delegitimized.

White gay contributions to the U.S. homophile movement, however, have been well-documented since the 1920s, with accounts of Henry Gerber and Frank Kameny's stories repeatedly told in its earlier moments and Harvey Milk's martyrdom told in its later ones. What we rarely hear about are the queer changemakers of color behind some of queer liberation's most groundbreaking moments, such as Silvia Rivera, Gertrude "Ma" Rainey, and Gil Mangaoang. In the 1970s, gay Filipino American activist Gil Mangoang went so far as to say that he felt he had "schizophrenia" as he was trapped between a homophobic Asian American community and racist queer community. "Initially," he said, "I felt that these two identities—Filipino and gay—were contradictory and irreconcilable" (Mangaoang 1994, 106–107). He later became an early member of the revolutionary Katipunan ng mga Demokratikong Pilipino (KDP)—in English, the Union of Democratic Filipinos—the first Filipino/a/x nationalist organization in the United States, and the only Asian American civil rights organization at the time to welcome LGBTQIA2S+ members (Toribio 1998).

It is clear that we are charged in this task with not only attempting to recall the Othering experiences of those with intersectional identities, but with restoring and reconstructing their importance as well. Jewish lesbian author and founder of Lesbian Herstory Archives Joan Nestle said of the early days of the U.S. queer movement, "I know that much of what I call history, others will not. But answering that challenge of exclusion is the work of a lifetime" (Jewish Women's Archive n.d.). The work done in bars, homes, jails, and on the streets is just as powerful and significant as the work done by those in the mainstream white homophile movement, who had access to formal organization and the ability to publish records of their happenings for posterity. It is important to recognize this, not just because small moments are important, too, but because not everyone has the privilege to be publicly known, even if they deserve to be.

A HISTORY OF LEGALIZED WHITE, STRAIGHT DOMINANCE AND QBIPOC CRIMINALIZATION

We previously discussed the racial construction of whiteness in the United States, including the shifting of white acceptability for certain groups, like Italian Americans, over time. However, some historically marginalized groups have never moved into acceptability, although they might have moved into greater "respectability" in relation to the white, straight mainstream. Rather, they have struggled against changing, but nevertheless oppressive, policies and legislation across history, which have served as guidelines for identity formation.

The Naturalization Act

Less than 100 years ago, the U.S. Supreme Court passed one such guideline, the Naturalization Act of 1790, a law that was created to determine who was white enough—that is, a "free white person of good character" to be a part of the national citizenry. Its passage denied access to citizenship for numerous communities already residing in the United States at the time, including Indigenous people, enslaved people, women, and free Black people (Neuman 1994). This served to narrowly define "Americanness" as a person of European ancestry with pale skin. It also kept political, economic, and social power in the hands of the privileged few, for citizenship not only granted the right to be considered a true American but also the right to vote (i.e., power to affect issues of import or interest to American public), sit on a jury (i.e., power to make decisions in the justice system), serve as an elected official (i.e., power to lead or participate in government), and own land (i.e., power to retain economic security and assets) (Menchaca 1997).

The Naturalization Act was reified over the next century by the justice system in a variety of ways, perhaps most famously in the 1857 U.S. Supreme Court *Dred Scott v. Sanford* decision, which effectively denied freedom to enslaved Black people, even while they resided in free states or territories, a right previously guaranteed to them through the 1820 Missouri Compromise. At the time of the ruling, the presiding justices wrote that Black folk "were not meant to be 'citizens' in the Constitution, and can therefore claim none of the rights and privileges which that instrument provides for and secures to the citizens of the United States" (Taney 1857). In other words, non-whites, regardless of residency status, had no claim on national identity—they would always be designated Other.

The Civilization Fund Act

The Civilization Fund Act of 1819—another such guideline which authorized then-president James Monroe "in every case where he shall judge improvement in the habits and condition of such Indians practicable" to "employ capable persons of good moral character" (Mannes 1996, 260)—ushered in an era of assimilationist policies, paving the way for oppressive legislation. One of these was the 1823 *Johnson v. McIntosh* U.S. Supreme Court decision, which asserted that Indigenous people had the right of occupancy, but not ownership, over land taken by the federal government (Williams 2006), effectively legalizing land thievery on a large scale.

Another was what is commonly referred to as the "boarding school era" for Indigenous people. In mainstream U.S. classrooms, the boarding school era, as intergenerationally traumatic as it was for Indigenous people in this country, is rarely discussed. Readers may thus be surprised to hear that it lasted for over 100 years, from 1860 to 1978 (Woolford 2015). During this period, Indigenous children were forced, by both the federal government and church leaders, to attend Christian boarding schools under the guise of introducing them to the "habits and arts of civilization" (Prucha 2000, 33). If we examine the rationales for the Civilization Fund Act (i.e., "habits and conditions of such Indians") and the boarding school era, it is obvious that the former was the precursor of the latter. As part of this "benevolent" process, Native people of all ages were forcibly stripped of their language, names, dress, religion, and other cultural practices, although not without resistance (Woolford 2015). Two-Spirit people were especially targeted, as missionaries in boarding schools and government officials on reservations enforced strict compliance for white Christian standards of conduct, including a rigid adherence to binary sexual and gender identities. The denial of these identities reinforced the traumatic impact of colonization for Two-Spirit people (Evans-Campbell et al. 2012).

By 1900, there were 150 boarding schools in the United States, with thousands of Indigenous children in attendance (Barnhart 2001). When the Carlisle Indian Industrial School opened in 1879, it became the first off-reservation Native American boarding school and the founding model for similar schools across the United States. Brigadier General Richard H. Pratt, the founder and superintendent of the school—which housed 50 children from the Só'taeo'o and Só'taétaneo'o (Cheyenne), Cáuigù (Kiowa), and Chatiks si chatiks (Pawnee) tribal communities, as well as some Filipino/a/x children (Hunziker 2020)—is now infamously cemented in history for proclaiming that the U.S. citizenry had a responsibility to "kill the Indian, save the man," implying paternalistically that Indigenous people were less than human, but might become more human through assimilation (Pratt 1892, 46–50). The policies developed in the U.S. boarding school era would become precedents for the policies of several U.S. colonial enterprises, including reeducation programs in the Philippines, where residents were also portrayed as tribal and uncivilized (Paulet 2007), leading the United States to rationalize agendas of domination.

The Chinese Exclusion Act and Panic of 1873

We can see this codified bigotry in the history of anti-Asian legislation as well. The Page Act of 1875, for instance, was created to ban immigration for Chinese women, forged from a moral panic about Asian prostitution and tension around labor shortages. Its provisions were expanded to men under the Chinese Exclusion Act of 1882, placing a moratorium on Chinese immigration for a decade, eliminating the chance for Chinese immigrants to become U.S. citizens, and promoting anti-Asian attitudes within the national body (Calavita 2000). The moratorium was extended in 1902 and remained in place until 1943 (Lee 2003).

In the late 19th and early 20th century, even more metropolitan San Francisco, a major point-of-entry for immigrants, was still reported as 95% white in the U.S. Census (Sueyoshi 2018), despite public officials often portraying it as an "international city." Indeed, San Francisco was a decidedly anti-Asian city in many ways, its prejudice catalyzed by the 1882 Chinese Exclusion Act, as well as the aftereffects of a devastating financial crisis, the Panic of 1873, which left many white workers unemployed (Barreyre 2011). Following the mass unemployment, several state and federal policies were introduced which targeted non-white communities, who were seen as "stealing" or replacing the need for white labor (Williams 2006).

When Chinese people first arrived in California after the 1848 discovery of gold at Sutter's Mill, they were highly valued for their bodies and willingness to take life-threatening, low-wage jobs on the railroad and in agriculture—jobs that no white laborer was willing to do (Sueyoshi 2018). Despite this reality, the "threat" of Chinese labor resulted in mainstream rhetoric labeling them as "inhuman," "heathens," and a sexual threat to white women, thereby condemning them to the label "Yellow Peril" (McClellan 1971) and all the consequences thereof. These attributions ultimately provided justification for anti-immigrant aggression, because surely "true Americans" would want to keep the United States from descending into immorality.

Sodomy Law and Sexuality

A vestige of Christian discourse and the 20th-century focus on "homosexual behavior," as opposed to "homosexuality," the criminalization of queers by means of sodomy law has since expanded to include sexual identity as well. Originating in the 17th century, sodomy law still exists in some states, and has historically been one of the most common legal methods for anti-queer discrimination. It was originally "part of a larger body of law—derived from church law—designed to prevent non-procreative sexuality anywhere, and any sexuality outside of marriage" (American Civil Liberties Union [ACLU] 2021). Prior to 1962, sodomy was a felony in every state, punishable by imprisonment, hard labor, and in some cases, the death penalty. It was wielded for several political purposes, but mainly to deny gay parents custody (e.g., cases in Alabama, Arkansas, Mississippi, Missouri, North Carolina, North Dakota, Pennsylvania, South Dakota, and Virginia), the ability to adopt (e.g., cases in Florida, Mississippi), or to foster children (e.g., cases in Arkansas, Missouri), as well as to justify refusing or terminating employment (ACLU 2021).

Further anti-queer discrimination was legitimized through the U.S. Supreme Court 1986 *Bowers v. Hardwick* decision, which expanded previous definitions of sodomy law to include "homosexual sodomy." The Federal Bureau of Investigation (FBI), for instance, announced that, according to the decision, it would officially consider queer identity a crime (ACLU 2021). Several states used the expanded definition to Other queer and trans people in uniquely reprehensible ways. Utah, for instance, has historically used sodomy law to reject the inclusion of LGBTQIA2S+ people as protected under hate crime legislation (Hoshall 2012, 233).

In 2003, the U.S. Supreme Court reversed its previously ruling when it struck down Texas same-sex sodomy law, arguing that "intimate acts" were protected under federal liberty rights (*Lawrence v. Texas* 2003). While this was an improvement, injustice is still pervasive at the state level. As of 2020, 15 states had yet to formally repeal their sodomy statutes. Idaho, South Carolina, and Mississippi, for example, still required anyone convicted before the *Lawrence v. Texas* 2003 to register as sex offenders, even if they engaged in consensual sex. Such a requirement can dramatically affect a queer person's ability to retain jobs, partners, and much more (Avery 2021).

THE FBI AND THE "LAVENDER SCARE"

Under the guise of simply complying with "law and order policies," federal and local law enforcement have made direct impact on the formation of Intersectional Otherness by means of brutality and harassment. Between 1947 and 1950, the FBI led by Edgar J. Hoover, began to more closely investigate and condemn queer people, partially due to media sensationalism over pedophilia at the time, and partially due to the increased visibility of queerness in society at large (Riemer and Brown 2019). The former incited a "moral panic," which eventually led Hoover to announce that "the most rapidly increasing type of crime is that perpetrated by degenerate sex offenders," referring to queer folks (Sutherland 1949, 543). His persecutory actions may have been fueled by internalized queerphobia, as several biographers and sources have indicated that he was sexually involved with other men at the Bureau (Summers 2012). The federal government persecuted gay men by targeting public sex, and in October 1947, the U.S. Park Police launched the "Pervert Elimination Campaign," which resulted in the arrests and apprehensions of hundreds of people (Johnson 2004, 144).

These issues were significantly magnified in 1950 when U.S. senator Joseph McCarthy began the federal crusade known as the Red Scare, which he justified by arguing that there were "hundreds" of communists working in the State Department as traitors to the state (Fitzgerald 2006). Politicians and the federal government used the country's fear of communism to amplify queer Othering during the Cold War era, which was seen as inherently linked to the "homosexual problem." Riemer and Brown (2019) wrote about this time that, to McCarthy, "homosexuality was the psychological disorder that led perverted minds to communism" (67). Indeed, McCarthy gave the Red Scare "a tinge of lavender" (Johnson 2004, 16).

As an Othering campaign, many queer scholars have expressed that the Lavender Scare was in many ways worse than its Red counterpart, although these attacks received much less media attention (Johnson 2004). Queer historian David K. Johnson (2004) noted that language played a critical part in Othering during this time period. He discovered, for instance, that contemporary historians often conflated "security risk" with the construct of "communism," rather than homosexuality, when finding the phrase in historical documents. In actuality, "security risk" was often a code phrase for "sexual deviant," as the government portrayed queerness at the time as mental or moral weakness. It wasn't so much that they thought queers were inherently enemies of the state, but more so that, by their calculations, mental and moral weakness made queers susceptible to blackmail (Johnson 2004).

Lumping the Lavender Scare in with the Red Scare harms more than it helps because the reality is that Othering for queer people was targeted and particularly harsh at this time, even compared to the infamous rooting out of communist sympathizers. By December 1950, every government agency came to the mutual understanding that "sex perverts in Government constitute security risks," and each had their own policies to identify and terminate the suspected "deviates" (Johnson 2004, 114). The federal government's stance toward queer people in the Cold War era effectively validated mainstream bigotry, as all companies hoping to do business with the government were forced to have similar anti-queer policies for employment. The result of this was that, by 1958, an estimated one in five employed adults had been subjected to "loyalty or security screening" (21–22). For queers in white-collar work, the threat of discovery was pervasive and frightening. The traumatic effects of these policies have arguably persisted ever since, making employment and disclosure of sexual identity a fraught relationship nationwide to this day.

HOMONATIONALISM AND THE "GOOD WHITE GAY"

Importantly, QBIPOC have been Othered not just by white, straight society over time, but also white, queer society as the latter has endeavored to be part of the mainstream and fulfill the role of the "good white gay." Indian American queer theorist Jasbir K. Puar's work *Terrorist Assemblages: Homonationalism in Queer Times* (2007) critiqued the use of sexuality and homonationalism as a tool of imperialism, arguing that the emergence of performative liberal "inclusion" toward white gay men in the United States is contingent on the rejection of those in the queer community who do not fit neatly into that category, narrowing their ability to access citizenship and acceptance. Although it may seem that the United States welcomes BIPOC into society's upper echelons, it does so largely when "the ethnic is . . . straight, usually has access to material and cultural capital . . . and is in fact often male" (Ahmed 2005, 243).

Indeed, to pursue "true" inclusion, or the American dream, Intersectional Others must learn to paradoxically love the nation which stigmatizes them. For instance, Asian American queers are often taught to project effeminacy and submissiveness so that they may be palatable and attain mobility. However, such a stance reinforces white queer dominance and disempowers Asian queerness. It also creates tension with Black queerness, as Asian stereotypes of effeminacy contrast with Black stereotypes of aggression and hypersexualization.

Out of this paradox, assimilationist ideology was born into the queer liberation movement, an ideology inherently at odds with the idea of "liberation" because it carried within it the primary goal of becoming part of mainstream society, and thus could never reach the utopic freedom the word "liberation" often signifies. The goal of assimilationism has been a source of division and antagonism between QBIPOC and white queer folks from the start of the U.S. homophile movement, leading the former to be excluded from membership, decision-making, and general participation in the homophile movement (Greer 2018; Peacock 2016). Ultimately, such a stance has meant less solidarity, visibility, and political power for queer communities at large.

THE (UNMISTAKABLY WHITE) EARLY HOMOPHILE MOVEMENT

Organized gay activism has existed far longer in U.S. history than most are aware of, with the first documented accounts in the early 20th century. Most documents have centered on Henry Gerber, although documentation has been dramatically skewed toward white queerness. In 1924, Henry Gerber, a white German immigrant and U.S. postal worker, who was also witness to the German "homophile emancipation movement," founded the Society for Human Rights (SHR), the very first homophile rights group in the United States, after reportedly becoming frustrated due to the persecution of "those who deviated from the established norms in sexual matters" in Chicago (Hogan and Hudson 1998, 244). Gerber appointed himself Secretary, among other white officers. A Black minister, Rev. John T. Graves, however, was appointed president (Kepner, Murray and Bullough 2002).

The significance of such an appointment seems lost on most queer historians, as it would make not only Graves the first chief officer to ever be recognized in the mainstream homophile movement but also the first QBIPOC to be in a leadership role within the movement. Unfortunately, SHR failed to garner much membership or political support aside from its founding members, even when attempting to collaborate with local reproductive justice advocates and was disbanded in 1925 after a police raid landed both Gerber and Graves in jail (De la Croix 2013). Gerber was posthumously inducted into the Chicago Gay and Lesbian Hall of Fame, but Graves is most often left with a single-line descriptor of his contributions, if he is present in text at all (Nichols 2000), demonstrating the profound effects of racism and homonationalism on historical memory.

Mattachine Society and the Shadow of Assimilationism

Beginning in the 1950s and 1960s, queer resistance became much more overt and moved away from the language of "homophile," though published accounts of these resistances were more likely to center white gay men

(Bérubé 2018). Many historians inaccurately cite the founding of the Los Angeles Mattachine Foundation in 1950, for instance, as the start of the gay rights movement, with Harry Hay as its pioneer. While the Mattachine Foundation—to be distinguished from the post-1953 Mattachine *Society*—became the largest and most well-known of the formal homophile organizations, it was formed by seven white gay men, and known to be highly exclusionary in its visions of QBIPOC, trans folks, and women (Peacock 2016). Because it prioritized assimilation strategies, it gained some political power within mainstream society, but at the cost of intersectional solidarity.

Gay Jewish astronomer Frank Kameny, often hailed as a gay rights icon like Henry Hay, who had lost his job with the U.S. army after being outed in 1957, quickly became a leader within the Mattachine Society after approaching the U.S. Supreme Court about anti-queer discrimination in 1962. He openly addressed Mattachine's New York chapter in 1964, with the speech, "It is absolutely necessary to be prepared to take definite, unequivocal positions upon supposedly controversial matters" (D'Emilio 1983, 152), and became the primary organizer of the 1968 North American Conference of Homophile Organizations (NACHO). He subsequently launched the "GAY IS GOOD" campaign, revolutionary at a time when gayness was blatantly vilified in mainstream society—importantly inspired by the earlier anti-racist, body empowerment "Black Is Beautiful" campaign—as part of what he felt was a necessary and "strongly positive approach, a militant one" for gay liberation (Riemer and Brown 2019, 50). Five years after the campaign started, the number of gay organizations in the United States had multiplied tremendously, from an estimate of 60 to over 2,500 (Riemer and Brown 2019). Many of these were still dominated by white gay and lesbian folks, however, as exclusionary practices were commonplace in the movement.

The Daughters of Bilitis and "The Ladder"

In 1953, Rose Bamberger, a Filipinx American lesbian who is often overlooked in queer historical literature, had been yearning for a non-bar lesbian space. She pitched the idea of expanding lesbian gatherings to some queer friends, Del Martin and Phyllis Lyon (Greer 2018)—the Daughters of Bilitis (DOB) was thus formed. What was originally conceived as a "secret society" by Bamberger grew significantly over the next couple decades to become a famed social and political group for lesbians (Riemer and Brown 2019). The lesbian femmes of the DOB actively discussed, from formation, the need to distance themselves from "vulgar" bar lesbians, and rejected potential members who appeared too masculine, or too dark, although this was not always explicitly discussed (Greer 2018). They aligned themselves with the more assimilationist Mattachine Society, as they were not attempting to define their identities as distinct from the mainstream, but rather appear acceptable to the mainstream, and "prove that lesbians and gay men are no different than other people" (Riemer and Brown 2019, 82).

Bamberger left the group by 1956, and only its white founders, Del Martin, Phyllis Lyon, and Noni Frey, remained. Some scholars theorize she left due to a desire to avoid the integration of men and straight women into the organization (Gallo 2006), as well as being outed as the DOB became increasingly public (Sueyoshi 2020). However, we can speculate that the decision to abandon ship may have also been due to a distaste for the increasingly white-centric atmosphere, as many QBIPOC commented on the prevalent whiteness of the group during this era. Ten years later, in 1966, this was still true when Chinese American lesbian activist Crystal Jang joined the DOB in an attempt to find community in San Francisco. She reportedly felt that it, along with the lesbian bar scene, was "all white," while the Third World liberation groups, which sought to gain power and rights for BIPOC, were "too male" (Sueyoshi 2019, 138). Thus, many Intersectional Others, and in particular QBIPOC women, were caught in an alienating double bind.

One of the DOB's largest contributors to lesbian visibility and destigma-tization was their monthly publication *The Ladder*, which was read across the United States as one of the homophile movement's main media sources. There were some problems with *The Ladder*, however, which stemmed largely from the fact that the DOB was not intersectional in the least. Many were hopeful about the publication, which was widespread within the homophile movement, raising visibility for lesbian and queer issues. Then-emerging Black lesbian playwright Lorraine Hansberry, author of the acclaimed tragedy *Raisin in the Sun* (1959), for instance, wrote optimistically to *The Ladder* staff in 1957, saying she was glad to find other queers and felt isolated in her non-intersectional experiences within the Black community (Riemer and Brown 2019).

In many ways, the publication *The Ladder* symbolizes the problem that arises when activism or discourse around liberation becomes exclusionary and siloed. As a group of predominantly white queer femmes, the DOB accomplished some important things—they created greater solidarity between (white) lesbians and (white) gay men, where previously the movements were segregated (Greer 2018). They also made genuine attempts to bridge the gap between the mainstream and the homophile movement, although they did this with a singular method in mind—assimilation. However, they simply did not have the wherewithal to truly gain traction with their ideas, because they relied on their whiteness, as well as binary gender and sexual norms, to get the job done. While they did attend a number of Mattachine events, for instance, their input was often ignored, which was likely at least partially due to stigma and discrimination against femmes by the gay men in charge (Riemer and Brown 2019).

Black queer activist and author Audre Lorde said of it in her autobiography *Zami: A New Spelling of My Name*, "One read *The Ladder* and the Daughters of Bilitis newsletter and wondered where the other gay-girls were" (Lorde 1982, 50). She continued, stating that, often due to exclusion and loneliness, QBIPOC had to "build community (of sorts) where they could" (Riemer and Brown 2019, 85), along with queer relationships with whomever they could find, no matter how "ill fit" the partners were due to the rarity of finding such a thing (Lorde 1982, 50). It was this sentiment that likely drove many QBIPOC organizing efforts underground, in bars and homes with the curtains drawn, meaning that formal organizations like the DOB and Mattachine Society lost out on some of the movement's most extraordinary voices, instead of joining forces with them.

By 1970, both Mattachine and the DOB had dissolved into smaller, disconnected groups, and the *Ladder* was no longer affiliated with them (Riemer and Brown 2019). After its dissolution, some radical West Coast activists wanted to continue the DOB's lesbian-centered group ethos, but with a greater presence for QBIPOC women. A new era of intersectional activism was born, including the work of lesbian feminists like Jeanne Córdova, a mestiza butch dyke who founded *Lesbian Tide*, a new-wave periodical that replaced *The Ladder* (Córdova 2011, 34–46) and was destined to become the voice for the radical lesbian feminist movement.

EXCLUSIONARY PRACTICES IN GAY BARS

After the Prohibition era, the gay bar became the central institution of (white) queer life, although many gay bars were mafia-owned, particularly in Manhattan (Carter 2004). Gay bars were simultaneously social centers and spaces for political consciousness to develop (Bérubé 1990, 271). They were places not only to form individual identity but also collective identity for white gays and lesbians (Kennedy and Davis 1993). Post-prohibition raids, therefore, became less about rooting out illegal booze than about rooting out "illegal patrons."

To stay in business, gay bar owners had to be quite discriminating about their location. They needed to strike the right balance between accessibility and invisibility, limiting the amount of ignorant passersby, police raids, and malicious reports on the establishment (Johnson 2001). In the rural United States, these issues were magnified, and gay bars often became clandestine operations. In fact, the gay tourist guide *The Lavender Baedeker* (1964) only had one bar listed for the entire state of Mississippi. The address for that bar The Cellar, however, was incorrect as its owners had moved locations to operate more quietly (Johnson 2001). Discretion was key to attracting business without also attracting those unknowingly wandering down the street.

Due to an increasing national focus on binary (i.e., gay-straight) sexual identity in the 1970s, queer politics began centering on sexual desire, rather than gender (non)conformity (Riemer and Brown 2019). It created an atmosphere whereby bi and trans concerns were minimized, as they didn't quite fit into the more definable categories that white cis-heteronomative society felt it needed to find and persecute an Other. It also minimized visibility for QBIPOC, who perceived gay bars to be unwelcome spaces (Chauncey 2008). In the 1970s and early 1980s, Black queer folks, in particular, were often asked to show multiple forms of identification to get into gay bars, while their white counterparts entered freely (Royles 2017).

RURAL OPPRESSION AND RESISTANCE

As the homophile movement grew in more well-documented urban neighborhoods, it also grew in rural America, although there is a dearth of research in this area for several reasons. One is that rural America is thought to be more repressive for marginalized communities; therefore, its historical and social relevance is often brushed aside by scholars. Another is that queer historians frequently depict culture formation as linked to urban capitalism. However, much of the association with urban living and queer formation is due to the fact that these urban areas are where queer historians live and work, not because these are the only areas where queer communities thrive (Johnson 2001).

Queer historian John Howard, professor of American Studies at King's College, argued in his book *Men Like That: A Southern Queer History* (1999) that queerness in rural areas was neither rare, nor isolated, and flourished especially in the 1950s when road-building proliferated, allowing for access to greater networks of queer desire. Howard found that once he expanded his definitions of queerness to include more fluid expression, such as homoerotic and nonconformist sexuality, in addition to the acts of those who identified strictly as gay, he was able to find numerous accounts of queer interactions. He further contended that, if we "reconceive silence" in queer history (Howard 1999, 31), we can find evidence that southern queers got creative in order to find safe meeting places, and often blurred the public and private by strategically using roadside rest areas, public restrooms, and even church recreation rooms for sexual encounters. Ironically, "southern indirection," the reluctance of southerners in the United States to discuss topics that might distress "polite company," he felt, may have also allowed queerness to flourish more readily at this time (Howard 1999, 67).

Unlike other scholars, Howard asserted that the "free love 1960s," not the "conformist 50s," constituted the largest amount of restriction on queer life by the government and mainstream society in rural areas. In 1965, for instance, Mississippi state officials launched a campaign to mass eradicate "sexual deviance," and quite literally ran queer men from Jackson's public restrooms and tearooms out of state (Howard 1999, 166). The crackdowns, which involved the ejection of low-, middle-, and upper-class residents alike, exposed the true prevalence of queerness in the state, and were heavily linked to the larger resistance of the white business class and white supremacists in the south to the passage of the *Brown v. Board of Education* (1954), Civil Rights Act (1964), as well as other attempts to dismantle Jim Crow (Howard 1999, 39).

The state government, to alleviate anxieties around the crackdowns, told the public that, if sexual deviancy did indeed exist, it was likely in sequestered areas already condemned by the white mainstream, such as the racialized "inner city" of Jackson, Mississippi. In doing this, southern U.S. governments effectively linked the oppressions of queerness and Blackness, making them both enemies of the state and targets of injustice. Howard (1999) wrote:

> By 1965 homosexuality was linked to the specter of racial justice—what white authorities understood as the most serious threat to the status quo. Queer Mississippians black and white found themselves in increasingly politicized positions. With the bravery earned in lives of local struggle and everyday resistance, they moved onto the public stage, determined to win a legitimacy and equity so long denied them. (xvii)

SPHERES OF RELATIVE CULTURAL AUTONOMY

Intersectional Others found ways to exist, and even revel, in the early 20th century. Despite the fact that they remained cautious, they built what one scholar referred to as "spheres of relative cultural autonomy" (Chauncey 1994, 2); that is, they developed ways to maintain power and control within the social circles that felt safe to them. In underground and nocturnal spaces, queer expression, in fact, thrived (Chauncy 2008). Indeed, queer history does not begin with Stonewall, nor does it begin with white gay men, as national media would have us believe. The early history of queer liberation and power extends beyond formal organizational efforts, like Gerber's, and includes more informal strategies, which were used to claim space within a hostile society (Riemer and Brown 2019).

"The Loop"

In Chicago, for instance, Intersectional Others claimed space in a business district known as "the Loop," which included Bronzeville on the South Side, the West Side, and the Near North Side. Bronzeville was the home to Black jazz and blues clubs, cabarets, and drag balls where racialized sexuality and gender were highlighted, and boundaries blurred to allow for more expressive freedom (Blattner 2021). During the 1920s and 1930s, the Chicago neighborhood around Rush and Clark Streets on the Near North Side was called Towertown, which emerged in the Prohibition era as a working-class lesbian and gay enclave. There, Chicago residents roomed together and were able to exercise sexual autonomy, discuss politics, and find entertainment. Within its limits, for example, one could find the Dill Pickle Club, whose patrons included queer folk, intellectuals, socialists, anarchists, and artists. It also acted as a stage where lecturers were known to speak on "radical" topics such as homosexuality and sexual freedom (Jessica 2020). The crossings of race and class lines at these locations are well-documented by sociologist Ernest Burgess, who encouraged his undergraduate students to explore Chicago nightlife for research purposes (Heap 2003).

The Tenderloin

The San Francisco Tenderloin, much like the Chicago Loop, has historically been a nexus of QBIPOC life, work, and resistance. It was a place where sex work sustained the livelihoods of street queens and trans people in the pre-war era, as well as a place where Intersectional Others developed intercommunity support. Photographs from the posthumous collection of Jiro Onuma, a gay Japanese immigrant who pressed laundry at Mercury Laundry and Cleaners in the Tenderloin in the 1930s, showed a vast array of social outings with other queer Asians in San Francisco, including one photograph taken at Moriyama Studio in Japantown, known for its artistic portraitures, which were popular at the time for middle- and upper-class residents. In it, he posed for a stately, yet intimate, photograph with two other Japanese American men, illustrating the ways in which the Tenderloin allowed working-class QBIPOC to transcend their class statuses and live out cosmopolitan fantasies (Takemoto 2014). Tamara Ching, mixed Chinese/Hawaiian American trans activist, remarked that drag queens lived and worked in the Tenderloin more than any other place in San Francisco in the 1960s. "Back then," she said in an interview with Stanford University historians, "everything was in the Tenderloin, everything. It started to ebb down towards Polk Street, and it didn't hit the Castro until the mid- to late-1970s, so the Tenderloin was it" (Ching 2018).

Formal homophile organizations in the 1960s, such as the Council on Religion and the Homosexual (CRH), which was formed by Glide Memorial Church and the DOB, debated, but ultimately decided against, coming to the aid of QBIPOC residents of the Tenderloin district—then called the "gay ghetto"—despite the fact that its residents suffered most intensely at the hands of police brutality, likely due to compounded oppression (Meeker 2012). It was quite telling, therefore, that the more visible assimilationist homophile organizations elected to ignore the suffering of Tenderloin queer and trans residents. Records indicate they likely saw the Tenderloin as a detour on their path to lift middle-class white queers, such as themselves, into upper-class mainstream society. This mindset created a growing division between veteran homophile organizations, such as DOB, and younger groups, such as the Society for Individual Rights (SIR), who were more interested in liberation discourse at the time (Riemer and Brown 2019).

Harlem and Queer Performativity

Recent scholarship (Schwarz 2003; Wilson 2010) has indicated that larger cultural movements, such as the Harlem Renaissance (1919–1935), would not have been possible without gay social networks as well as the support and upsurgence in creative expression from queer and trans women, despite the fact that it is largely known as a pivotal creative moment for Black men. The lesbian blues and jazz scene, for instance, was critical for the development of the larger lesbian community in the United States and brought with it solidarity and empowerment (Wilson 2010). While theater and performance circles were known to serve as spaces where queer Black creatives could freely express sexual desire, there were still issues with tolerance by the public, forcing queer intimacy to be separated from many performers' on-stage personas (Chen 2016).

Comments from celebrities at the time, like Black lesbian dancer Mabel Hampton, suggest that house parties were common spaces for exploration, sexual expression, and finding community, particularly for working-class Black folks, but due to the clandestine nature of these gatherings, it is hard to determine how frequent they were (Philipson 2011). Kevin J. Mumford, Black queer professor of history at the University of Illinois, described the ways in which queers connected with Black community in Harlem through their similar oppressive experiences, and folks questioning their sexuality, from all over, were drawn to Harlem to be a part of an intersecting community (Mumford 2008). As the mainstream embraced blues music, it indirectly heard and absorbed the messages about queerness embedded within the genre, affecting heteronormative society and the way it viewed racialized queerness.

The growing popularity of drag balls in the 1920s and 1930s illustrated the new visibility of queer society, which is different than saying society "accepted" them. Society was still actively stigmatizing and condemning queer identities. Rather, they accepted the performance and spectacle of them, and took pleasure as consumers who could come and go as they pleased. In 1929, Harlem's Hamilton Lodge Ball drew 7,000 visitors, all there to witness the main event *Parade of the Fairies*, which centered genderbending and nonconformity within the tension between queer and heteronormative cultures (Wilson 2010). The *Parade of the Fairies* was also featured at several other popular entertainment centers at the time, including Webster Hall in Greenwich Village (Lawrence 1989).

INTERSECTIONAL LIBERATORY CONSCIOUSNESS

As collective queer identities took shape in the 1960s and 1970s, so too did intersectional consciousness within the resistance. Black lesbian author and activist Audre Lorde said about the shift, "[I]mmediately within [any movement] you are going to get those people whose differences are not being articulated" (Riemer and Brown 2019, 22). As the gay liberation movement slowly moved closer to the mainstream, increasingly, white queers became invested in assimilationist ideology, no longer willing to make space for those who were racially Othered for fear that it would distance them from their goal of finding, as Audre Lorde called it, the "mythical norm" of white gayness (Olson 1998, 450–470). Gay Filipino American activism Gil Mangaoang wrote in his memoir that, in the 1970s, "Minorities who were members of these gay organizations were generally seen as subordinates reflecting the dominant racist attitudes in society" (Leong 2014, 108). These accounts have been corroborated by numerous QBIPOC activists throughout the era, including queer Japanese American activist Kiyoshi Kuromiya, who, during an interview for the PBS documentary series, *A Question of Equality* (1995), recounted several times when he was kicked out of Gay Activists Alliance (GAA) meetings after pointing out racism in the organization (Dong 1995).

Intersectional empowerment thus meant separating from the white faces of the gay liberation movement to form new organizations which addressed the specific needs of Intersectional Others in the United States. One such organization was the Third World Gay Revolutionaries in Chicago, a 1970 coalition between Black and Latino/a/x queers from the Chicago chapter of the Gay Liberation Front (Kisack 1995). Queer youth of color also formed their own organizations, such as New York Gay Youth, founded by Black queer and trans Stonewall rioter Zazu Nova, "The Queen of Sex." While Nova is less well-known, some believe she, and not Marsha P. Johnson or Stormé

DeLevarie, threw the first brick in the Stonewall uprising, though clearly, the accounts from that night are conflicting (Gay 2019). These splits from the larger banner of the gay liberation movement have shaped the landscape of queer activism, as they represent theoretical shifts in ideology and identity over time (Riemer and Brown 2019).

QUEER COMMUNITIES OF COLOR AND THE MILITARY-INDUSTRIAL COMPLEX

The development of the queer communities in the 1940s was fueled in part by the attack on Pearl Harbor and military policy. The U.S. Armed Services had, prior to the attack on Pearl Harbor in 1941, been a place where queer people could quietly find each other, as the peacetime draft was less strict about enlistees (Riemer and Brown 2019). However, a surplus around the time of the attack caused the military to set stricter standards, which included the specific ban of "homosexual persons," which later evolved into the language of "sexual psychopaths" (Loeser 1945). The screening was ineffective, thankfully, as only 5,000 people were excluded on this basis, out of the 18 million drafted. Studies suggest there were as many as 1.8 million queer servicemen alone, not even counting queer women and gender nonconforming folks who may have enlisted. In fact, evidence suggests that rumors spread through the armed forces about homosexuality, allowing servicepeople to find each other. Queer communities thus formed in military camps and fueled bar culture around them at the time (Riemer and Brown 2019).

Jackie Bross and Gender Policing

Gender and sexual expression were heavily policed during World War II, making gender nonconforming clothes a prime target for QBIPOC criminalization. In January 1943, 19-year-old-queer Cherokee American Evelyn "Jackie" Bross was arrested for "brazenly" wearing pants while walking home with a friend (Austin et al. 2012). While reports did not explicitly discuss racism, we cannot rule out the possibility that being BIPOC also played a role in her arrest, as Indigenous people were, and are, highly marginalized. Bross worked as a machinist at a World War II defense plant and had been on her way home. At Women's Court, Bross informed the judge that she wore pants—so-called "men's clothes"—because they were "more comfortable than women's clothes and handy for work," and then continued, "I wish I was a boy. I never did anything wrong. I just like to wear men's clothes . . . [but] everyone knows I'm a woman" (Jessica 2020, 232). Her sentencing included mandatory visits with the court psychiatrist for six months. The case marked a shift in city ordinance and a win for queer and other gender nonconforming folks, as Chicago City Council amended the 1851 regulation to exclude those people who did not intend to use clothing to "conceal their sex" (i.e., wore the clothing for work purposes). The event is cited as a major turning point in sexual and gender expression (Jessica 2020). However, it is worth noting that the Othering practice of policing and arresting "crossdressers" persisted throughout the rest of World War II. And the ordinance itself, although amended to allow for defense labor, was not repealed until much later, in 1973 (Meyer 1992).

As World War II began allowing queer women to wear slacks in order to more efficiently work within the military-industrial complex (Meyer 1992), new gender and sexual expressions around attire began to take shape, along with the development and expansion of lesbian community spaces—particularly lesbian-centered bars. Visibility from these spaces manifested a new kind of power for U.S. lesbians, resulting in a move from the butch-femme binary to what was often referred to back then as a "new kind of butch" or a "tough bar lesbian" (Kennedy and Davis 2014).

This "new butch" was seen as someone who assertively defended her space and set the standards for it based on her own desires, giving herself the power and position to maneuver within the larger queer community with a sense of individualism. The image also preemptively protected queers against straight patrons who attempted to enter the space confrontationally (Hankin 2002). While some historians argue that this created an untenable employment situation for the lesbian community at the time, as they were more easily identifiable, I submit that it actually increased power for future queer women, who were able to both more flexibly express their identities and benefit from the territorial rights gained by the dykes who came before.

A Queer Japanese Internment Story

In early 1942, approximately 110,000 people of Japanese descent—most American citizens and some Asian folks who were mistaken as Japanese due to racism—were forcibly relocated to internment camps, known on paper as "prescribed military areas," on President Roosevelt's authority via Executive Order 9066 (Nakanishi 2009). There are only a few records of queer Japanese internment survivors from this period in U.S. history. One such person was John Nojima, who was held at Manzanar Relocation Center in Independence, California, and later became an early founding member of ONE Inc., one of the most prominent homophile organizations (Lindsay 2018). However, most compelling were the unassuming records by Jiro Onuma, who was interned at the Tanforan Assembly Center (San Bruno, California) and Topaz (Delta, Utah) camps with his partner Ronald, which documented queer life and intimacy in confinement through photography (Takemoto 2014), perhaps the only photographs that exist showcasing these experiences. The collection illustrated the small joys queers in the camps derived from having their photos taken at the Topaz photo studio. It also captured the unique ways in which indulgences of this kind can be their own kind of resistance. In them, Onuma was pictured with Ronald and his friend Sasaki, posing with pleasant expressions, sometimes even with playful ones, taking a reprieve from daily realities of Topaz internment camp (Takemoto 2014).

One photograph in Onuma's collection, however, betrayed the loss queer Asian Americans faced while imprisoned—that of his partner Ronald and friend Sasaki, pictured without Onuma at Tule Lake Segregation Center, a depiction which indicated that Onuma and his partner had been separated for the duration of internment, and perhaps for good (Takemoto 2014). It is likely, given what we know of the internment configurations, that Sasaki and Ronald were determined by camp officials to be "disloyals"—also referred to as "no-nos," meaning they answered "no" twice to questions posed by the "loyalty questionnaire"—which asked Japanese Americans to renounce their allegiance to Japan and agree to enlist in the U.S. army if called upon (Lyon 2011). Tule Lake was used as a maximum-security prison for those who failed the questionnaire, a place where they were separated from their family and friends, and then subjected to even poorer conditions than the other internment camps (Funke 2008). Onuma's photographs likely survived camp surveillance because they appeared so ordinary, but they've become extraordinary accounts of a story untold.

Unfortunately, much of the history embodied through his personal effects cannot be commented on by Onuma himself. We can only speculate at these experiences through absence, as we must also do for much of the queer Asian American experience in the early homophile movement. This is partially due to the fact that many Asian American men during World War II felt the need to conform to American standards of white masculinity to prove loyalty, else face greater discrimination (Robinson 2016). Queer historian John Howard, for instance, found that because of an overrepresentation of wartime narratives featuring loyal Nisei citizens, patriotism, and traditional American family ideals, much of the existing literature on the concentration camps largely overlooked and ignored the wartime experiences of immigrants, women, political dissidents, and queers (Howard 2009).

Chapter 3

The Perils of the
Multiply Marginalized

Multiple Minority Stress and the
Health Impacts of Oppression

According to a report by the Movement Advancement Project (MAP) and Center for American Progress (2015), there are approximately 3 million LGBTQIA2S+ BIPOC in the United States. However, a large meta-analysis of demographic data found that, of the 3,777 articles dedicated to LGBTQIA2S+ health across multiple fields, 85% omitted information on the race or ethnicity of participants (Boehmer 2002). This grievous omission undermines our potential to assess the true impact of multiple marginalization and other social determinants on physical and mental health for Intersectional Others. A study by van Mens-Vulhurst and Radtke (2008) analyzed the use of intersectionality frameworks in mental health research and found that, at the time, only four studies mentioned "intersectionality" at all. Within studies examining identity characteristics without an intersectional framework for guidance, researchers noted a lack of recognition regarding the "complexity of social differences" (13). The report was published in 2008, from which we can conclude that the defined use of intersectionality theory in mental health is a relatively recent phenomenon.

There is very little written about the effects of multiple marginalization on the bodies and minds of Intersectional Others, but one thing is certain—the bodies of literature on queerness and race independently are not sufficient in describing them (DeBlaere, Brewster, Sarkees, and Moradi 2010). Early discourse on racial (Hardiman 1982; Helms and Cook 1999) and sexual (Cass 1979) identity development initially conceptualized race and sexuality as solitary aspects of social identity, rather than seeing them as interconnected parts of human experience (Jones and McEwen 2000; Wijeyesinghe 2012). However, many scholars have argued that unique issues, and overlapping oppressions, arise when someone holds two or more minoritized identities, such as in the experiences of a queer Black, Indigenous, or Person of Color (QBIPOC) or woman of color (Bieschke et al. 2008; Crenshaw 1989; DeBlaere et al. 2010).

MINORITY STRESS THEORY

"Minority stress theory" (Meyer 1995; Meyer 2003) proposed that marginalized people are exposed to additional stressors, such as stigma and discrimination, due to their minority statuses, which then disproportionately impact the health of those people. This body of literature therefore supports a biopsychosocial model of oppression-based experiences, whereby these factors interact to create unique constellations of experience for marginalized people (Ratts et al. 2016). There is now substantial evidence that minority stress is associated with poorer quality of life (Mays and Cochran 2001), increased psychiatric distress (Herek 1999; Ong, Fuller-Rowell, and Burrow 2009), substance use (Nawyn, Richman, Rospenda, and Hughes 2000), and health risk behaviors (Hamilton and Mahalik 2009) among many marginalized communities, not just those who are racially marginalized (Meyer 2003; Syzmanski 2005).

The resulting stress is likely compounded for Intersectional Others (Cyrus 2017; Nadal et al. 2017), which researchers have termed "multiple minority stress" (Balsam et al. 2011). Research in this area sometimes implies that stress is cumulative. In reality, stressors for Intersectional Others interact in unique ways that are far more than the sum of their parts. Mounting evidence, for instance, has demonstrated that a person's identity intersections have the potential to influence their mental and physical health (Conron, Mimiaga and Landers 2010; Hankivsky et al. 2010), indicating that our experiences of stressors, and our perceptions of these experiences, are multidirectional. This may be because Intersectional Others are subjected to multiple forms of oppression simultaneously—such as the effects of racism and sexism, or transphobia and ableism—causing them to be "doubly oppressed" (Kumashiro 1999), or, when forced to conceal their identities from their respective communities, live a "double closet life," presenting additional challenges (Leung 2016).

SOCIOCULTURAL BARRIERS
AS MINORITY STRESSORS

Oppression and social inequities deprive marginalized groups of their sense of well-being and safety, something often taken for granted by groups with privilege. It is true that some affirmative strides have been made toward decreasing systemic inequities affecting Intersectional Others, such as the

U.S. Supreme Court decision (*Obergefell v. Hodges* 2015) which legalized same-sex marriage on a federal level. However, countless socio-legal issues remain. It was only in late January 2021, due to an executive order issued by newly inaugurated President Biden, for instance, that federal protections were put in place to prevent workplace discrimination for queer and trans people. Prior to this, states were allowed the "freedom" to provide, or not provide as the case was in many conservative states, protections as they saw fit. Even now, the protections from this executive order have yet to be cemented into federal law, as the Equality Act has not been passed by the U.S. Senate (Human Rights Campaign [HRC] 2021).

According to data from the 2020 Gallup Daily Tracking Survey, nearly half of all queer and trans people lack state protections from discrimination in employment, education, housing, public accommodations, and credit (Conron and Goldberg 2020). It is easy to view these events, and pieces of legislation, as singular, though they are not. It can be helpful, instead, to understand that we are functioning off a status quo where the Equality Act is irregular, and that the fight over basic identity protections is not a stripping of freedoms, but instead an insertion of freedoms that never existed in the first place. It is a reality in the United States today that Intersectional Others can be evicted, refused medical care, and more in states where nondiscrimination statutes are not robust enough, as sexual and gender identities are not explicitly "protected characteristics" in some states. We are a country in which Othering is the norm, and "all" in "justice for all" does not include Intersectional Others.

Racism and Heterosexism

Intersectional Others are not immune to what minority stress literature has termed "objective prejudice events" (Meyer 2003)—real, observable phenomena that are experienced as stressors due to the adaptational demands they imposed on a subset of individuals, such as racial or sexual discrimination (Herek and Garnets 2007). According to a survey by the Human Rights Campaign (2018), four out of five queer youth of color experience racism on a regular basis, and more than half think about it "often" or "every day" (Khan, Johnson, Lee, and Miranda 2018). These youth also reported greater levels of harassment at schools, with 47% of Latino/a/x, 39% of Black, and 35% of Asian American and Pacific Islander (lumped together in this study) queer and trans youth reporting some form of bullying. Moreover, college graduation and attendance rates are lower, particularly for Latino/a/x and Black queer and trans adults, who report 15% and 17% graduation respectively, compared with 31% of the general population (Badgett et al. 2007).

Violence and discrimination, core stressors affecting Intersectional Others have been irrefutably linked to negative health outcomes in psychological meta-analyses (Pascoe and Richmond 2009). Specific stressors in U.S. history range from forced sterilization during the Progressive Era and beyond to the enforcement of sodomy laws punishable by imprisonment, castration, torture, and death, some of which still exist today (Meyer 2003). According to a 2017 poll by National Public Radio (NPR), the Robert Wood Johnson Foundation and the Harvard T.H. Chan School of Public Health, QTBIPOC are more than twice as likely as their white counterparts to say that they have been discriminated against while applying for jobs (32% versus 13%) and interacting with police (24% versus 11%) (Prichep 2017).

More recent work has attempted to expand research examining the effects of overt discrimination to include impacts of microaggressive behavior. "Microaggressions" are characterized as brief, regular assaults on marginalized individuals and can be social or environmental, verbal or nonverbal, and intentional or unintentional (Sue et al. 2007). They may not be perceived as discriminatory by perpetrators, who believe their actions harmless and do not understand their potential impacts (Sue 2010). Manifestations of microaggressive behavior for Intersectional Others include the use of problematic language or humor (e.g., misgendering, racial jokes), over-endorsement of heteronormative culture (e.g., parents reprimanding their child for not being "masculine enough") or the assumption of pathology based purely on sexual identity (e.g., believing "all queer people have HIV").

Sexual racism, racism perpetrated against Intersectional Others within LGBTQIA2S+ communities, is a commonly cited microaggression (Choi et al. 2011; Han and Choi 2018). Studies have highlighted rampant microaggressions in intimate relationships, for instance. Dang and Hu (2005) identified that 82% of queer and trans Asian Americans have personally experienced racism within the gay community, and Wilson and colleagues (2009) found that queer Asian Americans commonly reported seeing "No Asians" on dating applications like Grindr. Filipinx Gay and Lesbian Alliance Against Defamation (GLAAD) youth editor Andre Menchavez wrote about his experiences with sexual racism in LGBTQIA2S+ settings, saying, "'No fats, no femmes, no Asians' is a phrase in the queer community I am too familiar with. Similarly, I faced the complexity of both fetishization and isolation while dating as an Asian queer person" (Menchavez 2019).

Intersectional Others are acutely aware of the inherent vulnerability of identity disclosure, and that being "out" can lead to potential harm or rejection due to societal stigma (Mitchell and Means 2014). In fact, simply believing we hold a stigmatized identity—or multiple as the case is for Intersectional Others—is associated with stress and negative health outcomes. The stress of concealing one's sexual identity due to stigma, alone, has been found to be predictive of higher rates of anxiety and post-traumatic stress disorder (PTSD) in marginalized groups (Cochran et al. 2013), and these anxieties may be higher in certain communities than others. Studies have suggested that heterosexism in Black and Asian American communities may lead to a greater desire to conceal (Bridges, Selvidge, and Matthews 2003; Malebranche et al. 2009). This is important, considering just 4% of Black queer and trans youth and 5% of Latino/a/x queer and trans youth reportedly feel their racial communities are viewed positively by society at large, indicating they perceive significant racial stigma (Khan, Johnson, Lee, and Miranda 2018).

Income, Segregation, and Economic Security

Segregation in the United States is commonly thought to be a pre-civil rights issue, confined to Jim Crow. However, it persists today, and scholarship indicates it is likely growing (Chang 2016). LGBTQIA2S+ BIPOC have higher poverty rates than both straight, cis people and white queer and trans people (Human Rights Campaign [HRC] 2021). Black and Asian American queer and trans folks showed the most significant difference, 30.8% and 22.9% respectively, compared to 25.3% and 14.6% for their same-race straight, cis peers (Badgett, Choi, and Wilson 2019). The University of California, Los Angeles (UCLA) Williams Institute estimated that approximately 30% of QBIPOC and 40% of trans BIPOC live in poverty today in the United States (Badgett, Lau, Sears, and Ho 2007). According to a 2015 study by the MAP (2015), because Intersectional Others face a higher rate of lifetime poverty, they also face greater food insecurity. Fifty-five percent of Native queer and trans people, for instance, reported they worried about their ability to buy food, followed by 37% of Black and 36% of Latino/a/x queer and trans people.

Importantly, however, high rates of poverty are not created in isolation. They are formed through, and associated with, legalized discrimination (e.g., housing, credit, or employment discrimination), lack of family recognition (e.g., unfair taxation, inability to inherit), and hostile educational environments (e.g., inability to access financial aid, unsafe schools) (Badgett, Lau, Sears, and Ho 2007). In 2021, the HRC published a report that found 28% of queer and trans adults of color had no health insurance coverage. Only 79% of Black, 71% of Asian American and Pacific Islander (lumped together in this study), and 61% for Latino/a/x queer and trans folk had access to health insurance versus 82% for white peers (Badgett, Lau, Sears, and Ho 2007). Twenty-six percent reported that they needed to see a doctor at least once but could not due to the financial burden. And, compared with only 3% of cis straight youth of color, nearly one in five (17%) of LGBTQIA2S+ youth of color "usually" slept somewhere other than with a parent or guardian, in transitional housing or were homeless (HRC 2021).

George Lipsitz, professor of Black Studies and Sociology at the University of California, Santa Barbara (UCSB) and author of *The Possessive Investment in Whiteness* (2006), argued that

> public policy and private prejudice work together to create a "possessive invest-ment in whiteness" that is responsible for the racialized hierarchies of our society. Whiteness has a cash value: it accounts for advantages that come to individuals through profits made from housing secured in discriminatory mar-kets, through the unequal educational opportunities available to children of dif-ferent races, through insider networks that channel employment opportunities to the friends and relatives of those who have profited most from past and present discrimination, and especially through intergenerational transfers of inherited wealth that pass on the spoils of discrimination to succeeding generation. (vii)

Indeed, white folks in the United States are encouraged to invest in whiteness, to remain true to an identity that provides them with structured advantages. The flipside of these advantages are the inevitable disadvantages for margin-alized people in this country, who do not reap these benefits, and more so, are actively kept from them at a structural level.

Housing and Gentrification

In June 2021, the *What We Know Project* at Cornell University released a report which confirmed quantitatively what many of us invested in intersec-tional wellness have known for a long time—that Intersectional Others not only have higher rates of negative health outcomes, but also have higher rates of employment and housing discrimination. As a coalition between several social justice and advocacy groups, the project was able to break down results racially to better determine which intersections were most impacted by various types of discrimination. The results themselves were rather "painful," a senti-ment expressed by National Black Justice Coalition (NBJC) executive director David J. Johns after reading the report (What We Know Project 2021).

A study by the Pew Research Center (2016) found the median net worth of white households in the United States is about 13 times that of Black house-holds—a gap that has grown wider since the 2007–2009 Great Recession. "Affluence" as a construct provides stability and safety as much as it does luxury, experiences that may be taken for granted by those with privilege. As marginalized families contend with this wealth gap, and relocate to neigh-borhoods with lower cost housing, they become displaced. Trends like this have affected areas like San Francisco, now the most expensive city in the nation, where, after the "dot com boom" in the 1990s, a wave of white tech industry workers and corporations have systematically displaced those living in historically working-class Black, Brown, and immigrant neighborhoods, such as the Mission District (Nieves 2000).

From 1980 to 2013, the Latino/a/x population in the Mission District decreased from 44% to 38%. This was accompanied by an increase in white residents, from 36% to 43% (Cespedes et al. 2015). Studies show that active community organizing has resulted in a slower decline in the district than might have otherwise occurred, with notorious projects like the Mission Yuppie Eradication Project protesting gentrification in the area. The project gained heavy media coverage in the early 2000s due to the vandalization of new housing developments and expensive property, thought to belong to white, wealthy gentrifiers (Sharrok 2013); its actions represented a growing animosity from marginalized communities in the Bay Area.

A 2020 study by the National Community Reinvestment Coalition (NCRC) found that, of all larger metropolitan regions in the United States, the San Francisco-Oakland region was subject to the most gentrification and cultural displacement. Within gentrified areas, wealth abounded, but in what the report termed "opportunity zones" (i.e., neighborhoods to which marginalized residents were relegated near these gentrified areas), there was a stark contrast of low income, low home value, and low rates of home ownership. And despite the investment happening in the gentrified neighborhoods, marginalized communities did not have access to these resources, as they resided in the adjacent zone. The majority of opportunity zone residents were Black, and the NCRC correctly identified that this meant gentrification was a significant threat to marginalized people (Richardson, Mitchell, and Edlebi 2020).

Gentrification is just one example of the concrete ways in which strategic Othering over time can segregate wealth for those with marginalized identities, and ultimately disproportionately burden Intersectional Others with oppressive realities. Because there is a lack of recognition from the state and federal governments as to the legitimacy of queer families, they often reported additional costs for their households to accommodate. These included an average of $3,658 more in healthcare for partners, $2,525 lost in family safety net programs, and $3,760 in added income taxes (Badgett et al. 2007).

Employment Discrimination

The What We Know Project (2021) also found that queer and trans folks of color were more than twice as likely to experience anti-queer discrimination (e.g., verbal abuse) when applying for jobs than white queer and trans people (32% versus 13%). National surveys have indicated that between 75% and 82% of Asian American and Pacific Islander (lumped together in this project) queer and trans people report some form of employment discrimination, with 42% of Black peers reporting the same (Badgett et al. 2007). Queer and trans

immigrants may be particularly vulnerable, as they are subject to exploita-
tion, discrimination, as well as lack of access due to immigration status or
language barriers (Grant et al. 2011). Ultimately, this led to higher rates
of unemployment (15% for Black, 14% for Latino/a/x, and 11% for Asian
American and Pacific Islander [lumped together in this study] queer and trans
folks, as opposed to 8% for the general population) (Badgett et al. 2007).

A survey conducted by the IBM Institute for Business Value (2021), which
included responses from more than 6,000 U.S. professionals, found that 45%
of LGB people felt their employer discriminated against people based on
their sexual identities. More than two out of three people said they didn't feel
equipped to overcome the sexual or gender discrimination at their place of
work. Of LGB respondents, 9% of Black, 20% of Latino/a/x, 24% of Native
American, and 17% of Asian American respondents reportedly experienced
discrimination based on their sexual identity to "a great extent"—only 4% of
white LGB respondents agreed with this statement.

THE HEALTH IMPACTS OF
MULTIPLE MARGINALIZATION

We need no further proof of the consequences of minority stress than the
disproportionate impact of the novel coronavirus (COVID-19) pandemic on
Intersectional Others. For one, we know that Intersectional Others are disproportionately represented in the U.S. frontline workforce, with both sexual and
racial marginalization as factors known to greatly increase contraction of disease, based on minority stress studies (Balsam et al. 2011; Nadal et al. 2017).
A recent study by the UCLA on the Fall 2020 surge suggested that queer and
trans folks of color were contracting COVID-19 at double the rate of their
white cis straight peers (15% versus 7%, respectively) (Sears, Conron, and
Flores 2021). The significant difference we see between rates of infection is
not due to racial and sexual essentialism. Rather, it is due to systemic inequities, like an increased rate of poverty; a lack of access to COVID-19 education;
a distrust of hospitals due to traumatization or maltreatment by white straight
doctors in the past; and a higher rate of overall chronic stress due to systemic
oppression, which has led to overburdened bodies and immune systems.

This is obvious even in the same study (Sears, Conron, and Flores 2021),
which indicated there was also a stark contrast in financial strain during the
pandemic between these groups. Queer and trans folks of color had greater
difficulty affording household goods (29% versus 14%), struggled to pay
their rent or mortgage more often (26% versus 9%), and were generally more
worried about paying bills on time (63% versus 33%). They were also less
likely to trust the government and pharmaceutical companies' responses to

the global pandemic. This lack of trust may have been directly impacted by the large differences in COVID-19 morbidity in these communities; one out of three queer people of color said they knew someone who had died, whereas one out of five of their white cis straight counterparts knew someone who died from the disease (Sears, Conron and Flores 2021).

Intersectional Others and the HIV/AIDS Epidemic

The effects of Othering behavior by healthcare providers can be catastrophic for patient well-being, as medicine hobbled by detachment, bias, and incomplete patient knowledge runs the risk of diagnostic and therapeutic error (Halpern 2001). Prejudicial providers, for instance, may misdiagnose a patient, or even refuse treatment for serious illnesses, due to their own biases (Chandra and Staiger 2010). A recent study examining clinical decision-making showed that medical students with greater levels of heterosexist bias were less likely to prescribe pre-exposure prophylaxis (PrEP), a potentially life-saving medication which prevents those at high risk for HIV exposure from contracting it, to gay men, as they anticipated lower medication adherence (Calabrese et al. 2018). Lower rates of prescription were recorded for providers with racial bias as well (Calabrese et al. 2014). To help readers understand the true impact of this, approximately 50% of Black gay men contract HIV in their lifetime (Kelly et al. 2013). In other words, while modern HIV medications are increasingly effective at treating the disease, prescriber bias may cause barriers to receiving any treatment at all, resulting in unnecessary illness and fatalities.

Over the years, many QBIPOC activists have pointed to early depictions of AIDS as a "white gay disease" as rationale for why Black queer communities did not recognize the growing crisis sooner (Cohen 1999). However, the exclusion of Black gay men from high-profile AIDS groups in the early years of the HIV/AIDS epidemic was the result not only of their absence from early AIDS statistics but also of the racism and segregation which were endemic in metropolitan queer circles (Bost 2015). Groups like Gay Men's Health Crisis and the San Francisco AIDS Foundation, two of the largest HIV/AIDS organizations in the United States, grew out of the mostly white gay social networks, for example.

Because the neighborhoods where they operated were unwelcoming, if not outright hostile, to Black gay men—and because many had little experience working with Black, Indigenous, and People of Color (BIPOC)—they often failed to reach Black gay men with even the little information about the HIV/AIDS epidemic that was available (Kayal 2018). Within a few years it became clear that QBIPOC suffered disproportionately. Activists of color called on predominantly white gay AIDS groups, many of whom relied in part on public funding, to develop targeted outreach. There was some success in this area, with Gay Men's Health Crisis, the San Francisco AIDS Foundation, and ACT UP developing education programs for local Black and Latino/a/x communities by the late 1980s. However, the consequences of structural racism, as well as the delay in education and HIV/AIDS activism, were deadly for many (Wilton 2009).

In 2017, the *New York Times* ran a piece called *America's Hidden HIV Epidemic*, demonstrating the deadly consequences of Othering for QBIPOC in this country, which documented continuing struggles for Black bi and gay men in Jackson, Mississippi against HIV/AIDS (Villarosa 2019). According to a 2020 report by the Centers for Disease Control and Prevention (CDC), 42% of new HIV diagnoses were Black Americans, with the largest proportion being Black gay and bisexual men. Although the HIV/AIDS epidemic is often thought to be a thing of the past, it still actively affects QBIPOC today due to pervasive social inequities and Othering (Brooks et al. 2003).

Mental Health, Psychiatric Distress, and Substance Use

Intersectional Others are at higher risk than white, straight peers for both mental health issues and substance abuse as a result of racism and heterosexism (Xavier, Bobbin, Singer, and Budd 2005), and the risk may be especially high for queer women of color (Vu et al. 2019). One study found that psychiatric symptoms were associated with racist and heterosexist stressors for Black queer men (Zamboni and Crawford 2007). Another by Balsam and colleagues (2011) found that queer and trans Asian Americans reported significantly more microaggressions and psychiatric distress than queer and trans Black or Latino/a/x Americans.

A recent study (Human Rights Campaign [HRC] 2020) found that 35% of queer and trans youth of color are currently using alcohol, compared to 26% of straight, cis youth. They have also reported higher levels of depression (79%), hopelessness (73%), and anxiety (82%) related to their experiences of racial stigma and discrimination (HRC 2018). All of these may be impacted by a perceived need by Intersectional Others to sacrifice pieces of identity to find belonging. One mixed Asian American queer activist, Renee Nikolov, called this the "pendulum of identity" (Menchavez 2019), a phenomenon they felt affected young QBIPOC specifically.

Perhaps one of the more devastating mental health impacts of multiple minority stress is suicidality. A study by the HRC (2015) found that queer and trans youth of color were significantly more likely to attempt suicide (27%) when compared to white queer and trans youth (22%), as well as straight cis youth (5%) in the United States. Another study found that the rate of attempted suicide was especially high for Native queer and trans youth (31%; What We Know Project 2021). In a large national study, researchers identified that Native American, Pacific Islander, and Latino/a/x queer youth had significantly higher odds of an adverse suicidal outcome than white queer youth (Bostwick et al. 2014). These odds have been linked to discrimination in other studies looking at these age ranges (What We Know Project 2021).

THE DEFICIT MODEL IN HEALTHCARE

We have the responsibility to support the empowerment of Intersectional Others, and not simply highlight deficiencies, as healthcare professionals. However, often, fields like Medicine and Psychology simply add to the stigma and discrimination experienced by Intersectional Others by working from a Deficit Model. And what is the "Deficit Model" I discuss here? It is the tendency for researchers, practitioners, and educators to focus on the association between marginalized identities and negative outcomes such as those outlined in the Minority Stress Theory section. Identity pathologization has shaped the landscape of healthcare, so it is perhaps unsurprising that the preponderance of medical and psychological research to date would focus on these topics. And at a time when research—and thereby our understanding of the field—was historically limited to the descriptions of white cis straight people, these data were invaluable, as few studies focused on "minority" experiences at all, let alone the experiences of folks with multiple marginalized identities. In these ways, a deficit framework can be effective at communicating that there are differing needs based on the cultural identities and histories of people. But it is not enough.

While literature on minority stress is not without merit, its perspective is highly imbalanced, in effect ignoring resilience and the potential for power to manifest as a result of these experiences. A Deficit Model is singularly focused not only on the disadvantages of marginalized identities as a whole but also, often, on the disadvantages of a discrete identity or a discrete experience of discrimination. Arguably, it also reflects and perpetuates dominant white heteropatriarchal ideology, which has historically espoused the belief that marginalized communities are disadvantaged, dependent, and unhealthy in order to dominate them. This is further exacerbated by the fact that white straight researchers often act as the authors for this literature, creating a hierarchy whereby marginalized subjects are studied anthropologically without the ability to utilize their own voices for change, instead relying on researchers impacted by oppressive biases.

Systemic Imbalances Inherent in the Deficit Model

Rather than working within a pathologizing model, which is inevitably impacted by systemic oppression, we should instead ask ourselves in what ways we have been ignoring the power and change that has existed for centuries in the United States, which have been propelled largely by people at the margins of society. It is the privilege of the white straight elite and mainstream to assert its opinions, create structures, and define "normality" for the Othered. White straight society can do these things with a general sense of safety, knowing that its views are shared by other people in power and therefore at low risk of being rejected by peers and community leaders. Conversely, it is the privilege—or perhaps the burden—of those with marginalized identities to expose the weaknesses of these opinions, structures, and redefine what "normal" looks like for the benefit of all. In redefinition, however small, there is power—of vision, of progress, of a new system where marginalized people can rise higher than before because of the actions of one, or many.

The Deficit Model is rooted in preexisting systemic inequalities and perpetuated by a capitalistic healthcare system in which a Deficit Model is profitable. By consequence—and perhaps by necessity—researchers, clinicians, and even community members have developed a focus on community deficits, instead of focusing on community power, because the organizations funding projects on marginalized communities set the standard as such. A recent study by Viergever and Hendriks (2016) identified the largest public funders of health research across the globe. Of the top ten funding organizations they identified, the largest was the National Institutes of Health (NIH), which constituted 40% of the world's spending in this area, approximately $37.1 billion.

A division of the U.S. federal government, the NIH is more likely to approve funding for a project where empirical evidence is provided to demonstrate need. Very concretely, the NIH and other federal funding mechanisms, like the Substance Abuse and Mental Health Services Administration (SAMSHA), demand, and reinforce, a reductional approach to human experiences. The way this implicitly translates to health researchers is that they need to prove a community has increased rates of bodily disease, mental illness, and other social determinants of health, such as homelessness or income inequities, to get funded. In other words, they must adopt the Deficit Model or risk their project getting scrapped. Needs assessments have therefore become critical for marginalized communities not just for building awareness but also for gaining funds to sustain their communities' livelihoods. However, needs assessments only provide part of the picture. Most of the effort should be, but often is not, focused on bettering communities, growing power, and fostering life for the people that exist within.

Chapter 4

The (De)Colonization of Otherness

Decolonization in the United States is the difficult work of deconstructing colonial ideologies perpetuated throughout history which promote whiteness and straightness, while devaluing, exploiting, and pathologizing the histories and identities of those Indigenous to colonized spaces. Indeed, in the United States, every system—justice, healthcare, economic, and social—serves to reinforce the age-old bigotry embedded in our nation's founding as a colonial entity. It was built to serve not the colonized, enslaved laborers, but the white colonizers who came to this land. Their prejudicial vision and the resulting systems at work act as invisible webs which hold certain people, mainly white straight men, in power, while holding—nay, strangling—others away from it.

Although the process of decolonization has often been confused with the vague dismantling of socially unjust systems, it, importantly, has its own specific agenda, and should not be relegated to the metaphorical (Tuck and Yang 2012). Calls to "decolonize our schools" or "decolonize methods," while well-intentioned, may distract and detract from the true goals of decolonization. According to Unangax̂ (Aleut) scholar Eve Tuck and Asian American scholar K. Wayne Yang (2012), decolonization consists of two tasks. The first is contending with "the invisibilized dynamics of settler colonialism mark the organization, governance, curricula, and assessment of compulsory learning" and the other is contending with the ways in which "settler perspectives and worldviews get to count as knowledge and research and how these perspectives —repackaged as data and findings—are activated in order to rationalize and maintain unfair social structures" (2). In other words, we must first become aware of the true reach of colonialism, and then "unsettle" the oppressive norms which colonizers impose on Others.

THE REDEEMER NATION

By day, the United States masquerades as a sheltering land for immigrants, with a mission to propel them toward prosperity. By night, however, it does the opposite—oppressing, killing, and stealing from them—all in the name of humanitarianism. Our Statue of Liberty, perhaps the most recognizable symbol of the American Dream, has inscribed upon its pedestal a sonnet by author Emma Lazarus (1883), who wrote, "Give me your tired, your poor, your huddled masses yearning to breathe free." Lazarus, who worked with refugees at the time of authorship, was thought by scholars to have the welfare of immigrants on her mind as she wrote these famous words.

The sonnet is not immediately visible to Statue visitors, much as the concerns of immigrants and refugees are often forgotten by the U.S. social elite. In both the early 20th century and today, in 2021, we see the effects of this invisibility and fear, with anti-immigration advocates driving restrictive legislation like the Chinese Exclusion Act (1882) and Executive Order 13769 (2017)—known colloquially as the "Muslim Ban"—which suspended refugee immigration from seven predominantly Muslim countries. This discourse is driven by an affluent few, whose hold on it undermines the validity and visibility of marginalized voices in the country.

Ronald Reagan once referred to the United States as the "redeemer nation," with implications that, as a Christian country, it was the duty of our nation to spread global humanitarianism and American exceptionalism, "redeeming" or "civilizing" those who would come in contact with us. Indeed, for centuries, it was often considered the "white man's burden" to civilize those perceived to be less advanced across the globe, and any efforts to this end were moral imperatives intended to save the "barbaric" Others, such as in the case of the United States "liberating" (i.e., purchasing and dominating) the Philippines from their Spanish oppressor, resulting in the mass reeducation, oppressing, and militarizing of Filipino/a/x people (Ignacio, de la Cruz, Emmanuel, and Toribio 2004). All in all, it is far too easy to avoid dwelling on the consequences of our imperial pursuit of domination by telling ourselves that we are the moral purveyors of democracy. Eddie Glaude, African American Studies professor at Princeton University, wrote:

> American exceptionalism . . . allows us to contain our ugliness, to always narrate it in terms of the inevitable progress toward a more perfect union. . . So, the American ideology consistently allows us to let ourselves off the hook. The question is a perennial question of "is this America?" because of that aspirational claim that is built into the very self-understanding of who we are as Americans. (Glaude 2020, 52)

The progress we so pursue across the globe reflects the harm we have wrought. If we are ever to come to terms with our colonial past as a nation, and decolonize our thinking and future, we must not let ourselves off the hook. We cannot allow ourselves to be apathetic or ahistorical—we cannot allow ourselves to say the consequences of colonization are few. Colonization is highly consequential, and those consequences will be revealed in this chapter.

THE PHASES OF COLONIZATION AND DECOLONIZATION

The vast majority of scholarly literature on colonization uses Black Martiniquais psychiatrist and philosopher Frantz Fanon's Colonial Model (1961) as a theoretical framework for understanding the origins, impacts, and deconstruction of global colonization efforts. According to Fanon, we must understand the effects of colonization before committing to the intensive work of decolonization. He said:

> Decolonization, which sets out to change the order of the world, is, obviously, a program of complete disorder. But it cannot come as a result of magical prac- tices, nor of a natural shock, nor of a friendly understanding. Decolonization, as we know, is a historical process: that is to say it cannot be understood, it can- not become intelligible nor clear to itself except in the exact measure that we can discern the movements which give it historical form and content. (Fanon 1963, 36)

The four phases of colonization are described in detail in his seminal 1961 work *The Wretched of the Earth*. The framework's first phase involves the forced entry of a foreign entity into a territory with exploitative intent toward the Indigenous peoples of that territory. The second involves the establish- ment of a colonial society that is characterized by cultural imposition, dis- integration, and recreation of Indigenous cultures. These three things serve to impose a binary through which the colonizers are superiorized, while the Indigenous are inferiorized. In the third phase, this binary is further embed- ded through dehumanizing depictions of the colonized, labeling them "ani- mals," "savage," and in need of civilizing and domination by the colonizers. All of these eventually lead to the final phase, whereby colonizers establish a race-based system in which the political, social, and economic institutions in the colony are designed to benefit the colonizer and continually subjugate those who are colonized.

In a 2006 conversation with Native Hawaiian scholar and activist Poka Laenui, Virigilio Enriquez, the "father of Sikolohiyang Pilipino (Filipino/a/x psychology)," outlined what he felt to be the process of decolonization for Indigenous people. The first phase was rediscovery and recovery, the second mourning, the third dreaming, the fourth commitment, and the final phase action. Laenui and Enriquez both noted that the third phase, dreaming, was the most "crucial for decolonization" (4).

When recounting the conversation, Laenui discussed the fact that individuals and general society may be at different phases of these processes for different spans of time. He used the decolonization of Hawai'i as an example, which he claimed underwent several years of the first phase, rediscovery and recovery, socially. In 1978, a Kānaka Maoli (Native Hawaiian) criminal defendant made history by refusing to enter a plea in court, contesting the jurisdiction of the colonized Hawaiian government over the actions of Indigenous people (Laenui 2006). This steeply contrasted with the sociopolitical climate 20 years later—when most politicians and members of the general public supported Hawaiian sovereignty, demonstrating a progression in cultural recovery. Even so, some individual Hawaiians in 1998 disagreed. That is, depending on social strata or personal history, individuals might be in very different phases of the colonization and decolonization processes simultaneously (Laeneui 2006).

RACIAL AND SEXUAL COLONIZATION

A Brief History

The colonization of race in the name of power is evident from our country's very inception, which heavily relies on the narrative of liberation from tyranny, a nation "breaking free" from Great Britain. The irony of this narrative is not lost on queer Black, Indigenous, and People of Color (QBIPOC), as the United States is a settler-colonial nation-state, one founded on the backs of slaves, as well as the brutalization and marginalization of Indigenous lives. Whiteness and straightness, particularly of Western Europeans, were the identities valued highest among those who settled in what would 150 years later be the documented foundation of the "United States" (Grosfoguel 2004).

Colonialism has similarly hierarchized queerness throughout U.S. history. We may consider texts such as queer Indian American scholar Jasbir Puar's work *Terrorist Assemblages: Homonationalism in Queer Times* (2007), which introduced the construct of "homonationalism," posing the idea that the contemporary United States has a particular view on acceptable, racialized queerness, one which is linked inextricably with Americanness through the trajectories of imperialism and colonization. The U.S. projects itself globally as a progressive, gay-friendly nation, one which allows queer people to achieve upper positioning in social strata—if they meet certain criteria, that is. Indeed, historically, the queer subject may achieve pseudo-acceptance so long as they perform the "right" kind of gayness—one which intersects with whiteness, middle or upper economic status, and able-bodiedness—placing Intersectional Others lower on the socionational hierarchy (Rivera and Maglalang 2016).

A Settler-Colonial Nation-State

For the majority of the 17th century, the United States relied on Native slave labor, despite the fact that these were the people indigenous to the land white Europeans largely stole when they arrived. Innumerable Native people were murdered and infected by European diseases, including smallpox, measles, influenza, cholera, and even the bubonic plague. The first documented epidemic was a 1636 smallpox outbreak on Pueblo land, in what would later be called New Mexico. This, combined with a measles outbreak soon after, led to the deaths of approximately a quarter of the Pueblos living in that area. With increased contact in the next hundred years, and through the establishment of Spanish missions and settlements, the post-Columbian era brought even more death through colonization and its effects on Indigenous people (Martin and Goodman 2002, 65).

Tsalagi (Cherokee) Professor of Anthropology at the University of California, Los Angeles (UCLA), Russell Thorton, used historical records and statistical models to approximate the Indigenous deaths which resulted from the arrival of—and subsequent murder, violence, and impacts thereof by—colonizers between 1492 and the present. For the entire present-day United States, he estimated that the total number of Indigenous deaths for the contiguous United States was approximately 12 million, with an additional 790,000 deaths in Hawai'i, Alaska, and Puerto Rico (Thornton 1987). Other scholars have found that approximately 200,000 deaths have occurred since 1900 (Smith 2017). Using these data, genocide and the effects of colonization have taken a total of about 13 million lives since 1492. This horrific number is only a very small portion, however, of the genocide which occurred throughout the Western Hemisphere due to European colonizers, which appears to be about 175 million lives lost (Smith 2017). The calculations caused one historian to note that the almost inconceivable number of deaths caused by European settlers and their descendants constitute "the worst human holocaust the world had ever witnessed" (Stannard 1996, 146).

The systemic oppression of Native identity, brought on by European settlers, has resulted in intergenerational and colonial trauma for Indigenous communities. Those who were not killed by disease had their cultural histories delegitimized, and often erased, through the implementation of epistemic violence, such as the enforcement of Christian and Catholic boarding education, the destruction of cultural texts, land theft, and banning of cultural practices. During the boarding school era, white colonizers often went so far as to whip or kill individuals who spoke their tribal language, refused to wear European clothing, or rejected the practice of Christianity or Catholicism (Davis 2001). In many ways, the boarding school era was an attempt by white America to wage cultural warfare on Native people.

These struggles were not without resistance, however. There is documented evidence that, while some Native students did attempt to participate fully in the assimilative process, many did not, and often covertly participated in storytelling, held secret dances, and played Indigenous games with other students behind closed doors. Parents resisted as well, at times sending the "wrong" children to the schools in place of their own (Davis 2001), although obviously this was problematic for other reasons.

Oral histories recounted by queer scholar Will Roscoe (1998) have also documented Native queer resistances to targeted sexual and gender reeducation, including collective resistance by the Apsáalooke (Crow) people, who were "subjected to ongoing interference by representatives of the U.S. government," particularly over gender expression for "botés," those who identified as a nonbinary third gender. Recalling the treatment of one boté, Osh-Tisch ("Finds-Them-And-Kills-Them"), an Apsáalooke (Crow) participant, said that "former agents have repeatedly tried to make him [*sic*] don male clothes, but the other Indians themselves protested against this, saying that it was against his nature" (Morgensen 2010, 113).

Queer Indigineity and Biopower

Indigenous queer scholarship has examined the ways in which Indigenous identities, bodies, and sexualities are shaped by colonialism and biopower (Finley 2011). From the beginning, colonial and imperial expansions into the Indigenous Pacific, for instance, have been imagined as sexual events. In fact, some scholars have posited that Pacific Islander queer sexualities so powerfully informed 19th century white imaginings of masculinity that

> male homosexuality, as we have come to understand it, was constituted in no small part through the European collision with Polynesian culture, whose systems and activities of sexual attraction and desire were so different . . . as to throw the European observer into positions of reaction, denial and injunction that helped reify modern categories of sexual identity. (Wallace 2003, 8)

It is precisely because Indigenous queer sexualities were so exoticized and consuming that sexuality was weaponized. Upon encountering Native queer and Two-Spirit sexualities and genders, for instance, early colonists often marked them as "sexually perverse," in order to secure rationales for physical domination. Death often succeeded such a designation (Davis 2001), ensuring that, from the very beginning of the colonization, queerness was vilified and targeted. Even when death did not result, regulation was so harsh that erasure often followed (Morgenson 2010). It's unsurprising that sexuality was weaponized in this way, as many Indigenous communities were, and are, less rigid about sexuality and gender and thus did not fit easily into the hierarchy European colonists would have prescribed during that era and beyond (Morgenson 2012).

Diné (Navajo) scholar and professor of American Studies at the University of New Mexico, Jennifer Nez Denetdale, has pointed to the fact that queerphobia and heteropatriarchal attitudes are often equated with Native "traditionalism" in tribal nations, used then to justify the discouragement of Native women, queer, and Two-Spirit people in their assumptions of leadership roles. She wrote,

> While it is necessary for Native scholars to call upon the intellectual community to support and preserve Indigenous sovereignty, it is crucial that we also recognize how history has transformed traditions, and that we be critical of the ways tradition is claimed and for what purposes. (Denetdale 2006, 10)

The adoption of heterosexist attitudes toward marriage and nuclear family structures can be seen as a product of colonial trauma and imposition, as they are constructions of white heteropatriarchy, despite the fact that they are currently institutionalized in many Native communities (Denetdale 2006; Smith 2005). Several scholars have argued that colonialism and the heteropatriarchy purposefully hierarchize gender and sexuality, placing heteronormativity and masculinity at the top, else they fall apart (Finley 2011; Smith 2016). The sexualization of Native people effectively constructs them as incapable of self-governance without heteropatriarchal influence, which colonizers claim Native people do not "naturally" possess (Smith 2016).

Gay ethnographer Walter Williams (1986) recorded Lakota oral histories detailing the traumatic impact of the boarding school era on Native sexualities and genders. In one such recording, a participant said,

> By the 1940s, after more Indians had been educated in white schools, or had been taken away in the army, they lost the traditions of respect for winktes. The missionaries condemned winktes, telling families that if something bad happened, it was because of their associating with a winkte. They would not accept winkte into the cemetery, saying "their souls are lost." Missionaries had a lot of power on the reservation, so the winktes were ostracized by many of the Christianized Indians. (Morgensen 2010, 115)

The broadsweeping impact of the boarding school era traumas was devastating, and instituted mechanisms of control and silencing of non-heteronormative sexual discourse (Finley 2011). Although sexual shame and silencing are currently experienced around queerness in Indigenous communities, this shame was most likely incurred intergenerationally as a means of collectively surviving colonial trauma, and not as a "natural" occurrence due to Native traditionalism. It is easy for these perspectives to become distorted or lost due to structural oppression, making the inheritance and preservation of Native knowledge all the more important.

Indigenous queer and Two-Spirit activists are actively working on recentering decolonized perspectives on issues of gender and sexuality, combating the narrow definitions of gender and sexuality presented in colonial discourse and asserting queer modernities (Morgensen 2011). Expanding on Jaspir Puar's construct of "homonationalism" (Puar 2007), queer scholar Scott Morgensen (2010) argued that the development of settler homonationalism—a colonial interest in the specific depiction of queerness in the United States as white and gay—is a reaction to the introduction of Native queer modernities into settler-colonial nation-state. Because settler homonationalism promotes non-Native queerness as ideal, it simultaneously diminishes Native queerness and continues the colonization of Native land and people. The only way to subvert the effects of settler homonationalism, he felt, was to hold queer communities and systems in the United States accountable to Indigenous struggles for decolonization. We must all work together to end colonial interests and hierarchies which perpetuate unjust realities for queer and Two-Spirit Native people.

Black Subjugation and White Profiteering

Native lives were not the only lives affected by early U.S. colonialism; the "success" of the United States is also predicated on violence against Black people brought forcibly to the United States through kidnapping and enslavement. On August 25, 1619, transatlantic slave traders forcibly brought enslaved Africans to the state of Virginia. Slavery has since thrived under colonial rule, and its economic impact on the United States, and the rest of the world, is indisputable (Fields 1990). Most historical texts on Black subjugation at this time lack the specific experiences and perspectives of those who were subjugated. It is commonly believed in the United States, for instance, that slavery is a "southern thing"; however, slavery was ubiquitous across the northern United States as well (Farrow, Lang, and Frank 2006).

If you walk to the corner of Wall Street and Water Street in Manhattan today, you will see a small, few-foot-long plaque recently dedicated to the Municipal Slave Market, which operated from 1711 to 1762 (Alexander

2020). In fact, enslaved people built the wall that Wall Street is named after (Thomas 2019). Starkly contrasted to the Municipal Slave Market plaque, which represented the buying and selling of approximately 6,800 enslaved people—"legally," and even more illegally—in the city, is the 16-acre 9/11 memorial at the site of Ground Zero, which pays homage to the 2,977 people killed by terrorist attack on September 11, 2001 (Sturken 2015). The immense size disparity in these memorials is a direct reflection of, not only the priorities of the leaders dictating they be made and the memorial architects designing their external appeal, but also the immense structural inequities woven into the fabric of this country.

The signing of the Declaration of Independence in 1776 is often portrayed in textbooks as one of the nation's defining moments. Despite the fact that, in writing, it guaranteed equality for "all men," the Declaration did not extend those basic rights to the primary laborers of the country at the time of the signing, Indigenous or Black men, among many others. All to say, the founding of this country is not nearly as "equal," nor as "independent," as textbooks claim—unless you identify as a white straight man. When the Constitutional Convention was held in 1787, the white delegates in attendance specifically documented a difficulty reconciling the system's reliance on slave labor for economic growth with the immorality of human enslavement (Dougherty and Heckelman 2008). However, we cannot attribute too much altruism to the delegation, as they ultimately chose to continue their white profiteering despite its cost to marginalized communities.

Moving into the 19th century, colonization became the basis for the country's prosperity, and slavery the bedrock of the U.S. economy. From 1803 to 1937, cotton was the leading industry in the United States, an industry powered almost exclusively by Black labor. In 1790, we had just shy of about 700,000 enslaved workers in the country. By 1850, that number was 3 million, and demands for cotton were driving most of that growth (Dattel 2009). In fact, Black bodies were often used as collateral for loans, when capital was deemed lacking from banks without them (Rothman 2016). I say "bodies" because it was not their humanity that was valued, but their ability to work, produce, and export cotton as enslaved people across the United States, and to Great Britain, which financed and relied on U.S. slave labor for 80% of its raw materials, despite abolishing its own slave trade in 1807 (Desmond 2016). Rather than leveraging their homes or land, U.S. plantation owners leveraged Black lives.

The Reaping of BIPOC Land, Lives, and Futurities

Here is where the oppression of Black lives and Indigenous lives are joined, because their oppressive realities are linked. In the early 19th century, the United States continued to colonize and expand into what is now the lower South, an area home to several tribal nations, including the Tsalagi (Cherokee), Maskókî (Creek), Chahta (Choctaw), Chikashsha (Chickasaw), and Yat'siminoli (Seminole) nations (Krauthamer 2013). Meanwhile, the cotton industry had exploded in the areas already colonized and plantation owners were hit with a dilemma. Cotton production depleted soil relatively quickly, and they were soon out of land to produce—thus, profit—more. They put intense pressure on the federal government to perpetrate stealing the land they desired from the Indigenous people rightfully living there (Krauthamer 2013). What is often portrayed in U.S. history textbooks as simple thievery was actually a series of U.S.-led brutalizations and atrocities—not without enthusiastic support from President Andrew Jackson—which included the 1813–1814 war with the Maskókî (Creek) people, who did not agree to any "treaty" and lost 22 million acres of land in what is now known as Georgia and Florida (Nunez 1958).

There was clear evidence that the motivation of the federal government and judiciary at the time was to appease white settlers with little regard for the validity of Indigenous lives, nor the well-being of Indigenous people living on their rightful lands. In 1823, the U.S. Supreme Court ruled that Native people could live on U.S. lands but could not hold title to them (*Johnson v. M'Intosh*), effectively stripping Indigenous communities of their ability to live safely and securely, and paving the way for the 1830 Indian Removal Act, which falsely promised prosperity "in the West" to tribes willing to sign land treaties (Cave 2003). In his second annual message to Congress, arguing in favor of forcibly removing Native people from their territories, Andrew Jackson wrote that it would effectively

> relieve the whole State of Mississippi and the western part of Alabama of Indian occupancy, and enable those States to advance rapidly in population, wealth and power. It will separate the Indians from immediate contact with settlements of whites . . . and perhaps cause them gradually . . . to cast off their savage habits and become an interesting, civilized, and Christian community. (Jackson 1980, xii)

The amount of condescension needed to rationalize stealing from others as "relieving them of their lands"—and matter-of-factly imply that Indigenous lives were simply "savage" with hopes of becoming "civilized" and "Christian"—is beyond measure. We still hear echoes of these sentiments today.

There was one dissenting voice which perhaps (more) accurately portrayed the atrocities we know were about to take place. His name was Edward Everett, and he was a U.S. Representative at the time. In a speech to Congress, he said about the forcible removal:

Nations of dependent Indians, against their will, under color of law, are driven from their homes into the wilderness. You cannot explain it; you cannot reason it away. . . . Our friends will view this measure with sorrow, and our enemies alone with joy. And we ourselves, Sir, when the interests and passions of the day are past, shall look back upon it, I fear, with self-reproach, and a regret as bitter as unavailing. (Jackson 1980, xii)

Andrew Jackson noted this dissension and then went straight ahead with the removal. Many tribes disagreed and fought it—including the Maskôkî (Creek) and Yat'siminoli (Seminole) tribal nations, a resistance that goes under-discussed. Indigenous scholars have argued that there is substantial evidence that many tribes resisted by also working "within the system," actively challenging the framework of white colonizers by using the colonizers' own senses of paternalism, republicanism, godliness, and territoriality against them to negotiate treaties to benefit the tribes (Black 2009). These analyses of past events represent an attempt to decolonize historical accounts of settler colonialism.

Whether tribal governments did agree, out of fear of harassment by white colonizers, or did not agree, the outcome was largely the same. Their 25-million acres East of the Mississippi were taken—and, by 1837—46,000 Native people were forced across the country. More than 4,000 Tsalagi (Cherokee) people alone died of starvation, cold, and disease on the way to "the West," later termed the Trail of Tears. This left the settlers and plantation owners 25-million acres, through stealing and brutalization, on which to grow their cotton without worry of depletion. By 1860, the cotton industry became so absurdly powerful, and the number of enslaved people so staggering, that the combined value of slaves according to U.S. banks was greater than the value of all the railroads and all the factories in the United States (Desmond 2019).

Racialized Labor and Modern-Day Capitalism

If we closely examine the relationships between white slave owners and Black laborers, we begin to see origins of today's capitalistic reliance on productivity to the point of exhaustion and harm. Plantation owners regularly tracked their workers' hauls, resulting in severe beatings if someone felt short of their quota. It was a catch-22 for Black laborers, who did not want to gather too much, else risk increasing their quota the next time, but also did not want to gather too little for fear of being beaten. In severe cases, pregnant workers were required to lay down in divots to allow a whip to fall flat on their back during flogging (Desmond 2019).

In an interview with the *New York Times'* The 1619 Project, scholar Matthew Desmond, professor of Sociology at Princeton University, said,

"Slavery allowed this poor, fledgling nation to turn into a colossal power-house in the global economy. But what slavery also created was a culture in American capitalism that was incredibly brutal" (2019). As Desmond pointed out implicitly, but I'll make explicit here, colonial systems at their core harbor violence. Because they are defined through expansion and conquest, they devalue and dehumanize the targets they intend to conquer. Similarly, U.S. capitalism—as an extension of white, straight colonial efforts and dominance—dehumanizes the worker under scrutiny for production. Dehumanization and oppression have always been, and may always be, built into this country's very foundations.

ORIENTALISM, IMPERIALISM, AND ASIAN SEXUALITIES

Popularized by the theorist Edward W. Said in his 1978 book by the same name, "Orientalism" has become one of the founding principles of postcolonial and critical race theory. For our purposes, it may be defined as the essentializing or inferiorizing of the "Orient" (i.e., "the East") in direct opposition to the "Occident" (i.e., "the West"). As discussed by Said (1978):

> The Orient is an idea that has a history and a tradition of thought, imagery, and vocabulary that have given it reality and presence in and for the West. The two geographical entities thus support and to an extent reflect each other. (13)

Importantly, this relationship draws upon exaggerations of both Occidental and Oriental traits in order to create a fantasy that is a fictional recapitulation of both East and West. In Orientalism, Asia is not defined by what Asia is. Rather, Asia becomes a fictional version of everything the West is not, one that primarily serves to reinforce the West's own moral conception of itself through Otherness.

Hierarchizing cultures has long been a tradition of Western society, which tends to see the rest of the world through a colonial gaze of superiority (Said 1978). Western desire to exoticize and Orientalize Eastern cultures was highly prevalent in literature and art in the 18th and early 19th centuries, at a time when European imperialism was rampant and the East India Company colonized and exploited trade with East, South, and Southeast Asia (Lawson 2014). These exploitations made it convenient, and perhaps even necessary, for white imperialists to paint Asia—as well as its many cultures and its people—as less evolved or culturally static, an altogether patronizing perspective that devalued and dehumanized non-white global subjects. This is because, as discussed in chapter 1, imperialistic goals are also goals of global and cultural domination. Projecting attributions of inferiority or barbarism helps establish a rationale for that domination.

Indeed, because communications and physical travel between East and West geographical regions were immensely challenging prior to the 20th century, so-called Orientalist scholars often relied either on the stereotypical, fantastical stories conveyed to them by others, or those invented by their own imaginings (Yoshihara 2002). More contemporary Orientalist scholarship has its roots in ancient Greek texts, such as *Persians*, written by playwright Aeschylus, the "father of Greek tragedy," in 472 BCE, which described Persian people as slavish and emotional, opposite the rationality of Greek society (Hall 1989). Other popular texts, such as *Indica* by Ctesias, 15th-century BCE physician and historian, depicted Indian people as "dog-faced creatures," and even "creatures without heads" (Wong 1997, 417). These were hailed at the time as "invaluable findings," and they in no small part contributed to the exoticizing and dehumanizing of Asian people in Western medicine for centuries to come.

The Real-World Consequences of Orientalism

Although often portrayed in the white mainstream as an artifact of the past, much like Black and Native subjugation, Orientalism is not an innocuous scholarly artifact without real-world consequences. The moral inferiority and exoticization projected onto Asian subjects can be deadly. In October 1979, at the First National Lesbian and Gay March on Washington, lesbian Japanese American poet and activist Michiyo Fuyaka, representative of the Asian contingent said,

> We are called the model minority, the quiet, the passive, exotic erotics with the slanted cunt to match our 'slanted' eyes or the small dick to match our small size. But we are not. For years Asian Americans have organized against our oppression. We protested and were lynched, deported and put into concentration camps during World War II. We must not forget that the United States of America has bombed, napalmed and colonized Asian countries for decades. . . . It could rape and murder Vietnamese women, children and men, then claim that "Asians don't value human life." (Tsang 2001, 234)

More recently, in March 2021, six Asian women, four of them Korean Americans, were shot and killed near Atlanta, Georgia, by 21-year-old Robert Aaron Long, a white straight man who had systematically targeted massage parlors in the area (Ramirez 2021). The killings took place amid a surge of hate crimes against Asian Americans during the COVID-19 pandemic (Jeung, Yellow Horse, and Popovic 2021), a reminder that even so-called "model minorities" could be made subject to prejudice and brutalization with the flip of a white supremacy switch. The disproportionate targeting of Asian women and elders in these attacks are hypothesized to be due to racialized stereotypes of submission, which suggest they may be easily overcome or dominated (Ramirez 2021).

As we interrogate the motivation behind this attack, it is clear that these women embodied a racialized trope fetishized by white heteronormative culture in the United States—that of the "comfort women," a term sometimes conflated with "concubine" or "geisha" by those unfamiliar with the unique ethnic and historical origins of the words. It is a trope, I argue, Long knew would ring true with other white straight men, as he instantly named "sex addiction" as a reason for the shooting spree. Long's violent fetishization, then, is a direct descendant of Orientalism built into the nation's racial-sexual hierarchy, which has given white, straight men permission to objectify, sexualize, and dominate Eastern cultures and people (Said 1978).

The Historical Context of Orientalist Attitudes and Systems

There has been limited discussion of the ways in which Psychology and related disciplines maintain and reproduce Orientalist images of Asia and Asian subjects across U.S. history (Bhatia 2002), and queerness has only recently become visible in Asian American studies, with few publications appearing in the 1990s, if any at all (Sueyoshi 2016). Many scholars have pointed to Asian "conservatism" as the source of this dearth; however, in many Asian cultures, a spectrum of sexualities and genders have existed, and indeed, thrived, prior to Western imperialist influences (Alimahomed 2010). There is a dangerous tendency to assume a colonized perspective on Asian sexual and gender identity is the true cultural perspective, but these are false assumptions which invisibilize centuries of history prior to colonial rule and influence.

Asian Queer Criminalizations and "Oriental Depravity"

Orientalism did indeed affect governmental policies and legislation, beginning around 1900—this effect grew with each passing year. In 1900, California's first large-scale public protest against Japanese immigration and residents took place in San Francisco. The featured speaker was Mayor James Phelan, whose virulent anti-Asian attitudes were obvious in his speech, featuring the words, "The Chinese and Japanese are not bona fide citizens. . . . They are not the stuff of which American citizens can be made." In 1905, the *San Francisco Chronicle* launched an anti-Japanese editorial campaign, warning that an invasion of "the little brown men" constituted a grave peril to California (Kamiya 2014). Following suit, the S.F. Board of Supervisors that October ordered all Japanese and Korean students to join the Chinese students in what was renamed the "Oriental Public School." Public agitation around increasing Japanese immigration ultimately resulted in the Immigration Act of 1924, preventing any further Japanese immigration for the next four decades (Hirobe 2001).

In August 1918, San Francisco police officers pulled a body out of the San Francisco Bay, near Pier 28. It was reportedly unrecognizable, as the body had decomposed from water erosion, and the only physical feature noted in the ledger was the darker hair, which had stayed intact. Rather than log the identity as "unknown," however—because dark hair is hardly a feature specific to a single ethnicity—they wrote "John Doe Japanese" (Sueyoshi 2018). At the turn of the century, the (white) mainstream largely viewed East Asians as distinct from one another, often describing Chinese immigrants as "unassimilable" and Japanese immigrants as (at least slightly) more acculturated, although they continued to be targeted in other ways. This simplistic and inaccurate distinction, widely endorsed at the S.F. medical examiner's office, demonstrated the ways in which policing and criminalization manifested specific ethnic constructions. It also demonstrated the ways in which turn-of-the-century Othering directly contrasted with the later widespread conflation of all Asian people as pan-Asian "Orientals," an Othering of a different kind (Sueyoshi 2018).

Queer Chinese men in the 19th century, in particular, being the first wave of Asian immigrants in the United States as laborers, were affected by several oppressive factors—Orientalism, exclusionary practices, and anti-miscegenation laws, to name a few. These factors led to the creation of what many scholars have called "bachelor societies," social circles which forced Asian queer men into feminized occupations, such as laundry workers, domestic laborers, and cooks (Espíritu 1997). In examining early U.S. trade cards, Japanese scholar Yuko Matsukawa (2002) noted the visual and descriptive feminization of Asian queer men through various tactics such as infantilization and the equation of Asian labor with domestic work. Other writers, too, have rallied against these images, most notably the editors of *The Big Aiiieee!*, who lamented that, by the mid-1980s, Asian queer men in the popular media "[were] at their best, effeminate closet queens like Charlie Chan and, at their worst, homosexual menaces like Fu Manchu" (Chan et al. 1991, xiii). Asian queer men thus became highly gendered and desexualized to the white mainstream, as were they unable to vote, could not being citizens, could not work in "masculine occupations," and could not marry. When granted sexuality at all, Asian men were traditionally depicted as a deviation from the norm of white straight masculinity (Lee 1999).

There are few records of queer Asian experiences from 1890 to 1920; however, through the extensive criminalizing of QBIPOC, we have traces of their actions, albeit incomplete pictures of what their lives were like. Shortly after the Chinese Exclusion Act was passed in 1882, for example, there are records detailing the arrests of several Chinese laborers wearing gender nonconforming clothing in the San Francisco Bay Area. In 1908, one such resident, Chin Ling, was arrested in Oakland after reportedly dressing like a "handsome Chinese maiden of the better class" in hopes of allegedly "attracting a husband" for himself (Sueyoshi 2019, 130). Ten years later, in Sacramento, two queer South Asian men, Jamil Singh and Tara Singh, were arrested for soliciting sex from two other men. The myth of predatory Asians sexually pursuing young white (straight) men became so pervasive that criminal courts in the 1910s and 1920s often cited "Oriental depravity" as reason for degeneracy among transient white youth in California (Shah 2005, 703–725).

The Yellow Peril and Early Depictions of Asian Queers

Given the inherent power dynamics in the creation and dissemination of media images, it is not surprising to find that representations of the "East" have a lurid history in Western society. In nearly all existing literature from 1860 to 1900, queer Asians in America existed as a discursive device in public health records and leisure culture that painted them as morally deviant (Lee 1999). If we look at evolving media representations of Orientalism over time, for instance, we see that the earliest depictions of Asianness were highly fetishized and animalistic (Ma 2000), such as the introduction of the "Yellow Peril" motif in 1897 by Russian sociologist Jacques Novikow, which served to integrate three fears: "Western anxieties about sex, racist fears of the alien Other, and the Spenglerian belief that the West will become outnumbered and enslaved by the East" (Leung 2014) and presented Asian men as predatory, mystical, and primitive (Shek 2007). It can feel in recent years that changes are afoot, with movies like *Minari* (2021) and *The Half of It* (2021) portraying more realistic encounters. However, while changes do exist, Orientalism still commonly manifests today, resulting in projections that are fundamentally foreign and threatening (Sun et al. 2015).

Moving into the 20th century, the Yellow Peril motif transitioned to routine portrayals of Asian men as meek houseboys or asexual sidekicks who largely existed to fill feminine acting roles when Asian women were scarce (Hamamoto 1994). Several scholars have noted the Orientalist exoticization of Asian American sexualities in the United States, including the desexualization of men and hypersexualization of women. Queer Asian American scholar Rosalind Chou (2012) wrote that

[w]hile all men of color face racist, gender-specific constructions, there is something clearly unique about the construction of Asian American men that makes emasculating public humiliation seem safer to the assailants. East Asian-looking men are constructed as physically weak and nonthreatening in the white racial frame. (105)

Indeed, it seems that Asian women are sexualized for the same reason men are asexualized—both support the white man's virility and superiority in the context of Orientalism (Kim 1982, 70). In other words, the evolving discourse and representations of racialized and sexualized Others is socially and politically dependent on the positionalities of white straight persons defining that discourse. These analyses become more complex as we look at gender and sexual constructions and their intersections with QBIPOC identities.

Orientializing Queer Intimacies and Desire

Queer intimacies and sex, although obviously affected by Orientalism, seemed nearly absent in early Asian American histories in the United States, despite the fact that we know they did exist and perhaps thrive in many respects. Kosen Takahashi, an illustrator for *Shin Sekai*—a pioneering 19th-century Japanese American newspaper in San Francisco—publicly declared himself at one time "the most queer boy among all Nipponese" to a local journalist in 1899 (Sueyoshi 2012, 80). Takahashi's intimate relationship with Japanese American queer poet Yone Noguchi is well-documented, as is Noguchi's many escapades with men in Oakland and Los Angeles in the early 20th century, including white queer poets Joaquin Miller and Charles Warren Stoddard, well-known creators in their own right (Sueyoshi 2020). These queer intimacies existed within a larger social context in California, where it was common to flaunt white interest in Asian men, what might be considered today "yellow fever." Referring to Asian queer sexual partners as "brownies," white men at the time wrote of their somewhat fetishistic "social favors" to Asian men, such as invitations for long-term residencies at their homes (Sueyoshi 2019), which may have been advantageous for Asian queers hoping to temporarily elevate their social statuses.

Orientalized Desire and "M. Butterfly"

Depictions of Intersectional Others in performance can be a window into contemporary mainstream views on racial-sexual tensions. We can see these complex tensions acted out in the Tony award-winning production *M. Butterfly* (1988), by Chinese American playwright David Henry Hwang, for instance, which peers into the complicated romantic and sexual relationship between Chinese opera singer Song Liling and white French civil servant Rene Gallimard—the play was inspired by Puccini's *Madama Butterfly* (1904). As women were banned from acting on stage in China during the time, Liling, a queer cis man, took on the role of a woman in his opera, and met Gallimard without dropping the pretense. Although Liling and Gallimard fall in love and remain together for 20 years in total, Gallimard is somehow "taken by surprise" by the end of the production when he finds out Liling was a queer cis man all along, and a spy to boot (Hwang 1988).

Hwang commented in an interview with *Huffington Post* that "the lines between gay and straight become very blurred in this play, but I think [Gallimard] knows he's having an affair with a man. Therefore, on some level he is gay" (Young 2016). Although Gallimard ultimately rejects Liling and they separate, he dons Liling's kimono, makeup, and wig in the final act and commits suicide—the insinuated attachment to Liling and gender performance of the scene caused many who watched the production to assume Gallimard was actually a closeted queer himself. While Hwang's production is a commentary on the performance of gender and its intersections with race, theater critics have pointed out that it stops short of any "foray into nonbinary or transgender identities" (Lewis 2017), an exploration that may have lent to the complexity of gender constructions in the production, but instead was absent. In fact, Hwang reportedly interviewed several gender nonconforming people prior to the first performance, and concluded Liling was gay, and not trans (Lewis 2017).

The production is an illustration of the way in which Orientalism pervades the imaginations of the white mainstream, constructing an overtly feminized version of Asian queerness. In the play, Liling said, "The West thinks of itself as masculine—big guns, big industry, big money—so the East is feminine—weak, delicate, poor." He continued, "I am an Oriental. And being an Oriental, I could never be completely a man" (Hwang 1988, 83). That is, Gallimard's resistance to see Liling as anything other than a woman, despite the long-term nature of their relationship, is not truly due to Liling's deception, but rather it is undergirded by the East-West binary constructed through colonial and Orientalist histories. Due to the financial and critical success of the play, we can conclude that these beliefs are not only entertained but likely shared by the mainstream.

Contemporary sexual racism within queer communities is an extension of the *M. Butterfly* metaphor. Under Orientalism, Asian queer racial, sexual and gender constructions inform each other, with racial markers often defining what the mainstream considers "feminine" and "masculine," or "sexual" and "asexual." The effeminate projections of the white mainstream onto

Asian men is also present perhaps even more so, for Asian queer men. One study demonstrated that white drag performers, for instance, felt that Asians in drag "passed" more easily, and thus had a greater chance of winning competitions due to what they felt was a higher level of innate femininity, referring to their smaller stature and features (Han 2006, 83). The performers therefore bought into was society's Orientalist feminized constructions of Asian queer men.

Orientalism and the "Terrorist"

The projection of foreignness is perhaps most saliently seen in the projection of terrorism on Brown Asian, Arab, and Muslim lives and bodies. Xenophobia and Islamophobia, which refers to the unfounded fear, negativity and hostility toward immigrants and Muslims, respectively (Johnston 2016), are parts of Orientalism that manifest as opposites to constructs of United States nationhood and citizenship. The manifestation of xenophobia and Islamophobia provides justification for atrocities against Brown communities, and ultimately has a negative impact on the health of those affected. A study by Haque, Tubbs, Kahumoku-Fessler, and Brown (2019) on Muslim American mental health identified several repercussions as a result of constantly having to defending Islam, such as stress and isolation when confronted by peers and co-workers, feelings of overwhelm at being a token minority, as well as general anxiety and fear for safety due to public perceptions of Muslims in the United States. Propaganda and prevailing negative sentiments toward Islam likely contributed to the internalization of some of these sentiments.

In July 2008, during the presidential campaign season, the former presidential family, Barack and Michelle Obama, were featured in a satirical cartoon on the cover of the *New Yorker*, dressed as radical American flag-burning Muslim terrorists, Osama bin Laden in tow. The cartoonist depicted what the country already knew to be true, that Muslimness and Brownness had become tied, without question, in the U.S. mainstream imagination to un-Americanness (Rahman 2010). There is a common misconception that 9/11 created the stereotype of the "Arab terrorist." In actuality, propaganda related to this event only intensified the prejudicial rhetoric that already existed (Whidden 2000), aggravating stereotypes about Muslims as being terrorists and violent by nature (Haque 2004).

As noted by queer theorist Jasbir Paur, there is a strong association between U.S. expectionalism, Islamophobia, and queerness. This was perhaps most obvious in the national reactions to the 2004 Abu Ghraib torture scandal, in which photographs were released showing evidence that guards forced prisoners to perform "homosexual" acts (Puar 2018). She said,

The Abu Ghraib saga demonstrates that sexuality is at once absolutely crucial to the production of the geopolitics of American exceptionalism, and despite this critical role, or perhaps because of it, it is an undertheorized, underrated, and often avoided aspect of the debate on the war on terror. (124)

Prior to the 2004 scandal, national organizations, like National Gay and Lesbian Task Force (NGLTF) and the Human Rights Commission (HRC), were far more concerned with gay marriage rights and gays in the military than the war on terrorism and welfare of Brown queer people.

There is considerable evidence that terrorism in the United States is driven primarily by radicalized, conservative white, straight individuals and groups (Beltran 2020), rather than by the Black and Brown communities who are most often allotted the stereotype. Two false narratives abound due to Orientalism, perceived threat, and prejudice. One is that "terrorists are always (brown) muslims." The other is that "white people are never terrorists" (Corbin 2017, 455). Of course, neither of these is true, and the binary this creates only serves to perpetuate prejudicial realities. When a white Christian individual commits violence in the name of God, they are portrayed humanely, and we strive to understand the nuance of that individual's family background and mental health (Stern 2003). Conversely, when a Brown Muslim person commits violence in the name of God, they are immediately categorized, judged, and condemned by society (Jarvis 2016).

THE PSYCHOLOGICAL LEGACY OF COLONIALISM

Several works have attempted to discern and define the United States' postcolonial legacy for marginalized people. Discussing this topic, Black Martiniquais revolutionary psychiatrist Frantz Fanon (1961) states that "[i]mperialism leaves behind germs of rot which we must clinically detect and remove from our land but from our minds as well." He elaborated that colonialism's systematic denigration of the colonized person and the continuous denial of the colonized person's humanity led to self-doubt, identity confusion, or feelings of inferiority among the colonized. Later, Tunisian Jewish author Albert Memmi (1965), in his book, *The Colonizer and the Colonized*, added that the colonized might eventually come to believe they possessed an identity consistent with the colonizer's negative perceptions of them.

Perhaps the most relevant recent body of literature is that of Filipino American scholar and University of Alaska professor of Clinical-Community Psychology E. J. R. David's "colonial mentality," defined as the adoption and internalization of the colonizer's value systems, culture, behaviors, and oppression by the colonized (David 2008; David and Okazaki 2006). Echoing these sentiments, professor of Art Studies at the University of the Philippines, Felipe de Leon Jr. (2014), wrote of Filipino/a/x connectivity:

> The moment we began to view ourselves through Western eyes, what we held sacred suddenly became worthless, our virtues turned into vices, our strengths turned into weaknesses, and our triumphs into failures. We could no longer be proud of anything truly our own and began to regard anything native as primitive and undeveloped. Anything indigenous became a source of embarrassment and uneasiness. (1)

Much of colonial mentality research has specifically targeted the impacts on Filipino/a/x Americans, who have been, and continue to be, greatly affected by the U.S. imperialist regime, which colonized, militarized, and reformed the education system in the Philippines, leading to what one Filipina American scholar has suggested is an ongoing cultural identity crisis and confusion on what constitutes "genuine" Filipino/a/x culture (Cordova 1973). Perhaps unsurprisingly, after developing the Colonial Mentality Scale and surveying participants in the United States, David and Okazaki (2006) found that colonial mentality was associated with internalized racism.

Recent scholarship has used findings from Fanon and Memmi's work to identify associations between colonization and modern-day sociostructural inequities and mental health. It has found between colonization and increased substance use and domestic violence among Native people (McBride 2002; Braveheart-Jordan and DeBruyn 1995), as well as the denigration of culture, intra-community discrimination, and oppression tolerance of Filipino/a/x Americans (David and Okazaki 2006). Some Indigenous scholars have even described the pain of colonization as a deep "soul wound," one which continues to affect Native communities intergenerationally today (Duran and Duran 1995, 27). It may be that, indeed, all communities historically Othered by colonialism have soul wounds such as Duran and Duran (1995) described, for the effects of colonization not only pervade the bodies of the colonized but also their psyches and, more deeply, their spirits.

THE ROLE OF LIBERATION IN DECOLONIZATION

Writing in the context of Algerian liberation, psychiatrist Frantz Fanon noted first-hand how prevailing knowledge and practice in Psychology and related fields tended to reflect and serve the interests of colonialism. In *Wretched of the Earth*, Fanon (1961) charged that it is the duty of researchers and practitioners in power to decolonize intellectual discourse, to reject the "caricature" of white colonial mentality, and to seek out other ideologies. However, because we are a country of colonizers and colonized, our understanding of race, sexuality, gender—and indeed psychological science itself—are limited by the colonial lens.

We could argue that Fanon's critiques remain largely unfollowed. Mainstream research continues to promote the work of highly educated, affluent, white, cis, straight individuals (Delgado 1984; Heinrich, Heine, and Norenzayan 2010)—the privileged among us. And by consequence, whenever research is directed toward understanding marginalized groups, that research is heavily framed by the lens of these privileged folk, resulting in literature that exoticizes and dehumanizes groups that are unlike them. The question then remains—is it even possible to decolonize, or liberate, notions of "race" or "sexuality"? And if so, how can we do this? Black lesbian author and activist Audre Lorde (2003) noted this double-bind when she wrote that "the master's tools will never dismantle the master's house. They may allow us to temporarily beat him at his own game, but they will never enable us to bring about genuine change" (27).

Liberation of the colonial system and oppression are the true goals of the colonized, as each is constrained by white supremacy and suffers from the traumas colonization brings with it. But as idyllic as liberation sounds, it is much more difficult to achieve. During a 2020 interview with Trevor Noah on *The Daily Show*, Eddie Glaude Jr., chair and professor of African American Studies at Princeton University, remarked, "Here we are in a moment of moral reckoning, where the country can be otherwise, but every single time we try to give birth to a new nation, the umbilical cord of white supremacy is wrapped around its neck" (Shilcutt 2021). The paradoxical image of an infant restrained by its own parent's cord is a comment on the constant tension today between white supremacy and those who would be free of it. It may not ever be possible to entirely "cut the cord" of white supremacy, but liberation theorists can guide us toward a more liberatory future.

Recognizing the Coloniality of Power, Knowledge, and Being

In her book *Purpose of Power*, Black queer cofounder of Black Lives Matter, Alicia Garza (2021), wrote:

> When people come together to solve problems, they do not automatically become immune to the distorted ways society and the economy are organized. We bring the things that shape us, consciously and unconsciously, wherever we go. Unless we are intentional about interrupting what we've learned, we will perpetuate it, even as we are working for a better world. (201)

Living in a colonial entity like the United States, we are all held within the constraints of what some scholars have termed the "coloniality of power"

(Quijano 2000, 534), as well as its sequelae, the "coloniality of knowledge" (e.g., definitions of knowledge and subjectivity), and the "coloniality of being" (e.g., definitions of race, gender, sexuality) (Mignolo 2002, 451). That is, we exist in a world with hierarchical organizations of society and its people, historically and discursively placing Western ideology on the top of that hierarchy and condemning all other people and their ideologies to marginalization and invisibility. That power hierarchy also leads to a hierarchy of learning and definitions, as well as one of identities (Mignolo 2002). We are not all equally regarded in U.S. society but defined through the histories that have brought us to this point.

Therefore, the first mechanism of liberation is acknowledging that our "everyday reality" is biased and in fact not a natural reality at all—it is a contrived reality that serves dominant pedagogy and those in power (Martín-Baró 1994, 16–25). The subjects that we consider "worth studying," our notions of how we "should be practicing," and even the establishment of data norms, are all embedded within this biased system. If we accept these critiques, it is not a reach to say that our everyday realities are racialized and sexualized to disempower Intersectional Others. Rejecting the normality of these assumptions, then, is essential to critically evaluating the construct of "power" itself, those in power, and those disempowered.

Part of this is the decolonization of language, as colonizers create and impose language for the colonized through their own experiences, a concept known in scholarship as "linguistic imperialism." This is partially done through the imposition of educational systems, such as boarding schools for Native Americans (Haag 2007), which perpetrated the erasure of tribal languages through threats of mental and bodily atrocity. When we use the colonizer's language, to define our own identities and conversations, we in essence trap ourselves in our own internalized oppression. Deconstructing and reclaiming the language of the colonized prior to assimilation can do significant work toward decolonizing our minds and livelihoods.

In his work *Decolonising the Mind* (1986), Ngũgĩ wa Thiong'o, a Gikuyu communication scholar who initially published his works in English but committed to solely publishing in Gikuyu after writing the aforementioned book, said of this topic:

> Language carries culture, and culture carries, particularly through orature and literature, the entire body of values by which we perceive ourselves and our place in the world. . . . Language is thus inseparable from ourselves as a community of human beings with a specific form and character, a specific history, a specific relationship to the world. (15-16)

Because colonization is accompanied by the silencing of the colonized by the colonizers to diminish the likelihood of them regaining power and selfhood, language reclamation and abrogation—the rejection of the colonizer's language as dominant and normal—become all the more important, as they are, in effect, "de-silencing" and, therefore, acts of empowerment. Language and culture are inseparable, as are language and power.

Recovering Historical Memory

Second, we must recover our historical memory (Fals-Borda 2013, 155) by recognizing that history itself is set by those in power. It is a fallacy to assume that history is factual by nature. To believe history is made exclusively of facts is to take the word of the oppressor at face value. In reality, history is determined by subjective evidence. The victor of a war will determine what is written about their conquests. Prevailing narratives of such a war will therefore portray the motivation and outcome of the war not as cultural violence but as cultural progress.

Conquerors are by nature invested in collective forgetfulness, because not doing so is admitting atrocities inherent to any colonial system—rape, murder, and cultural erasure. It is for this reason that governmental bodies, such as the former Trump administration, and other systems in U.S. white heteronormative culture, are heavily invested in the idea that the nation is an equitable, just society, because to not invest would mean admitting systemic injustice may be the true narrative of our country. As human beings, we all resist the notion that we are bearers of injustice. It is much more comfortable to label ourselves the bearers of "progress" and "civilization."

Assimilation and Its Bearing on Historical Memory

Assimilation is not a neutral concept, despite its use interchangeably by some sociological and psychological experts with acculturation—also not a neutral concept, importantly. I can distinctly remember studying for graduate school exams and having these terms defined in text for me, devoid of their aggressive associations. Swiss psychologist Jean Piaget defined "assimilation" as "a process whereby people of a culture learn to adapt to the ways of the majority culture" (Ginn 1995, 10). This definition is a great example of the ways in which oppressive pedagogy may pervade our field—the connection to trauma goes undiscussed and the definition is therefore divorced of its true meaning.

When the United States instituted the Civilization Fund Act of 1819, which authorized missionaries and church leaders to "civilize" Indigenous people, the boarding school era began (Haag 2007). Native families who did not comply with assimilation immediately, and even those who did, suffered physical consequences, including documented reports of sexual abuse (Irwin and Roll 1995). Some children or families went missing. Some were killed

(Little 2017). The boarding school era carries with it a traumatic legacy of loss, brutalization, deep sadness, and rage. Yet, these events are rarely known outside the Native community, as the U.S. educational system neglects to mention them, leading non-Native children to believe the narratives they were given—that colonization efforts were more akin to peaceful treaty negotiation, not a slaughter. To recover historical memory, intentional efforts must be made by researchers to seek outside narratives and to see such narratives as equally valid.

Empowering the Disempowered

Third, to achieve liberation from colonization, we must bring awareness to, and uplift, marginalized voices. This requires a significant shift in the priorities of Psychology and related fields, however, which have historically pathologized Intersectional Others. Therefore, it is not enough to include those who have been pathologized. The term "inclusivity" implies that marginalized people are being seated at the table, or at least exist somewhere in the room, with those making decisions. While this is an improvement over exclusivity and invisibility, it does not mean the voices of the disempowered are heard.

Making marginalized voices the center of conversation and the owners of their own experiences is the only true path forward and the only means through which we can decolonize intellectual discourse. The "indigenization" of psychology is an example of this—the active work of infusing therapy and research with cultural practices of local tribes, destigmatizing and empowering Two-Spirit identity, consultations with Native leaders and community members, and the promotion of Native leadership within, or importantly *without*, an organization or system. What we are looking for, then, are equity and justice—not simply the inclusion of a marginalized person in the room where decisions are being made—but providing access and actively promoting opportunities for QBIPOC at every level, particularly at the highest levels. This means restoring rights, memory, and privilege to marginalized people, as well as their humanity.

SELF-DETERMINATION AS
DECOLONIAL RESISTANCE

It is only natural that conversations around decolonization and social power have risen due to the immense efforts of Indigenous voices. Native queer and Two-Spirit activism challenge settler colonialism and white queerness by recalling legacies of resistance and forming Native modernities, communities, and politics that affirm the survival and resurgence of Native peoples. One of the primary mechanisms for decolonial resistance is the *insistence* of self-determination for Indigenous people. We can think of self-determination as a force that sits between the personal and social, a space in which much of our freedom, as human beings, lies. Several queer scholars have written about the possibilities for activism that exist between the personal and social realms (Jones and Adams 2016; Quesada, Gomez, and Vidal-Ortiz 2015).

For Indigenous folks, self-determination is an issue tied innately to sovereignty—its importance was recognized by the United Nations (UN) and ratified through Article 1 of the 1945 UN Charter, although loosely defined, stating, "All peoples have the right of self-determination. By virtue of that right they freely determine their political status and freely pursue their economic, social and cultural development." Beginning in the 1950s that formalized definition became an important social and political tool for decolonial efforts and was successfully grafted onto ongoing talks about human rights norms in the UN (Reus-Smit 2013). The fight for self-determination thrives in places like Hawai'i, where the unrightful overthrow of the Hawaiian Kingdom in 1893 is heavily contested by Kānaka Maoli (Native Hawaiian) people, with significant public support (Kauanui 2008).

Indigenous scholars have argued that self-determination and indeed the very essence of cultural identity are intertwined with a decolonizing responsibility (Alfred 2015; Corntassel 2012), as well as the invocation of Native peoples' personal and collective relationships with the land. Kanien'kehá:ka (Mohawk) scholar Taiaiake Alfred (2015) wrote that these methodologies are

> symbolic of the social and cultural force alive among Onkwehonwe [Indigenous peoples] dedicated to altering the balance of political and economic power to recreate some social and physical space for freedom to re-emerge. Wasáse is an ethical and political vision, the real demonstration of our resolve to survive as Onkwehonwe and to do what we must to force the Settlers to acknowledge our existence and the integrity of our connection to the land. (Alfred 2005, 19)

Resurgence and Regeneration, *Not* Recognition and Reconciliation

It may be problematic to rely on government support of the right to self-determination, as it is the U.S. government which created systems of colonial dependence to the detriment of Intersectional Others historically. Tsalagi (Cherokee) scholar Jeff Corntassel (2012) argued that any mobilization strategy "premised on state recognition of Indigenous self-determination, will not lead to a sustainable self-determination process that restores and regenerates Indigenous nations" (92).

Indeed, simply calling upon others to *recognize* (Coulthard 2007) Indigenous rights to self-determination is not enough to change the underlying structures at play in Indigenous disenfranchisement and violence, nor is *reconciliation* enough to do so (Corntassel 2012). This is because recognition and reconciliatory discourse are based on a premise of inclusion by the colonial state, rather than the idea of revolutionizing or deconstructing it. One common instance of reconciliation strategies is the "grand apology," a gesture often offered by the head of a settler-colonial entity for optics, and to further bring Indigenous and other people into the proverbial fold.

In June 2006, for instance, then Canadian prime minister Stephen Harper issued an apology in the House of Commons to Chinese Canadians who had historically been impacted by racist policies in the country. He said, "We fully accept the moral responsibility to acknowledge these shameful policies of our past," and then stated, "On behalf of all Canadians of the government of Canada, we offer full apology to Chinese Canadians for the head tax and express our deepest sorrow for the subsequent exclusion of Chinese immigrants" (House of Commons 2006, iii). Twenty thousand dollar was also given to the last remaining Chinese Canadian elders who paid the "head tax," but few at the time were alive to receive the settlement (Wong 2019). Ultimately, while the elders accepted the settlements, the acceptances gave the Canadian government an ability to optically claim they appealed, and were forgiven, for the longstanding bigotry. While reparations are certainly deserved, relying solely on strategies such as these further enshrine colonial histories and aid in colonial agendas of assimilation.

To this effect, Diné political theorist Glen Coulthard (2007) said, "the politics of recognition in its contemporary form promises to reproduce the very configurations of colonial power that Indigenous peoples' demands for recognition have historically sought to transcend" (437). Indeed, harkening back to the earlier Audre Lorde quote, we cannot seek to tear down the master's house with the master's tools (Lorde 2013). Instead, it is important to seek community-based resurgence (Alfred and Corntassel 2005) and *regeneration* (Alfred 2009), and find ways to implement changes in our everyday lives. If colonization is a disconnecting force, then resurgence is about reconnecting with homelands, cultures, and communities. Both decolonization and resurgence facilitate a renewal of our roles and responsibilities as Indigenous peoples to the sustainable praxis of Indigenous livelihoods, food security, community governance, and relationships to the natural world and ceremonial life that enables the transmission of these cultural practices to future generations (Corntassel 2008).

Michi Saagiig Nishnaabeg (Alderville First Nation) artist and scholar Leanne Betasamosake Simpson (2008) pointed out, "Indigenous Knowledge is critical for resurgence" (75). Resurgence *must* include the grassroots efforts of Native activists, elders, and teachers who understand that Indigenous teachings must be centered in decolonization. Change of this magnitude tends to happen in small increments, "one warrior at a time" (Alfred and Corntassel 2005, 613). Elders and teachers, as mentors grounded in Indigenous knowledge, may take up renewed responsibilities of assisting others in their reconnections to land, culture, and community. Resurgence and regenerative praxis may also include the use of ceremony or community-building, such as in the Kanien'kehá:ka (Mohawk) war dance ceremony, Wasáse, or the concept of "digadatsele'i," a Tsalagi (Cherokee) word which holds the sentiment of "we belong to each other." Digadatsele'i, as a way of being, breaks through colonial definitions of the nuclear family, instead assuming the need for a "series of radiating responsibilities," as well as active reciprocation within Indigenous communities to guarantee the well-being of the collective (Simpson 2008).

Chapter 5

Dehumanization and Power

To understand how to empower ourselves, we must first understand the need of the oppressor to dehumanize the Intersectional Other, for without this understanding of the oppressor and their systems, we will also not understand how to dismantle them. What is oppression but the extraction of humanity and value from those who are Othered? For instance, racism and homophobia take from their targets—they take their livelihoods, their safety, their labor, their futures, and their family's futures. They do this by means of several factors, including the social systems which have been built to dehumanize Intersectional Others over time, such as mass incarceration in the prison system; housing inequality and resegregation; degradation and invisibility in the media; as well as police brutality and legal injustice.

When former president Donald Trump was running for the first time in the Republican presidential primary, a myriad of scholars, leaders, and members of the public expressed concern at the dehumanizing language he used to describe marginalized people (Oh 2020; Pavetich and Stathi 2021; Warnock 2019). Immigrants were the first on the chopping block, starting with the Mexican "rapists" at a 2015 campaign event, who he claimed were crossing the border illegally at "high numbers" (Saul 2017). Then, in 2016, he publicly referred to Syrian refugees as "trojan horses" for terrorists hoping to enter the United States (Rucker and Phillip 2017). In 2020, he regularly tweeted that Black Lives Matter protesters were "thugs" and called the novel coronavirus the "Chinese virus" (Beer 2021). A pattern of dehumanizing behavior and rhetoric was thus established. But, despite the outrage Trump encountered on a national level, many of Trump's supporters seemed unfazed, leading some researchers to conclude that dehumanization was actually a foundational element of his base (McElwee and McDaniel 2016).

Dehumanization is by no means a strictly internal process—it has far-reaching, detrimental psychological and societal consequences. Research has found, for instance, that dehumanization may motivate the development of hostile policies toward marginalized communities, such as the incarceration and separation of immigrant families at the border, the Muslim ban, and police militarization, to name a few (Cassese 2021; Kteily and Bruneau 2017). Indeed, one study on this topic drew a striking association between blatant dehumanization of Muslims and Mexicans in the United States and membership in the Republican Party, even controlling for political conservatism (Kteily and Bruneau 2017). If we can draw these types of associations, it may imply that dehumanization is far more widespread than reported in the literature, as most studies focus on public displays, not the personal beliefs of party members and individuals.

EXPLICIT AND IMPLICIT DEHUMANIZATION

Dehumanization often proceeds, and is used to justify, prejudicial and oppressive behavior toward Intersectional Others. It has been historically defined as the denial of full humanness, as well as the cruelty and suffering that accompany it, and frequently involves a perception of the Other as incapable of self-restraint or impulse control, having minimal intelligence, and being devoid of culture and morality (Haslam 2006). Researchers have found that dehumanization can manifest both implicitly and explicitly (Kteily et al. 2016), both of which have been used to Other marginalized people historically.

When dehumanizing perceptions by (white) mainstream society, for instance, lead to the imposition of damaging stereotypes and behaviors on the Othered, dehumanization moves from implicit to explicit in nature. A consistent theme of explicit dehumanization is the likening of people to animals, as in calling them "savages" with primal appetites. Experimental research has shown that the use of animal metaphors in Othering is associated with feelings of degradation or disgust on the part of the perpetrator(s) (Hodson et al. 2014). Haslam and Loughlan (2014), for example, identified that the act of likening a group of people to "apes" or "dogs"—as is common in racist tropes toward Black folks—was often associated with degradation, while likening a group to "rats" or "pigs"—common in racist tropes toward Asian and Jewish folks—was associated with disgust. Other types of explicit dehumanization include perceptions about the Other being "deviant" or "enemies" (Jackson and Gaertner 2010).

Implicit dehumanization, on the other hand, may involve the same associations, but they are not at the conscious level. Goff and colleagues (2008) conducted an interesting series of studies focused on the implicit dehumanization of Black Americans. In the first study, they measured reaction times for participants who were primed with images of either Black or white faces, and then tasked the participants with staring at the fuzzy image of an ape. They found that, hands-down, participants more quickly identified the ape when they were primed with Black faces. In contrast, those primed with white faces took longer to identify the ape. The difference was about six frames on average. The source of the association was unclear, so researchers conducted the same experiment again, but used both an ape and African cat image, testing to see if it was simply the African continent, not apes, that participants associated with Black faces. The result was repeated, demonstrating that the association was, in fact, with apes, specifically.

The results of the last two studies in the series were even more disturbing. In one, participants were shown a video of Rodney King being beaten by the police and told either the victim was Black or white. They were either primed with ape words or cat words. Every participant reported that the police brutality was unjustified, except those in the group primed with ape words, who were told the victim was Black. The link between Blackness and racialized dehumanization was clear. In the last study, the researchers wanted to see how this might translate to the criminal justice system. They researched 183 death penalty-eligible court cases over a 20-year span and coded for ape-like words, such as "beast" or "jungle." They found that, not only did Black defendants have significantly more ape descriptors ascribed to them, but that the more ape descriptors they had, the more likely they were to be put to death (Goff et al. 2008).

The technologies we create share our biases. Most recently, in June 2021, Facebook artificial intelligence labeled a video of Black folks "primates," and prompted viewers to continue "seeing videos about Primates." In 2015, Google's artificial intelligence similarly auto-tagged Black photos with "gorillas" (Lyons 2021). Both companies issued apologies, but clearly demonstrated dehumanizing bias against Blackness. Even outside our conscious awareness, these acts of dehumanization can have real, even fatal, impacts on the Othered. It is altogether too convenient to blame political leaders, like former president Donald Trump and Republican congress members, for increasing levels of dehumanization. The reality is, dehumanization—such as that seen in chapter 1 when we discussed scientific racism—has been used as a tool for centuries to more effectively subjugate marginalized people. Its legacy, as Goff and colleagues (2008) have shown, is far-reaching and furthers discrimination and oppression in U.S. society today.

Infra-Humanization

As human beings, we all experience the same basic emotions—fear, anger, happiness, surprise, disgust, and sadness (Ekman et al. 1987)—though the expression of those emotions is culturally bound. However, there is evidence that we attribute uniquely human emotions (UEs)—more complex feelings, such as love, regret, or nostalgia—solely to our ingroup, but do not grant the outgroup the same (Leyens et al. 2008). The frightening result of this phenomenon, called "infra-humanization," is that we believe outgroup members are just a little "less human" than we are.

In the same way an authoritarian parent might call their child "weak" for crying or being "overly emotional," emotional suppression has historically been used by society's oppressors to invalidate and make unavailable a basic human need for Intersectional Others. Stripping Intersectional Others of their emotional capacity and expression—and attaching negative stereotypes or character attributions to normal emotional experiences—is a common, insidious method of dehumanization rooted in infra-humanization. One study suggests, in fact, that this phenomenon is so robust that ingroup members, even presented with evidence to the contrary, will actively avoid incorporating the contrary evidence into their outgroup concept (Leyens et al. 2008). That being said, we can still bring infra-humanization into conscious awareness. It just means that enacting change and preventing harm may be more challenging than simply telling ourselves to do so.

DEHUMANIZATION IN PSYCHOLOGY AND MEDICINE

The fields of Psychology and Medicine have historically been dominated by white straight men, with roots in dehumanizing and oppressive policies and practice. More recent studies suggest that racism and queerphobia are still prevalent in the experiences of Intersectional Others accessing healthcare (Howard et al. 2019). From the Tuskegee experiments—in which Black Alabamans were injected with syphilis, many perishing under the guise of free medical care, from 1932 to 1972—to the pathologization of "Homosexuality" as a disorder by the World Health Organization until 1992, when the International Statistical Classification of Diseases and Related Health Problems (ICD-10) was finally published eliminating the diagnostic category, there had been a strong bias against viewing queer Black, Indigenous, and People of Color (QBIPOC) as "normal" and "medically well" (Johnson et al. 2004). I want all readers, including therapists, to consider how it would feel to seek treatment from an institution you know has a history of Othering you in this manner. How trusting would you be? How safe would you feel? We cannot ignore the pathologization our fields have historically created for marginalized people, because these will inevitably impact our stances, choices, and feelings as providers.

Psychotherapeutic Othering

Mental health professionals, as cogs in an oppressive medical machine, act as gatekeepers for identity affirmation. There are several problems associated with this. The first one is that therapists are not neutral or apolitical entities. We hold just as much bias as any other person, and that bias can lead to a stigmatic reaction in therapy, not to mention detrimental consequences for our clients. Psychotherapy may be rooted in an ethos of care for the common good, but it has, for the most part, been a white, straight privileged profession. Hence, training and treatment has focused on these populations as well. For marginalized patients, this manifests as a profound inequality in the lack of access to therapy services and disproportionate risk for developing mental health issues, particularly depression, trauma, suicidality, and psychosis (Bostwick et al. 2014; Williams et al. 2018). For therapists, we see a therapy workforce that is majority white, straight, and cis, which creates a challenging situation for therapists with marginalized identities who are available as they easily become overwhelmed with requests and higher risk cases (Miu and Moore 2021).

A 2013 study by the American Psychological Association (APA) Center for Workforce Studies revealed a startling trend—83.6% of psychologists were white, with Black psychologists comprising only 5.3% of the workforce, Latino/a/x only 5%, and Asian American only 4.3% (Lin et al. 2015), despite the fact that studies have shown identity-matching (i.e., when your therapist's identities mirror your own) matters in therapy (Meyer, Zane, and Cho 2011; Thompson and Alexander 2006). Native American and Pacific Islander therapists were not parsed out in the APA study, but lumped into the Other category, an oversight that likely indicates that they are both extremely underrepresented, as well as the fact that there is bias in the field toward cultural erasure of Native and Pacific Islander people. These disparities have an impact on the quality of therapy for marginalized clients, who have unique needs.

Studies have indicated that there is often a large disparity between therapist and client ratings of psychotherapeutic services. One study found that, while 75% of therapists believed that their services met the "cultural needs" of their Black, Indigenous, and People of Color (BIPOC) clients, only 10% of their clients felt the same (Khan 2020). Other studies have similarly found that queer and BIPOC clients have a general distaste for their therapy prospects when looking for a provider (Crawford et al. 2016). These are not just due to the mismatch in client-therapist identities but also manifestations of Othering that occur as a result, such as the use of therapeutic modalities that are not well-suited for the complexity and types of stress that marginalized patients bring to the table, a lack cultural humility, cultural disaffirmation, or even active stigmatization or discrimination against clients, either due to implicit or explicit bias (Lee et al. 2018; Shelton and Delgado-Romero 2013). Common examples of these include misgendering, refusing to treat QBIPOC people, or succumbing to racial stereotypes, such as the fact that Asian Americans must excel academically or don't deal with discrimination because they are a "model minority."

Queer therapists of color are even more underrepresented. As of August 2021, there are only 30 therapists in the entire San Francisco Bay Area, for instance, listed on the National Queer and Trans Therapists of Color Network (NQTTCN) directory, the largest of its kind. Class also plays a large factor, because everything in therapy—from the language we use to conduct therapy to expectations—is organized around middle-class, what we might think of as "mainstream," values. This contributes to an often-inhospitable therapeutic environment for not just marginalized patients, but marginalized students training to be therapists, both of whom may have higher dropout rates. People who share these experiences will feel "at home" with the framework espoused by their therapist, but people who do not may feel alienated, misunderstood, and unseen.

CBT and the Ethics of Neutrality

Sigmund Freud was the first to introduce the idea that therapists should be a "blank slate" when conducting psychotherapy, allowing for a pure reflection of a client's internal process. With increasing awareness of social inequities due to Black Lives Matter activism, many professions are reevaluating their stances on social issues, politics, and neutrality. Unfortunately, Psychology graduate programs still often portray the neutral therapeutic stance, with little to no self-disclosure, as the "best" way to conduct a relationship with a client (Gelso and Kanninen 2017). But, if you listen closely to the experiences of queer clients of color, you will hear that identity simply cannot be blank. In fact, pretending that a therapist can hold illusory blankness when their identities (a) are visible to the client, (b) may help or hurt a client due to mirrored oppression, or (c) may contribute to their actual therapeutic practices could easily be labeled willful ignorance. Even the "blankest" of therapists will react to the oppressive realities of our world through their speech, appearance, nonverbal expression, and importantly, their biases (Smith, Chambers, and Bratini 2009). Ultimately, Intersectional Others have needs that require affirmation, openness, and nuanced understanding. They may not feel safe expressing their needs to (white straight) therapists who choose to embody Freud's "blank slate."

The insistence of neutrality in mental healthcare persists in other forms, including the use of the Cognitive Behavioral Therapy (CBT), a popular modality of individualistic therapy which focuses on present symptoms, negative thought patterns, and behaviors (Rothbaum et al. 2000), rather than oppressive histories that may contribute to a marginalized person's psyche and struggles. Perhaps at the heart of the CBT issue is the assumption that whatever distress the client may be experiencing can be resolved by shifting these thought patterns, or "maladaptive cognitions." There are significant limitations to a modality which focuses on the notion that a person's interpretation of an event, which may be socially located and produced, can reduce their distress. Peter Kinderman, Clinical Psychology professor at the University of Liverpool, wrote, when serving as acting president of the British Psychological Society,

> CBT can rightly be criticised for adhering to an outdated and unscientific model of mental "illness," for continuing to locate the blame for our distress inside our heads (rather than looking to social or even political root causes), and for sometimes implying both that people are responsible for "thinking errors" and that "positive thinking" can solve our problems. (Kinderman 2017, par 5)

It may be that, even more important than this question of "Do CBT and behavioral modalities fit the problem set marginalized people are bringing to therapy?" is the question of

> Is it even ethical to tell someone they should change their emotional response or interpretations of injustice, when these emotions are valid and a result of a societal issue that is inequitable and should be the target of change itself?

While there are beginning to be calls from BIPOC and LGBTQIA2S+ therapists to "decolonize therapy" (Singh, Appling and Trepal 2020; Varanasi 2021), there continues to be little commentary on this in our field, which is more invested in defining the effectiveness of an intervention.

As a therapist who uses intersectionality, liberation, and social justice frameworks, I have observed that some of the most powerful therapeutic interventions have been validating and sharing in the anger, devastation, and sense of helplessness that we experience as Intersectional Others in this country. Often, a client will look profoundly relieved and say that this is their first time they have experienced such a response—it is a moment of solidarity and community in the room. We, as healthcare professionals, often rely on the notion that our practices are "evidence-based" to validate ourselves. However, the reality is, we need to be critical about our methods and the evidence we are using to inform our decisions. Are we using biased norms? And if we decide that we are going ahead with a treatment modality regardless of how a patient is living, feeling, and what is relevant to them in the moment, is that truly an ethical decision to make?

Our Research Is Too "WEIRD"

Psychological and medical research have been problematic over time, as the majority has been conducted by Western, Educated, Industrialized, Rich and Democratic (WEIRD) scientists on WEIRD participants. One analysis (Heinrich, Heine, and Norenzayan 2010) found that as many as 80% of samples in social and behavioral science studies fit into the WEIRD category, despite the fact that these folks represent only 12% of the world's population. It is not skeptical to say that forecasting based on these participants may not be accurate or generalizable, as they could be outliers, despite appearing "normal" to the research team. Other researchers have proposed that it is not just the sample we should be critical of but also the experiments themselves and the ways in which we interpret results based on cultural differences (Baumard and Sperber 2010). What this serves to reinforce is a bias that moves from scientific study to the real world, where research is often used to inform education, policy, and program development. Those programs are then also biased as they come from a similar origin.

I have observed the WEIRD phenomenon as a researcher myself, and it was most potent for me in graduate school. I completed my graduate training in Palo Alto, California, home to some of the whitest, richest, most educated communities in the United States. According to the 2019 United States Census, the median household income in Palo Alto was $157,271, where the median income in the United States the same year was $62,843 (Semega, Fontenot, and Kollar 2020). Looking at assigned articles, it became clear that Psychology had only one population in mind—white college students. Sexual identity was, at the time, unaccounted for in the sample demographics. Another key variable was appallingly absent—participants with mental health diagnoses, especially comorbid diagnoses. Weren't we, providers in a "helping profession" no less, intended to work with the most vulnerable of society? Shouldn't our samples be normed on those who did struggle with mental health and marginalization, not those who were already privileged, mirrored the researchers' lived experiences, and were simply the easiest to survey? What I felt to be an enormous oversight was rarely commented on by faculty, as if they saw it as an unimportant detail. This made me feel like an unimportant detail, too.

It is not necessarily the researchers' faults that this type of bias exists. We often blame researchers for being too "removed," anthropological, and dehumanizing. And they may well be, but that's not the point. It is the system which causes them to treat their subjects in this manner because they are penalized (implicitly) for seeing their subjects as powerful. Ibram X. Kendi, author of *How to Be Anti-Racist*, speaks to this issue when he says:

> Americans have long been trained to see the deficiencies of people rather than policy. It's a pretty easy mistake to make: People are in our faces. Policies are distant. We are particularly poor at seeing the policies lurking behind the struggles of people. (28)

Indeed, we like to blame the individual, when, really, it is colonialism, nationalism, and the white heteropatriarchy which create the very people we choose to despise and scapegoat.

THE SOCIAL CYCLE OF DEHUMANIZATION

Despite the fact that marginalized people are typically the targets of dehumanization, most research to date has been conducted on effects for majority group members. It was previously thought that marginalized people might minimize, or even accept, dehumanizing behavior from majority groups, because they held relatively "little power" socially to change the system they existed within—this was referred to as the "system-justification hypothesis" (Miranda, Gouveia-Pereira, and Vaes 2014). However, emerging research points to the fact that marginalized people do, in fact, recognize that their cultural groups are strongly dehumanized by specific party policies and attitudes, such as those of the Republican Party after the 2016 U.S. presidential election (Kteily and Bruneau 2017)—big surprise.

It may be that the dehumanization process is one lens through which to see the cycle of oppression in the United States, as studies suggest that the dehumanized often become the dehumanizer, turning to "reciprocal dehumanization" after being harmed (Kteily, Hodson, and Bruneau 2016). Brazilian educator and activist Paulo Freire (1968) wrote of this phenomenon:

> But almost always, during the initial stage of the struggle, the oppressed, instead of striving for liberation, tend themselves to become oppressors, or "sub-oppressors." The very structure of their thought has been conditioned by the contradictions of the concrete, existential situation by which they were shaped. (45)

Those who recognized they were targets of dehumanization in the study often exhibited aggressive thoughts or behaviors, such as wishing Donald Trump harm or wanting the Republican Party to "fall apart." Latino/a/x and Muslim participants in the Kteily and Bruneau study (2017) who felt dehumanized by the U.S. mainstream were more likely to report a sense of marginalization, greater emotional hostility, support of collective action, and less trust toward law enforcement agencies.

DEHUMANIZATION IS THE PRIMARY TOOL OF THE OPPRESSOR

The psychological literature on dehumanization often gives the illusion of false equivalence between those who are Othered and those who do the Othering, as both may be prone to dehumanization under specific circumstances. However, the dehumanization committed by the white, straight majority will always be most impactful on the marginalized, as they are disproportionately affected by dehumanization as a result of systemic injustice. Stereotypes that result from dehumanization reflect the values and beliefs of those who create them and work to maintain the privilege of those who deploy them for use. They tend to tell us more about those who manufacture them than those who are stereotyped.

While it is true that all groups, even those on the margins, can create and deploy stereotypes and explicit dehumanization for personal advantage, not all groups have the power to make their stereotypes come to reflect a "reality"—this is a privilege allotted to the powerful. Brazilian educator and activist Paulo Freire (1968) said of this dynamic:

> It is not the tyrannized who initiate despotism, but the tyrants. It is not the despised who initiate hatred, but those who despise. It is not those whose humanity is denied them who negate humankind, but those who denied that humanity (thus negating their own as well). . . . For the oppressors, however, it is always the oppressed (whom they obviously never call "the oppressed" but — depending on whether they are fellow countrymen or not —"those people" or "the blind and envious masses" or "savages" or "natives" or "subversives") who are disaffected, who are "violent," "barbaric," "wicked," or "ferocious" when they react to the violence of the oppressors. (56)

The false equivalence in literature of the experiences of the oppressor and the oppressed only serves to exemplify the bias inherent in the literature of the U.S. majority (Henreich, Heine and Norenzayan 2010). To the white straight majority, the animalizing of Intersectional Others will always seem rooted in empiricism and history. The main problem with this is that such a history is dehumanizing.

Dehumanization by Restricting Anger and Grief in the Face of Trauma

Intersectional Others have every right to be angry with oppressive systems and their contributors, but often feel the need to suppress anger, else risk being seen as a threat (Archer and Mills 2019). Psychologically, we can see anger as our body's mobilization mechanism, manifested in response to injustice and disempowerment. Everyone has it, although people who are Othered are often subjected to injustice more frequently and more intensely. Stereotypes, such as the "angry Black femme," not only invalidate these experiences but also racialize and gender a basic emotion that we all experience and portray that emotional expression as inherently aggressive. They are unfairly unidimensional and ahistorical, suggesting that nonviolent means aren't almost always a first line of defense against injustice. To the contrary, countless marginalized people use nonviolent methods to engage oppression every day, but these instances are overlooked or willfully ignored. When we stop trying to see an entire race or an entire gender as monolithic, we begin to see their emotional complexities as similar to our own. This is critical for combating implicit dehumanization.

After being acquitted and released from incarceration in 1972, Black queer activist Angela Davis was faced by a white reporter who asked if she condoned the violence used by the Black Panther Party. Her response was one of pointed irony, as Black and other marginalized folks have faced violence at the hands of white oppressors for centuries. She responded, saying:

[W]hen someone asks me about violence, I find it incredible because it means the person asking that question has absolutely no idea what black people have gone through and experienced in this country from the time the first black person was kidnapped from the shores of Africa. (Bakare 2020)

It is offensive to suggest that—after generations of kidnapping, genocide, police brutality, deprivation of basic rights, and inequity—those who are Othered should accept "their place" quietly. Yet, there is an expectation, and even a demand, to behave with passivity in the face of suppression. This double standard has been noted by many as a hallmark of systemic oppression. Black queer author and activist, James Baldwin, said:

When a white man in the world says "Give me liberty or give me death," the entire white world applauds. When a black man says exactly the same thing, word for word, he is judged a criminal and treated like one and everything possible is done to make an example of this "bad nigger" so there won't be any more like him. (Peck and Strauss 2017)

We consume a great deal of mental energy trying to balance authenticity, confidence, and perceived prejudice and ultimately get burned out doing so. This is not the fault of QBIPOC, but the system's fault, because it places undue oppressive burden on the Othered, who are then forced to continuously juggle these issues internally, often without recourse. And if these stressors are mentioned in academic or workplace settings, those same people will be perceived as paranoid, overly anxious—or, my favorite—"sensitive." It's a catch-22 anyone in their right mind would feel unhappy about. After all, in the last words of Heather Heyer, who was killed in 2017 by white supremacists in Charlottesville, Virginia, while protesting a Unite the Right Rally, "If you're not outraged, you're not paying attention" (Cuellar 2017).

Anger and Activism

Anger can be a powerful catalyst for activism (DeGagne 2018). In a 2021 interview with the community and online media platform *them.*, Alan Pelaez Lopez, queer Afro-Indigenous poet, activist, and scholar at the University of California, Berkeley, said about the power of anger in intersectional movements:

> I come from a place of anger—particularly on social media, where people who are oppressed talk about their embodied knowledge—but my anger is rooted in the fact that my human limits have been met. . . . Anger is generative and a source of empowerment. Only when we are angry can we do something to address what makes us angry.

We can see this power in the Movement for Black Lives, where video recordings have consistently forced the public to face the trauma of victims, causing a collective grieving to occur across multiple communities (Garza 2020). In the case of 13-year-old Adam Toledo, for instance, who was killed by Chicago police in April 2021 after being chased down an alleyway, body cam footage led to national mortification as people from coast to coast could bear witness to the killing of a Latinx youth who had his hands up, unarmed, complying with police orders (Nickeas 2021). Then there was the death of 20-year-old Daunte Wright, earlier that same week, who was killed during a routine traffic stop. His mother, Katie Wright, was recorded speaking to a crowd that gathered at the site of the incident soon after, in anguish, stating that Daunte was afraid as he spoke with her on the phone prior to interacting with the police, due to their history of targeting Black and Brown people (Lavoie 2021).

The location in which Wright was killed was a stone's throw away from where George Floyd died, in Minneapolis, a fact that many were haunted by as they watched the news (Lavoie 2021). The connection goes even deeper, betraying the emotional intimacy that is inevitably part of every single death, though not often acknowledged by those outside of the victim's community—George Floyd's partner Courteney Ross was, at one time, Daunte Wright's high school teacher (Mencia 2021). The emotional nuance of the incidents, as well as the recordings and interviews in their aftermaths, enabled the nation to collectively humanize and relate to the victims and their families in ways that it may not have wanted to, but, nevertheless, could not avoid doing.

It is not a humanistic stance, nor within the right of the oppressor, to insinuate that injustice due to rage, like white violence, should be met with politeness. When a family member is killed or brutalized by a police officer, the natural response is not to shake that police officer's hand and sheepishly request they stop. The natural response is to demand they stop. To feel enraged and devastated that the brutalization occurred at all. To feel enraged that this brutalization was only one in a long list of the same. And to hate that anyone, including police, thought so little of your family that they felt entitled to harm them. This is the righteous anger of the Othered—and it deserves to breathe. Black queer activist Peniel E. Joseph, author of *The Sword and the Shield: The Revolutionary Lives of Malcolm X and Martin Luther King Jr.* (2020), wrote in a *CNN* opinion piece, "While it is too late for Daunte Wright, we can save Black lives in America by ending our blind allegiance to systems of law enforcement apparently unable to recognize Black humanity" (Joseph 2021).

Dehumanization through Oppression Denial

Denial in the face of the marginalized person's suffering is a true privilege of whiteness and straightness. To deny the obvious effects of your actions and the actions of those who look like you is to deny a marginalized person the ability to confront you. To gaslight the very people you oppress can only be considered heinous because you deny them the right to be human beings. In his 1963 novel *The Fire Next Time*, Black queer author James Baldwin wrote, "[I]t is not permissible that the authors of devastation should also be innocent. It is the innocence which constitutes the crime" (5). He was commenting on the destructive capacities of oppressors invested in their own denial.

Oppression denial may manifest as denial to the self or to others. It may consist of a refusal to believe that those who oppress have contributed to the cyclical and intergenerational violence that affects those who are marginalized. It might look like defensiveness and include accusations of "emotional overreactivity." It might even manifest as anger at being confronted at all or centering the oppressor's own feelings rather than keeping the focus on the issue brought to their attention. It might also mean literal denial, as in those that say, "Oppression isn't real," or say, "I have this wealth because I worked hard and if other people weren't so lazy, they'd have it, too." In March 2021, Filipino American scholar E. J. Ramos David commented on the longstanding tradition of oppression denial toward Asian Americans by tweeting, "Forgetting, disregarding, and minimizing anti-Asian racism is as much of an American tradition as anti-Asian racism" (David 2021). That is, intertwined with prejudicial behavior are the oppressors' tendencies to avoid acknowledging its effects on those they are prejudicial toward.

In a 2020 conversation with Black feminist author Rebecca Carroll on the podcast *Come Through*, Robin DiAngelo, author of *White Fragility* (2018), stated that she was frequently called upon to lead anti-racist trainings at institutions across the United States, at which time she would ask the question of BIPOC staff, "When have you, as a person of color, had feedback received well, when your peer inevitably makes a white comment?" The most common response from those people was "Never." Let that sink in, because it is core to oppression denial, and one of the main factors that perpetuates institutional stigma and discrimination for marginalized people. When peers are finally confronted about racist remarks or interactions, those people—the same ones who claim to be part of an institution that cares about "diversity"—react with fragility, denial, and anger, rather than attempting to process the information they hear and change their behavior.

In the interview, she went so far as to say that white progressives operating out of denial and privilege were perhaps more dangerous than overt white supremacists (Carroll 2020). QBIPOC scholars have discussed this issue as well, particularly in the context of intersectional microaggressions (Nadal et al. 2017). Microaggressive harm is more insidious, and the comments may feel harder to navigate. Intersectional Others impacted by their statements or acts may therefore be left to wonder, "Should I just endure this treatment, or should I confront it?" and ultimately decide to leave it be. While DiAngelo's words were intentionally provocative, there was some truth to them, because, while former president Donald Trump may, for instance, traumatize QBIPOC on a national scale through threats of restrictive legislation and outright bigotry, the daily traumas we endure from friends, colleagues, and strangers compound quickly and consistently over time. Ultimately, we may be able to resolve the traumas we can see, but the microaggressive cuts that harm us are not easily resolved and could result in additional cumulative harm.

Nathan and Isabel: A Brief Illustration

I, like many QBIPOC, can identify with DiAngelo's statement, because these insidious daily cuts are a part of our normal everyday lives in the United States. I once confronted some white straight friends of mine—who I no longer consider friends, but that comes later—after I saw them flaunting geisha attire at a bizarre family gathering. The photo was part of a series, and, in another frame, a family member sat in a Native headdress, beading, and fringe-laden tan clothing. There was clearly a theme of "culture as costume" being had. My white straight cis male friend—we'll call him Nathan—had decided to complete his geisha outfit with a black wig and servile hand gesture, his hands clasped in front of him, ready to do the bidding of his master.

He and his partner—we'll call her Isabel—had proudly posted pictures of the occasion, presumably because they thought it was fun and exotic, the same reasons most people choose to appropriate other cultures and perpetuate colonialism. It was 2016 and I decided to reach out. After all, we were all young and I was hopeful that they would be understanding about my concern. I sent the message with context on the feelings, including education on "yellowface" and a link for them to learn more. It was more than was necessary—we could get into "minority tax" and the undue burdens placed on marginalized people to educate the privileged, but let's leave it there.

The message was met with blatant disregard and accusations of sensitivity, a speech on the freedom of expression, the downplaying of anti-Asian racism, a denial of the very existence of cultural appropriation, and the assertion that, as a Russian person, Nathan was distantly linked to Mongolian people, and therefore somehow justified in his actions. Isabel, on the other hand, did not see fit to respond. For context, these were people I considered good friends at the time. I invited them to my baby shower. Nathan was supposed to be a member of our wedding party. He was one of my partner's best friends. It was honestly devastating to receive this response.

I found out later that they publicly mocked the incident on social media, which could only lead me to conclude that they had privately mocked it with others. It was the latter situation that was the clincher which ultimately caused me to end my friendship with these "progressive" friends of mine. I said it before, and I'll say it again—oppression denial is one of the worst things you can do to a marginalized person because it denies them the ability to pursue justice. It also denies them the compassion and thoughtfulness that every human being deserves in return for telling you the truth of their experiences or pain. And I do not blame any person for their decision to end a relationship with someone who chose denial over humanity.

"Oppression Doesn't Exist"

Throughout the 2000s, you continued to hear droves of (mostly white) folks openly proclaiming that racism was dead—that our society was decidedly post-racial—a proclamation that became even more common after Barack Obama was elected as U.S. president in 2008 (Neville et al. 2016). The fallacy of the white progressive movement is that most people are "doing their part" to end systemic injustice, and that white liberals are helping along the societal curve slowly bending toward equity. But the reality is otherwise. In fact, prominent members of society still espouse the idea that racism is factually unreal.

Faced with allegations of police brutality and calls for lawmakers to denounce racism in the police department after officer Derek Chauvin murdered George Floyd in May of 2020, several Republican congressmembers sung this old refrain. GOP Pennsylvania representative Scott Perry, in a September interview of this kind, was recorded as stating, "What is systemic? . . . If there's a system, someone had to create that system. Someone had to nurture and operate that system. I don't know who in the country is doing that" (Moreno 2020). After the interview, his office spokesperson tried to walk the "controversial" statement back to the press, but the ignorant remark was already out there for all to see. This is by no means an isolated incident, but representative of whole swaths of U.S. society who believe oppression is a topic better dropped. And with these beliefs, what are the chances that white straight men will take responsibility for their part in the system that they do, actually, "nurture" and "operate"?

Dehumanization through Identity Blindness

Akin to oppression denial, but not quite the same thing, is "colorblindness." Colorblindness is denial's more ignorant, but ever-so-slightly more well-intentioned, cousin—the false assumption that acting as if marginalization does not exist will somehow increase the level of equity in society. I was raised to be colorblind as a mixed Asian American living in a mostly white neighborhood growing up. If it said something that my parents chose to move us to this particular white community in the Bay Area, I wouldn't have known it at the time. Colorblindness was a teaching popularized in the 1990s which pervaded the U.S. educational system and accompanied the notion that the United States was a cultural "melting pot," within which cultural identities, histories, and traumas "dissolved" and became integrated until a single national identity was left (Apfelbaum, Sommers and Norton 2008).

My parents brought the colorblind ideology into our home and largely ignored issues of race unless a class project on "cultural pride" came up. Such an assignment typically prompted a quick, easily digestible conversation on Chinese heritage which involved Chinese New Year and red envelopes. It was very much focused on downplaying any differences I might have from any other white classmate. That's the fable of colorblindness—it somehow manages to preach acceptance while also being reductionist and devaluative of any non-white life experience.

Sexual identity was even more invisible growing up, partially because Asian American families, even mixed ones, so rarely discuss sex due to cultural taboo, and partially because my parents thought if they mentioned gayness, I might get contaminated by it somehow, a strange dilution of their Christian upbringings, although my brother and I never went to church as children. The contamination debate resulted in several arguments during my college years, especially once I realized I was queer and had been queer all along. I'm sure they would flatly deny that these conversations ever happened, because that is the danger of colorblindness. It causes collective forgetfulness that nevertheless injures those around you, whether you remember doing the injuring or not.

Operation Varsity Blues and Affirmative Action

When Operation Varsity Blues, the 2019 college admissions scandal, hit the headlines, it quickly became a showcase of white privilege. Pictures of *Full House* actress Lori Laughlin and *Desperate Housewives* star Felicity Huffman graced the front covers of national magazines and news outlets across the country, sparking outrage about the 40-some odd parents who paid counselor Rick Singer to get their kids into elite colleges and universities (Thelin 2019). Hidden deep within this scandal is white fear, a fear that white elitism is no longer enough to dominate the college admissions game, higher education, and success in this country.

Sitting opposite this scandal, and so many undiscovered inequities like it, is the conversation on affirmative action in this country. "Affirmative action" first appeared as a legal term in the 1935 National Labor Relations Act; however, it was largely unused until former president John F. Kennedy issued Executive Order 10925 in 1961, declaring that government employees must be treated "without regard to their race, creed, color, or national origin" (Whalen and Rubin 1977). Historically, policies like affirmative action have been proxies for conversations about identity without ever needing to speak the word "race," partially due to this original legal definition. The national debate around the legitimacy and effectiveness of affirmative action policies can therefore be seen as a reflection of the push-and-pull leaders, institutions, and individuals feel about identity blindness and systemic oppression.

Opponents of affirmative action often argue that our "post-racial society" has rendered the need for a leg-up useless, and that affirmative action is "reverse racism" (Chang 1995). Proponents have pointed to situations like Operation Varsity Blues as evidence that there is a continuing need to support marginalized access and opportunity in the government and other institutions. For how can we change an obviously biased system if we turn a blind eye to it? The true danger of identity blindness is that we, in our ignorance, become the carriers of, and bystanders to, injustice. That injustice doesn't disappear simply because we decide to do nothing.

Keeping Up with the Kardashians

Kim Kardashian has often stated in the media that she "doesn't see color," but her actions belie her words. *Keeping Up with the Kardashians* (2007–2015) and Kardashian's subsequent brand have exoticized, and financially profited from, aesthetics for which Black women have historically received criticism—these aesthetics have run the gamut from cornrows to larger buttocks (Appleford 2016). In 2017, her sisters Kylie Jenner and Khloe Kardashian were accused of stealing designs from independent Black creators, like Destiney Bleu, designer at *Good American*, who was able to provide evidence that Kardashian bought out every single one of her designs only to reproduce identical items for her own shop (Lawrence 2017). There has always been a vampiric relationship between white-straightness and those they Other, yet another reason "not seeing color" is not only unhelpful but harmful. Helen Neville, Educational Psychology and African American Studies professor at the University of Illinois, said on colorblindness,

> When we adopt these racial blind beliefs, they actually don't help us in moving our society forward, in terms of promoting racial equity. In fact, they actually reinforce that inequity. So, within this context, one of the things that is important is that people begin to educate themselves about the history and experiences of black folks [and] the history of white supremacy. (Neville 2020)

We Must See Our Otherness for What It Is

I was miserable growing up in an identity-blind environment, and, looking back, it's so easy to see that at least some of my misery could have been prevented had they just let me come into my own power, rather than trying to mold me into something I simply couldn't be. I now see that they wanted me to be a "good" child and citizen, someone who followed the rules and easily adopted the narrative fed to me by white straight education, that success could only be reached through assimilation. It was a commonly held desire in immigrant families at the time, and perhaps even more commonly held in mixed families, though there is little data to support this speculation.

The truth was, I could never be that pull-yourself-up-by-your-bootstraps kid who conformed to the model minority myth and questioned nothing. And it sent me into a tailspin for most of my young adulthood, because their visions of me inevitably clashed with my reality as a hapa queer person walking through the world. Upon talking to other queer Asian Americans,

I realized how ubiquitous it was to feel oppressed and trapped in our own homes. In the case of fellow East Asian Americans, rigid expectations around race, gender, and sexuality were strongly enforced through filial piety—we were taught to accept and show deference to our elders, and especially our parents. Not one of us had the language for what we were experiencing until much later in our lives. To realize our power as the Intersectional Other, we must first exist in conditions where we see our Otherness for what it is. In *Pedagogy of the Oppressed* (1968), Brazilian educator Paulo Freire spoke to this idea:

> Only as they [the oppressed] discover themselves to be "hosts" of the oppressor can they contribute to the midwifery of their liberating pedagogy. As long as they live in the duality in which *to be* is *to be like,* and *to be like* is *to be like the oppressor,* this contribution is impossible. (48)

Our power comes first from the realization that we are part of the system of oppression, and that we participate in that system, often willingly. Liberation and power are not easily achieved, because we were built to compare ourselves to the oppressor, a comparison by which we always come out deficient. We are deficient in attractiveness. We are deficient in intelligence. We are deficient in charisma. We are deficient in will. Our parents and teachers are the conduits of these deficiencies as they push us toward assimilative "success." They do this at times with the best of intentions—an intention to help their children fit in, to be safe, and to eventually elevate the whole family's success. It can be painful to realize the "facts" we chose to believe most of our lives, entrusted to us by people we love and admire, are mythologies. Accepting this pain as part of our reality, however, is the first step to manifesting our power in the mid of an oppressive society.

JEOPARDIZING OUR OWN POWER

It makes sense that, as Intersectional Others, we would see ourselves through the lens of deficiency. After all, we have been the subjects of compounded deficiency rhetoric for generations, which has led to extensive internalized oppression. We have been told we are not good enough—not beautiful enough, not smart enough, and completely unsuited for power. Without our own communities, we are subject to sexual racism and gatekeeping. While these projected deficiencies are untrue, it is understandable that emotions and beliefs surrounding not-good-enough. Black lesbian activist and politician Stacey Abrams wrote in her 2018 memoir *Lead from the Outside* that "we must cease being participants in our own oppression" (Abrams 2018, 136). Sadly, this is easier said than done, because while Intersectional Others may strive for a liberatory future, we are stuck in a double bind crafted by our society. We can either succumb to invisibility and the expectations of our oppressors and mainstream society, or reject those expectations and risk losing individual power, collective power, and our livelihoods. If this is truly the bind we are in, how can Intersectional Others hope to affect change?

Power cannot hope to be achieved by Intersectional Others until we can break free of the constraints placed on us by, and effects of, systemic oppression. We may be able to create small shifts within the system, for instance, but because we are using the tools of an oppressive system, our lives will be bound by it. Without rejecting norms forced on us, there is no real way to enact change. We will only reinforce the cycles that ultimately oppress us and other marginalized people. Because we are caught in a system that subjugates us, we are prone to subjugation not only from the dominant groups of society but also from ourselves and those in our communities. We become self-oppressors and self-dehumanizers.

Jeopardizing Power by Internalizing Oppressive Ideals

As Intersectional Others who exist in the diaspora, there is an understandable temptation to gain acceptance, because the American Dream is a powerful projection that lures global residents to the United States in hopes of change, upward mobility, and success through ambition and hard work. We are told that anyone is capable of this dream, and in particular, that this dream is possible in the United States like nowhere else in the world. But the American Dream is a lantern fish illusion. Much like the lantern fish, the American Dream shines bright from afar, but the closer you are, the larger its teeth become. Those who choose to believe in it are often victims of its duplicity, because the truth is that only some of us can take advantage of the mobility we are promised. And who wouldn't want to take part in the American Dream after hearing such promises? I charge you to find someone who wouldn't want to believe that anything is possible for them, particularly after experiencing trauma in their home country or family of origin.

Becoming the Oppressor

One of the most potent lies of the American Dream is the impossible idea of belongingness. This is not to imply that Intersectional Others can't find communities to belong in—they can and do. But the illusion of total acceptance in the upper echelons of white straight society is just that. To gain this belongingness and sense of social worth, we may do all sorts of things that jeopardize our own power. We may, for instance, jeopardize or diminish our power by attempting to become the social elite, rather than choosing to find power within and uplifting queer communities and communities of color. Bell hooks (1989) told the following story:

> Once mama said to me as I was about to go again to the predominantly white university, "You can take what the white people have to offer, but you do not have to love them." Now understanding her cultural codes I know that she was not saying to me not to love people of other races. She was speaking about colonisation and the reality of what it means to be taught in a culture of domination by those who dominate. She was insisting on my power to be able to separate useful knowledge that I might get from the dominating group, from participation in ways of knowing that would lead to estrangement, alienation, and worse assimilation and co-option. (36)

It serves those currently in power to keep marginalized communities aspiring to become them. Because to encourage Intersectional Others to become the most powerful, decolonized, socially conscious versions of themselves would mean those currently in power might lose that power.

There is a real pressure for Intersectional Others to conform to hegemony, to get as close to whiteness and straightness as possible. We are taught from an early age that we shouldn't expect greatness, that the social elite don't look like us. This is embedded in everything we see and do. We see it in movies, as we watch white straight leads save the day, and often, the world (Meyer 2020). We see it in beauty commercials showcasing white thin femmes (Deliovsky 2008). We see it in dating applications focused on promoting straight relationships (Hanson 2021). We are exposed to these messages ubiquitously, and with each passing advertisement, it becomes harder and harder to reject those messages. They are thus normalized.

Consuming messages about white straight heroics, power, and physical attractiveness can create a dichotomy whereby Intersectional Others begin to see themselves as less powerful, less attractive, and less capable of achieving major accomplishments. Indeed, many researchers have expressed marked concern over what is known as the "immigrant paradox"—the counter-intuitive reality that children of immigrants who are more assimilated, or "Americanized," are actually more at-risk for negative psychological outcomes and health behaviors, such as increased substance use, unprotected sex, and delinquency (Garcia-Coll et al. 2012). However, it is important, as we discussed in chapter 3, to consider not only the social and psychological "tax" of marginalization or assimilationism, such as minority stress, but also the sources of these outcomes. The immigrant paradox is a phenomenon which exists precisely because internalized oppression pierces the psyches of those who choose assimilation without understanding its hidden cost.

Freire's "Self-Depreciation"

It is easy, in a system built by someone else for their own kind and not us, to buy into the belief that we will never hold power, because we can never be them. To minimize this dissonance, we internalize white straight ideals of selfhood, and, simultaneously, the internalization of hatred for our minds and bodies as the Othered. Brazilian educator Paulo Freire described this phenomenon as "self-depreciation." He wrote,

> Self-depreciation is another characteristic of the oppressed, which derives from their internalization of the opinion the oppressors hold of them. So often do they hear that they are good for nothing, know nothing and are incapable of learning anything—that they are sick, lazy, and unproductive—that in the end they become convinced of their own unfitness. (Freire 1968, 63)

Self-depreciation is expressed in varying ways in practicality. We might subscribe to colorism and buy skin-bleaching products (Banks et al. 2016). We might get plastic surgery to emulate traditionally white features, such as double eyelid surgery (Heyes 2009). We might feel that our bodies are at a deficit because our curves don't match what we see from thin white influencers, or worry we aren't feminine enough as we gaze at straight women on Instagram (Deliovsky 2008). When we idealize the bodies and aesthetics of white heteronormativity in our lives and devalue others, we let colorism, queerphobia, and self-depreciation jeopardize our power.

In addition to self-depreciation, we also subscribe to the opinions of our oppressors because we are so often told that white straight society is the standard by which we must always compare ourselves. That is, while we hate our bodies, minds, and selfhoods, we also idealize that which we can never be, and often collectively forget that our ancestral legacies and identities should be prized. Filipino author and activist José Rizal, who was executed in 1896 by the Spanish government after rebelling during its colonial period in the Philippines, wrote about the effects of Spanish colonization on the psyches of Filipino/a/x people more than a century ago. It still rings true today. He said that

> little by little they lost their old traditions, the mementos of their past; they gave up their writing, their songs, their poems, their laws in order to learn by rote mother doctrines which they did not understand, another morality, another aesthetic different from those inspired by their climate and their manner of thinking. Then they declined, degrading themselves in their own eyes; they became ashamed of what was their own; they began to admire and praise whatever was foreign and incomprehensible; their spirit was dismayed and it surrendered. (Rizal 1912, 130)

Self-depreciation in this context does not occur in a vacuum, but was, and is, created through the forceful indoctrination of Indigenous people into colonial mentality and society (David and Okazaki 2006).

The Effect of Self-Depreciation on Queer Intimacies

Unsurprisingly, one aspect of internalized oppression that has been identified in the literature lies in the unique constellation of queer intimacies that accompany oppression and intersectional experiences. For instance, some literature on QBIPOC intimacies have pointed to a prevalent attraction to white queer folks, perhaps partially due to the desire to become to which we have eluded here. Until very recently, there has been a near absence of queer Asian men in national media, even gay media production. The few portrayals that have appeared were submissive and presented mainly for white gay consumption, such as in gay porn, marginalizing queer Asian American experiences (Fung 1996).

One study analyzed gay print media in 2005 and found that the relative marginalization of Asian gay men was especially evident in *The Advocate*, the largest gay and lesbian magazine in the United States, which only featured them one time. It was also evident in the content of *OUT* magazine that year, which published an article entitled *How to Gab in Gaysian.* One term on its "vocabulary list" was "dogeater," defined as a "gaysian who unapologetically uses men for all their emotional, sexual, and financial worth because they feel men are dogs by nature" (Han 2008, 841), a term which also plays off the prejudicial stereotype that Asian Americans consume domestic pets. The ubiquitousness of negative representations in Western media caused one queer Asian Canadian scholar, Maurice Poon (2000), to note that "such images certainly will have a negative impact on gay Asian men's self-esteem and self-worth" (47), particularly when masculinity is valued over femininity, aggressive over submissive, and white over color.

Michael Kimmel, professor of Sociology and Gender Studies at Stony Brook University, said that U.S. masculinity which "defines white, middle-class, middle-aged, heterosexual men is the masculinity that sets the standards for other men, against which other men are measured, and more often than not, found wanting" (124). He posited that these definitions made masculinity an inherently homophobic construct (Kimmel 1994). By that logic, it is also a racist construct. By design, expectations like those that Kimmel describes ensure that non-white, non-straight, and non-cis people will consistently fail to achieve conventional norms of "attractiveness," "virility," or "manliness," not only from the white mainstream but also from themselves as they contend with internalized racism, queerphobia, and transphobia.

The Pulse Nightclub Massacre

In a more extreme example of the ways in which internalized hatred can affect our self-image and actions as Intersectional Others, we can look at circumstances of the 2016 Pulse Nightclub shooting, in which Omar Matteen, who was known to have frequented the nightclub himself, killed 49 people and injured 58 others late on a Saturday night, the gay bar's Latin Night. It is now known as the deadliest LGBTQIA2S+ shooting in U.S. history; the majority of the victims were queer and trans Latino/a/x people. The club was an important fixture in Orlando for QBIPOC; it reportedly acted as a nexus for HIV prevention and immigrant rights activism (West 2016). Several customers remembered seeing Matteen at the club prior to the shooting, and one, Jim Van Horn directly commented in an interview over the next couple weeks that "[Omar Matteen] was a homosexual and he was trying to pick up men" (BBC News 2016).

No one can be sure of Matteen's exact motives, as he is no longer alive to tell us, but his ex-wife, Sitora Yusufiy, reported that he had homophobic tendencies during their relationship (Barry et al. 2016) and we can speculate through the pieces of evidence available to us. One of the most disturbing pieces is the connection between Matteen and his victims. Matteen was Afghan American, and therefore racially marginalized like his victims, in addition to the fact that he came from an immigrant family, attended the club, and may have been queer, though was likely closeted if so. In many respects, he mirrored the identities of the people he killed.

I do not believe this is an accident, but rather that the intense anger Matteen must have felt to perpetrate such heinous violence tells us something far more intimate about his internal state—that he secretly harbored hatred, not toward any specific victim, but toward himself. There are no known records of any personal vendettas, and the chances of knowing every victim he wounded or killed are low. One can only conclude that Matteen projected his internal state onto his victims that night. At its core, internalized oppression teaches Intersectional Others that we are lesser than, and that we deserve the hatred of our oppressors. Without conscious awareness of these internalizations, their hold on us can be devastating.

Jeopardizing Power through Respectability Politics

As old as hierarchized oppression are the myths of the "good negro," the "model minority" and notion of "respectability politics"—the belief that cultural and national divisions can be resolved if only marginalized folk just improve their behavior. We can define "respectability politics," and the willing adoption of titles like "model minority," as attempts by individuals within marginalized communities to police their own members in order to prove to the mainstream that their community's values are compatible with hegemonic values, rather than challenging the status quo. The ideology behind respectability politics is misleadingly simple. What is often left out of discussion is the meaning behind this so-called "behavioral improvement." That is, what does "improved behavior" even look like, and who is determining when it has improved enough to merit goodness? Just as a parent might scold or lecture a child about social "appropriateness" when they act out, the answer to this question is implicitly that those at the top of the oppression hierarchy should both decide and be the measuring stick for this decision.

The truth is our worth should never be defined by how respectable we appear. We inherently have worth, and we alone should have the power to define our worth as we move through the world. Social respectability is thus a tool of the oppressor, as it causes the Othered to constantly question their worth and police their own actions in order to gain approval that will never be received. By contrast, straight white middle-class people in the United States may question their worth, but a violation of social norms rarely means "disappointing their community." Rather, these violations are viewed as acts of individuality and not representative of their communities as a whole. Respectability politics holds within it the potential to diminish individual and collective power if used to limit mobility, individuality, and engagement by the self and others within oppressive systems.

It is a code of silence, which plays out in subtle ways, but also overtly over national media. When Philando Castile was killed by the Minnesota police in 2016, Charles Barkley, former NBA athlete, tweeted soon after: "I've always said we as black people, if you want respect, you've got to give each other respect. You can't demand respect from white people and the cops if we don't respect each other" (BET News 2016). His response was immediately condemned, especially by younger generations who eschewed the idea that respectability was the way to achieve success and change.

From Geraldo Rivera's comments that Trayvon Martin's hoodie was to blame for his tragic death (Castellanos 2012) to 7-year-old Tiana Parker being forbidden to display her natural hair at school because it was an inappropriate "fad" (Persch 2013), the message is clear—if you remain a respectable minority, and play by the rules of the (white) mainstream, you may be granted a reprieve or immunity from prejudice and thus be welcomed with open arms by mainstream society. However, this reprieve comes at a deeper cost, the cost of buying into oppressive ideals. That is, it requires buying into the tainted belief that to be born with darker skin, coarser hair—to be who you are, or to love who you love—is to be inherently inferior. In this manner, respectability politics not only stifle self-expression but self-worth.

This phenomenon is not contained to communities of color—queer people also police other queers. Often, this policing has significant repercussions for QBIPOC, who are deemed "less respectable" than what the state portrays as the dominant, acceptable version of queerness—the image of white gay men. Scholars have pointed out that there has been a pervasive whitening in the media, politics, research, and social perceptions of gayness and queerness (Bérubé 2016), which is intertwined with respectability politics for Intersectional Others. In a personal account of his social justice work, queer Chinese American activist Daniel Tsang (2001) wrote of what he called the "reformist" inclinations of Asian queers:

> For too long, gays have refused, or strategically delayed, confronting Asian American straights about their homophobia. This conspiracy of silence (and acquiescence in our own oppression) occurred under the mistaken notion that by not rocking the boat we would gain the respect of the dominant culture. . . . Such a reformist orientation naturally left unchallenged the sexist, heterosexual character of Amerikan society. (228)

We can see traces of respectability politics historically in events such as Stonewall and the same-sex marriage movement, which were both highly racialized and dominated by media imagery and stories of white cis gay men and women, by design.

There has also been the reverse—an investment in heteronormative and masculinized stories for BIPOC—such as the heavy reliance on Black masculinity (e.g., Steve Harvey) and faith leaders (e.g., Martin Luther King Jr.) to make the notion of social change for Black queer folk less threatening to the mainstream. These dichotomous representations are oppressive mechanisms for Intersectional Others, who then have their stories, struggles, and needs obscured (Story 2016). Most of us, for instance, are familiar with Martin Luther King Jr. and his iconic *I Have a Dream* speech at the 1963 March on Washington for Jobs and Freedom, which called attention to continuing racial inequities rampant within the United States a century after the emancipation of slavery. A much smaller number are familiar with the monumental efforts of two Black queer activists Bayard Rustin, one of primary organizers of the March on Washington and the Journey of Reconciliation (i.e., the first Freedom Ride), and Ella Baker, cofounder of the Mississippi Freedom Democratic Party (MFDP) and the Student Nonviolent Coordinating Committee (SNCC). Adam Ewing, associate professor of African American Studies at Virginia Commonwealth University, said in an interview with *Associated Press*,

> With all due respect to King, the most important figure in the civil rights movement was Ella Baker, who was organizing communities in the 1940s and 1950s,

hosting leadership conferences, making contacts throughout the South, and generally doing the work. (Williams 2020)

The erasure of Rustin and Baker's contributions is not coincidental, but part of a larger trend of QBIPOC erasure in U.S. historical literature. We can see the impact of this erasure, and the detriment of respectability politics, if we look closely at the person responsible for barring Rustin from receiving credit for his contributions to the march. Ultimately, it was the National Association for the Advancement of Colored People (NAACP) chair, Roy Wilkins, who objected to Rustin receiving credit, calling his queerness a "liability" for the cause. He instead appointed A. Philip Randolph, head of the first predominantly Black labor union, Brotherhood of the Sleeping Car Porters, as the director of the march (Life Magazine 1963). The visibility of Ella Baker's contributions, on the other hand, were often thwarted by Martin Luther King Jr. himself, with whom she was known to have conflicts during her tenure at the Southern Christian Leadership Conference (SCLC). Many scholars have noted the sexism in the civil rights movement, as well as King's particular tendency to downplay, and take the credit for, Baker's important work (Elliot 1996; Ransby 2003). It is, therefore, not only erasure from larger U.S. history which often thwarts the successes of QBIPOC but also erasure from inside our communities.

The Ancestral Trauma Embedded in Respectability Language

If we lean in and intently listen to the ideology behind respectability politics, we can hear ancestral trauma embedded within. It harkens back to the concepts like that of the "good negro," a pejorative designation developed in the early 20th century by white society to signify that a Black person was doing what was "expected of them." It was a term that rose to prominence as Black folks began to join the middle and upper classes in the South, at a time when being seen as a "bad negro" could jeopardize one's social position. In other words, if the Black upper class did not "control" other members in the community well enough, they were collectively affected by white retaliation, which included economic intimidation, segregation, and violence (Mixon 1997). Respectability in this context becomes a kind of adaptability, not unlike code-switching and learning to chameleon oneself in different environments to attain greater success or avoid harm.

We can acknowledge the traumatic roots of respectability politics—but to fall into the trap of believing we will be fully accepted into white straight society if we only behave, talk or look a certain way, and then shaming others for choosing to challenge these notions—only ignores the sacrifices our ancestors have made so we can achieve individual and collective liberation.

In an article on the subject for ESPN, Brando Simeo Starkey, author o*f In Defense of Uncle Tom: Why Blacks Must Police Racial Loyalty* (2015), beautifully wrote:

> We owe it to ourselves to press for racial progress outside the white gaze, an opportunity available because of those race warriors who once battled for racial progress inside the white gaze. Their bloodshed sapped white supremacy's power, allowing black people to foster a positive racial self-identity that serves as the launching pad for a better existence. This can only happen if we renounce respectability politics and heal the psychological carnage white supremacy has wrought. (Starkey 2016)

When we hear a marginalized person use the language of respectability politics, two assumptions can typically be made. The first is that they hope that the U.S. social elite will notice their efforts and bring them into the fold. The second is that they believe that pursuing the route of respectability has the potential to further the interests of their community. Both assumptions are illusory, as they hold high assimilation as the answer to oppression, while ignoring the detriments associated with such an answer.

We may choose to refuse subjugation from dominant white straight society (e.g., protest and stand up to an employer) if we feel the cost of doing so is worth it to us, but sometimes that cost feels too high. Each of us has a different threshold for defiance, notions of safety, and idea on the relative success of our defiance. An Intersectional Other may choose to say nothing, even while experiencing abuse from authority, for instance, not because they don't want to stand up for themselves, but because they know doing so will jeopardize the safety or power of a collective group.

An Intersectional Other may get pulled over by the police for speeding—get berated or abused by the police, and still choose to remain silent even if they individually want to speak out in their defense—because they know the cost of rebellion may be death, further trauma, or the pain of their loved ones (Garza 2020). An Intersectional Other may also choose to assimilate into straight or white society and separate from their family or community, move into a more privileged area, or emigrate to the United States from another country, all to give future generations more resources (Sangalang and Vang 2017). In sum, respectability, code-switching, and self-policing are complicated endeavors that may diminish individual power temporarily, but may preserve safety, future power, power for family, and power for community. There is a temptation to dichotomously assess and judge whether someone is too colonized; too closeted; and whether they've sold out or become "whitewashed" beyond repair. In reality, each of us may make the decision to accept or refuse a mainstream acceptance based on a combination of factors and that decision is anything but easy.

Jeopardizing Power by Believing We're Less Qualified

A viral tweet from Sarah Hagi in 2015, "Carry yourself with the confidence of a mediocre white man," has become a staple phrase in feminist and intersectional circles. It is the sentiment that white men—even queer white men—often get away with putting in less work, or having less resolve, than marginalized people, yet still retain confidence and success as a result of their privilege. Whole books are now dedicated to this topic, such as the 2020 novel *The Dangerous Legacy of Mediocre White Men*, written by Black queer author Ijeoma Oluo.

Imposter Syndrome

Most often discussed in the context of one's career or academia, "imposter syndrome" refers to the psychological pattern in which an individual doubts their skills, talents, or accomplishments and has a persistent internalized fear of being exposed as a "fraud," no matter the individual's actual qualifications for a role. The original construct of "imposter phenomenon" has been around for a few decades (Clance and Imes 1978) and is widely accepted today as a legitimate barrier to performance and self-esteem. Initially conceived as a plague only on nervous, perfectionistic "high-achieving minds," it is, in actuality, a syndrome that widely impacts marginalized people of all kinds and therefore is much more common than previously suspected (Holliday et al. 2019).

As a therapist who specializes in work with Intersectional Others, I can attest that most of my clients suffer from imposter syndrome in one way or another, and it has a significant effect on their self-perception. The sources are various, but most cases are definitively caused by social stigma and discrimination within specific institutions. Yes, imposter syndrome can co-occur with anxiety or low self-esteem (Wolfe 2021), but the bigger picture points to a lack of positive representation for marginalized people, less resources, higher levels of oppression, and negative portrayals of diversity in an institution. The perceived stigma that influences a person's development of imposter syndrome is very much a microcosm of the social stigmas marginalized people experience in their everyday lives. Alicia Garza (2020), activist and cofounder of Black Lives Matter, wrote of imposter syndrome and its impact on her experiences:

> Imposter syndrome is a symptom of a larger phenomenon where Black women, especially queer Black women, seem to belong nowhere. We don't belong at the front of social movements, organizations, Congress, city councils, businesses, classrooms, or anywhere else you can name. Black women have always been the stepping stone for someone else to take their so-called rightful place at the front of the line. We are taught we belong nowhere. (198)

Much of the existing narrative around this syndrome involves individual fixes, rather than a focus on its systemic roots. The bias toward these fixes is evident in the research, which focuses on traits like perfectionism, rather than roots like systemic inequity, as the source of imposter feelings. This has led researchers to suggest fixes like mindfulness or self-care (Mullangi et al. 2019). While these strategies may be helpful in the short-term, they are not the true cause of imposter feelings, which only leaves room for these feelings to recur. Even worse, when these "fixes" don't work, a person experiencing imposter syndrome may blame themselves for the lack of success.

The Imposter Lawyer: An Example. I have a queer nonbinary Vietnamese American client—we'll call them Hai—who came to me after seeing a white straight cis psychiatrist for a couple years. They felt intense imposter syndrome at their law office, to the extent where the focus of every session became this issue for a month. Whenever they entered the office, they reportedly fell silent, after being socially active, and conscious, in most other spaces in their life. Their gregarious nature was apparent from the first moment we met. They were also extremely capable, facilitating workshops and assuming leadership roles in queer and Asian community spaces. Their psychiatrist had chalked their imposter feelings up to social anxiety and a general lack of adjustment to the new work environment. What they could not see—likely at least partially due to the fact that they were not queer, nor trans, nor BIPOC—was that my client was now in an environment where they perceived their authentic self to be wholly unwelcome. Some of this was due to misgendering and other microaggressions, but some of the stress they felt came from a more obscure source. Overall, they believed the intentions of their coworkers were good, and they had yet to receive negative feedback about their performance.

Despite a lack of "evidence," Hai felt they were incompetent most of the time they were at the office, and were convinced their supervisor would, any second, call them in to report their failings for the record. The anticipation of this hypothetical reprimand was so strong that it infected other areas of their life, causing them to feel depressed and encumbered most days. It took a focused conversation about stigma in the legal profession for my client to realize that their imposter syndrome was actually a reflection that their deep beliefs in social justice and anti-racism felt inconsistent with the dehumanization in their intended profession.

Hai announced to their parents that week that they would not be applying to law school after all and would instead go all-in on community organizing before transitioning to teaching as a career. Their anti-anxiety medications were utterly unhelpful for this issue. Ultimately, they needed to talk to another Intersectional Other who truly heard and saw them. Their relationship with their parents was temporarily strained due to family expectations but is now more authentic than ever. Last week, I listened as Hai said joyfully that they've never felt closer to, or so grateful for, their parents. Without this deeper level of exploration, it's hard to say if the same authenticity would have ever been achieved.

Imposter syndrome causes us to doubt our abilities, and indeed our senses of being, when interacting with social circles in which we feel we must perform well. It is this doubt that is a true jeopardy to the power of our Otherness. A mentor in Boston once told me that imposter syndrome is really "a fire waiting to be born from within." That fire may cause discomfort because its bearer recognizes their thoughts and behaviors are distinct, out-of-the-box, and may not be received well by those invested in institutional norms. But this fire doesn't need to be perceived as a flaw. Instead, we may see it as a signal that we harbor ideas and perspectives previously unshared, a way of doing things in ways that have been previously undone. In some cases, it may mean we have entered a situational context where our voice is not intended to be heard. Sensing that our voices will be muted can, and should, cause great anxiety. In these cases, imposter syndrome may be an indicator that we need to leave an unsafe, oppressive institution, and search for institutions that seek to enhance our power instead.

Chapter 6

De-Vilifying the Other

Part of owning our power as Intersectional Others is owning our goodness, even in the face of social conditions which vilify and dehumanize us. Queer Black, Indigenous, and People of Color (QBIPOC) have long known they don't deserve to be vilified, despite pressures to internalize otherwise, and have resisted vilification across history (hooks 1989; Davis 2016; Lorde 2012). But is it even possible to decouple the idea of badness and minority status given how entrenched our biases have become? Black queer producer and activist Erika Alexander (2020) asked about this on NPR's podcast *Throughline*, "How do you create a moral space for yourself inside a space you know is amoral?" It was rhetorical at the time, but I do feel, in many ways, this is the core question the book is trying to answer.

Arguably, the field of Psychology has not only created an amoral space for racialized and sexualized Others, but an immoral one, as it has perpetrated Othering systemically. Brazilian psychologist Elisa Lacerda-Vandenborn said of this history of Othering, "Psychology is implicated in this process because this field created the language, tools and practices to individualize problems that are social in nature. . . .This individualism-focused mental health system is further perpetuating the oppression of particular groups" (Varanasi 2021). Indeed, as psychologists, we are culpable for our field's history and continued vilification.

There are three answers for this, which I believe are central to understanding the full reclamation of power for Intersectional Others. The first is humanization, the natural reversal of dehumanization. By humanization, I do not mean empty gestures of "diversity" and "inclusion." By humanization, I mean genuine attempts to empathize and deepen our understanding of difference and the various intersections of QBIPOC identity and experience. Society at large must see Intersectional Others as complex human beings worthy by virtue of living, else it will never truly be capable of de-vilifying Otherness.

The second is the intentional recentering of intersectional stories. By recentering, I mean the reinjection of intersectional ideas, faces, and voices in national history, storytelling, and media of all kinds. What has previously been erased, overlooked, and silenced by trauma must be recognized and uplifted. The third is the recentering of self-reflection and social consciousness, so we may bring awareness to our contributions and positionalities within an oppressive system. This includes the intentional decentering of whiteness and straightness, which may be among our positionalities, and are absolutely among our social expectations. All three of these are necessary to subvert a dehumanizing and oppressive system, thereby reassociating goodness with Otherness.

Being Othered creates an indelible impression not easily removed. It undermines our sense of possibility and can leave us feeling traumatized and shaken. Power and humanity are intertwined and to reform one must also mean to reform the other. Those with societal power are often disinvested in the reformation process because to do so would mean losing their hold on superiority, virtuosity, as well as their sole—and very presumptuous—claim on humanity. To de-vilify means to decouple whiteness and goodness just as much as it means to decouple Otherness and badness. De-vilification of the Other must continue to be an aspirational goal for future generations to claim, else we risk liberation for us all.

THE COMMODIFICATION OF "DIVERSITY"

Diallo Shabazz was a student at the University of Wisconsin-Madison when he stopped by the admissions office in 2000. He was approached by an admissions counselor, who said, "Did you see yourself on the admissions booklet? Actually, you're on the cover this year." Shabazz quickly realized something was off. His face appeared on the cover all right—a cheerful freshman beaming in the bleachers behind a slew of white fans cheering at a UW football game. The problem, however, was simple. Shabazz had never been to a football game in the entirety of his undergraduate education. His face had been photoshopped into the cover photo and transposed, presumably to give the illusion that the campus was more diverse than it actually was (Prichep 2013).

Behind the scandal, an even bigger problem was afoot. The college's Multicultural Student Center was just two floors below the Admissions Department (Prichep 2013). The department had no need to steal and photoshop Shabazz's face; it could have reached out for authentic, consensual photographs of student life on campus. The incident quickly became a national example of the lengths to which academic institutions would go in order to market diversity to its audiences, whether those audiences were marginalized prospective students or white liberal parents hoping to send their kids to a "well-rounded" school (Chang 2016). Shabazz complained but little was done until he sued and won a 10-million-dollar settlement for the violation. It became clear through this process that Shabazz' Blackness was a commodity, and that the institution cared little about actual equity, inclusion, or the feelings of its marginalized students (Roediger 2005). Until they lost face and capital, the institution was unwilling to change.

The Pitfalls of Diversity Training

We often make the mistake of thinking we can solve institutional inequities through simple diversity training. The constructs of "diversity" and "inclusion" are helpful as building blocks for de-vilification, but not as helpful as people give them credit for. When these terms first emerged in U.S. corporations and academic institutions around 2010, they proliferated quickly, adopted by liberal white administrators and leaders as a means to "improve" the environments of their organizations. By 2015, the terms were being used ubiquitously in the United States (Jansen et al. 2016). Whole university departments were being given titles with these terms in them. Type "Stanford diversity and inclusion" into Google, for instance, and you will immediately find at least four departments on the first page with websites dedicated to these terms. Prospective applicants began seeing them stamped ubiquitously on the bottom of job applications. Often, they are used interchangeably, without much understanding of their differences, or their limitations.

Why do I bring up diversity training in relation to the assimilative pretense I mentioned? Because they are not dissimilar. Much like identity blindness, diversity initiatives give applicants the illusion of acceptance or potential belonging. Let's think about the term "diversity," for example. Here, we refer to the presence of different identities in a room. In practical terms, you can think of this as the number of marginalized folks allowed into a space, which effectively "diversifies" that space. "Inclusion," then, can be defined as the sense of belonging, value, or acceptance a person has when they enter a space. If diversity is the party Intersectional Others were invited to attend, inclusion is being asked to dance at that party.

While the lack of diversity and inclusion is a problem, it is not the problem. The real problem is a resistance to diversity and inclusion, and an insistence on maintaining power for those with privilege (Kumashiro 2001, 11). What if, instead of asking who has yet to be included, for example, we ask why certain voices were silenced in the first place (Scott 1993)? Theoretically, in an environment promoting diversity and inclusion, white straight coworkers will value, provide access for, and uplift the work and voices of QBIPOC so that equity and opportunities are achieved by all. However, as a Harvard study (Chang et al. 2019) would indicate, corporate diversity training may affect attitudes toward marginalized folks, but not behaviors. The study revealed that when targeting bias toward BIPOC and women, the people primarily impacted were junior women at an institution, who sought mentorships with senior women at their companies after the training—great. However, it's telling that the typical targets of diversity training, those in power like white straight men, did not attempt to increase access or opportunity for their marginalized peers when prompted to do so.

The training mainly increased awareness of bias for already-marginalized women in the company, causing them to look for ways to gain upward mobility by utilizing connections with more senior members of the company. What does this imply? It implies what marginalized folk already suspect with diversity training, which is that lip-servicing that you want "more diversity in a company" or "a greater sense of inclusion in the workplace" does not actually yield substantial change to the barriers at play here. Barriers are structural and pervasive, from the lowest level in the pipeline (e.g., the recruitment process) to the highest level (e.g., who occupies the senior-most leadership role, such as CEO), and every step from here to there.

Tanya Golash-Boza, Peruvian American scholar and professor of sociology at the University of California, Merced, wrote on the hypocrisy of diversity initiatives when she posted on Twitter:

I have worked on diversity in faculty hiring for several years and have studied racism for decades. I can thus tell you with confidence that the #1 reason Black, Latinx, and indigenous people are under-represented among faculty is that people on search committees are racist. (Golash-Boza 2021)

Good intentions and positive attitudes are not enough to change the oppressive structures that exist within such a system, because that oppression is entrenched in a multitude of ways, ways that diversity training just doesn't touch. It is not enough to allow QBIPOC into a boardroom meeting, for instance. They must also have a voice at the table, not in the back. They must also help design and create the projects discussed at the meeting. They must also help validate and give feedback about those projects, and have their feedback heard and valued. And they must also be able to lead the meetings, the team, and the company. Being allowed into a space is one thing—being truly heard and prized for your work and self are another.

THE FIRST STEP TO DE-VILIFICATION
IS HUMANIZATION

Kimberlé Crenshaw, Black feminist legal scholar whose work *Demarginalizing the Intersection of Race and Sex: A Black Feminist Critique of Antidiscrimination Doctrine, Feminist Theory and Antiracist Politics* (1989) coined the term "intersectionality," wrote that literature on Blackness was simply not sufficient to understand the experiences of Black women in the justice system, nor was the literature on being a woman sufficient to describe those experiences. She said,

> With Black women as the starting point, it becomes more apparent how dominant conceptions of discrimination condition us to think about subordination as disadvantage occurring along a single categorical axis. . . . In other words, in race discrimination cases, discrimination tends to be viewed in terms of sex- or class-privileged Blacks; in sex discrimination cases, the focus is on race- and class-privileged women. This focus on the most privileged group members marginalizes those who are multiply-burdened and obscures claims that cannot be understood as resulting from discrete sources of discrimination. (140)

"Demarginalization," although a helpful construct, implies that our aim is to bring someone back to the mainstream—potentially even to reintegrate them into the system that marginalized them in the first place. I argue the first step toward de-vilification must be humanization, not demarginalization, as Crenshaw argued. We cannot simply seek to demarginalize this country—we must ultimately seek to de-vilify and re-own goodness for Intersectional Others. To do this necessitates the exposure of the nation' history of dehumanization for the Othered, as well as intentional efforts to reestablish the humanity of those it has previously sought to dehumanize.

We can, however, use Crenshaw's logic to understand the vital importance of an intersectional perspective for humanizing and empowering QBIPOC. Since Crenshaw's introduction of "intersectional" terminology, it has become an invaluable concept in understanding compounded systemic issues across many disciplines, including sociology, psychology, anthropology, history, and law. "Intersectionality" at its coining (Crenshaw 1989) may not have been an attempt at de-vilifying marginalized identity, but it has since been adopted by organizers, artists, and other community players to highlight the compounded nature of oppression in this country.

We spoke in the last chapter about the intent, pressure, and actions of oppressive systems to dehumanize the Other. Humanization after lifetimes of dehumanization is not easy, as it requires a subversion of everything that is "known" about marginalized people. It is important to recognize that histories of dehumanization and humanization in this country cannot exist without each other. It is precisely because we are dehumanized that we strive for our humanness. It is perhaps this tension that causes those who are dehumanized to then attempt to dehumanize their perpetrators, a cycle that has been captured in literature (Kteily and Bruneau 2017). In essence, they are shouting, "We are human, too!" Paulo Freire, Brazilian educator and activist, wrote in *Pedagogy of the Oppressed*:

> The struggle for humanization, for the emancipation of labor, for the overcoming of alienation, for the affirmation of men and women as persons would be meaningless. This struggle is possible only because dehumanization, although a concrete historical fact, is not a given destiny but the result of an unjust order that engenders violence in the oppressors, which in turn dehumanizes the oppressed. (1968, 44)

Freire called attention to the fact that dehumanization, as a process, is more so an outcome of systemic injustice than it is, on the whole, driven by individual perpetrators. Social justice and equity are impossible without bringing the humanity of the Othered into collective consciousness, for to dehumanize an individual or group is to inherently believe that they are not worthy of such things (Freire 1968).

Intersectionality before Crenshaw

Importantly, "intersectionality" was not a concept created in isolation, but one crafted by the minds of activists and scholars working in tandem to combat the oppressions experienced by Intersectional Others and their communities. Black and Brown queer feminists, in particular, discussed and wrote about intersectionality well before the term was coined by Crenshaw in 1989, although Crenshaw's work brought new publicity to the topic through its explicit naming. Sojourner Truth, for example, in her poignant 1851 speech, *Ain't I a Woman*, shone light on the ways in which being Black intersected with gender identity and enslavement.

Black lesbian playwright Lorraine Hansberry may have also been one of the first theorists on intersectionality, as her writing for rallies and theater productions, her communications with other members of the queer community, and pan-African community building—working with WEB Dubois, James Baldwin and others—belied her radical thinking of the time, as well as her deep understanding of Black queer feminism before there were words for such a thing, which was revealed in her posthumous personal documents (Carter 1980). She wrote a letter to the Daughters of Bilitis (DOB) staff in 1957, which stated that particularly as one raised in a cultural experience (I am a Negro) where those within were and are forever lecturing to their fellows about how to appear acceptable to the dominant social group, I know something about the shallowness of such a view as an end in itself. (*The Ladder* 1957)

Black queer Professor of History at the University of Illinois, Kevin J. Mumford (2016), believed that by "juxtaposing the progress of the civil rights movement against the question of lesbianism," Hansberry "compared the dictates of black respectability to the homophile's pursuit of a kind of respectable integration" (17). Hansberry, who also had a vision of unified otherness for all who were oppressed, wrote later in the letter to the DOB that "what ought to be clear is that one is oppressed or discriminated against because one is different, not 'wrong' or 'bad' somehow" (Riemer and Brown 2019, 84). She died from pancreatic cancer at age 34, and her intersectional works and more radical ideologies of the time are rarely recollected in scholarship on queer history and ethnic studies (Raymos 2020).

In 1969 and 1970, respectively, Black feminist scholar Frances Beale introduced the concept of "double jeopardy" and intersecting oppressions, while Black queer feminist Toni Cade Bambara (1970) edited the anthology *The Black Woman*, which featured contributions from several prominent BIPOC feminists at the time—Grace Lee Boggs, Alice Walker, and Audre Lorde, to name a few—covering the intersections of race, sexuality, gender, and class. In 1977, the Combahee River Collective wrote a public statement on their experiences as Black lesbians, stating within,

> We often find it difficult to separate race from class from sex oppression because in our lives they are most often experienced simultaneously. We know that there is such a thing as racial-sexual oppression which is neither solely racial nor solely sexual. (4-5)

Black queer author bell hooks (1981) also published well-received written works on intersectionality, such as *Ain't I a Woman: Black Women and Feminism*, followed by Xicanx queer activist and writer Cherríe Moraga and Chicana dyke-feminist Gloria Anzaldúa, who wrote extensively on the intersections of racial histories, sexuality, and gender in their book that same year, *This Bridge Called My Back: Writings by Radical Women of Color*, an anthology which included voices from Black, Native, Asian American, and Latina/x activists. In it, Anzaldúa poetically wrote of her own experience:

> I am a wind-swayed bridge, a crossroads inhabited by whirlwinds . . . "Your allegiance is to La Raza, the Chicano movement," say the members of my race. "Your allegiance is to the Third World," say my Black and Asian friends. "Your allegiance is to your gender, to women," say the feminists. Then there's my

allegiance to the Gay movement, to the socialist revolution, to the New Age, to magic and the occult. And there's my affinity to literature, to the world of the artist. What am I? . . . They would chop me up into little fragments and tag each piece with a label. (Anzaldúa and Moraga 2015, 204)

As the author stated, these siloed "allegiances" and "labels" can never fully define Intersectional Others, just as language can never fully capture the whole of human experience. Even without the word "intersectionality," there remains a clear understanding of its meaning and the effect of its existence. In her 1987 book *Borderlands/ La Frontera: The New Mestiza*, Anzaldúa described the fluidity of intersectional realities in relation to what she termed "transgressions" of physical, communal, historical, and psychological "borderlands." QBIPOC have always been on the front edge of intersectional discourse.

Intersectionality Versus Integrated Relationality

For our purposes, intersectionality provides a framework for understanding how identity can be used to explore factors relating to racial and sexual identity. Society's tendency to rely on incomplete understandings of discrimination that stem from single cultural identities (e.g., racism or heterosexism) ultimately obscure, and completely miss, the complex nature of Intersectional Others' experiences. And although the intersectional framework may be the best one we have to discuss QBIPOC identities, there are still limitations. Embedded in the framework is the notion that cultural identities act as discrete categories which merely "intersect," rather than occupy an "integrated relationality" (Wong and Santa Ana 1999, 172). Queer Asian American scholars David Eng and Alice Hom (1998) discussed this conflict, writing that, while they were concerned with "the intersection of racial and (homo) sexual difference," they also had an "unwilling[ness] to bifurcate identities into the racial and sexual" (1) due to the fact that doing so would inevitably provide an inaccurate read on those intersections.

Indeed, some scholars, such as queer Latinx scholars Queseda, Gomez, and Vidal-Ortiz (2015) even implied there might be a merging, rather than intersecting, of various identities. They wrote in *Queer Brown Voices*,

Brown is not a mere color but a way of seeing (and of being seen by) the world; it is a form of identification that supersedes both "Hispanic" and "Latino" ethnoracial categories . . . Brown (capitalized) often becomes queer. (i)

It is difficult to say which conceptualization is most accurate. The truth is that intersectionality is a messy construct, despite scholarly attempts to parse it out. However, it is the best construct we have to date for addressing the needs of QBIPOC as they exist simultaneously.

An Empathic Understanding of the Othered

Because dehumanization takes place when Intersectional Others are told they must "be respectable" and restrict their emotional expression for the sake of mainstream society, humanization must mean allowing the full breadth of human emotion to be expressed, and therefore processed and dealt with. Beyond simple empathy, which is a shared understanding or feeling for another human being and their circumstances (Elliott et al. 2011), we must also humanize by allowing for authentic emotions, even uncomfortable ones, in the face of injustice and systemic inequities. Shining a light on the complexity of human emotion powerfully brings to visibility that which was previously invisible, even in the most minute circumstances. Joy, grief, anger—yes, even boredom—are all necessary components of understanding the depth of a person's humanity.

In social sciences research, empathy is often offered up as the primary solution to dehumanization, but little is discussed of exactly what this means and how to do it (Haslam 2006). There have been studies on empathy-related constructs which do seem to be effective countermeasures for prejudice, however, which may be a good proxy for reducing dehumanization. For instance, we know that direct, or even imagined, contact with members of an outgroup can create positive perceptions of that group. This phenomenon is called the "contact hypothesis" and is often considered the foremost method to reduce prejudice among the social sciences (Pettigrew and Tropp 2006).

Unfortunately, more recent studies show contact specifically aimed at improving interracial conflict may yield weaker effects (Paluck, Green, and Green 2019). One might speculate that this weaker effect is seen at least partially because it is not increased contact alone which reduces conflict, prejudice, and dehumanization, but, perhaps more importantly, an empathic understanding of the Othered, which may or may not be achieved through contact. Thus, personal relationships—such as friendship, familial ties, and coworker connections—are likely much more helpful for reducing prejudice, as they often involve the cultivation of compassion, kinship, warmth, and empathy.

A study by Stephan and Finley (1999) found that prompting participants to empathize with immigrants significantly reduced the amount of prejudice they felt toward them. Other scholars have indicated that increased intergroup contact (Stephan and Stephan 2000), emphasizing shared humanity (Allport 1954), and providing education on the outgroup (Berryman-Fink 2006) may also serve to humanize the Othered. If providing education, there should be effort made to educate from the point-of-view of the outgroup members, such as white folks learning about Black-centered history in the United States in *The New York Times'* The 1619 Project. These methods may not extinguish prejudice, but may provide a starting point for discussions on otherness and reduce the impact of perceived threat, stigma and propaganda.

An under-discussed part of taking an empathic stance is an openness to receiving the emotional experiences of others, even if they are different from your own. Often, we talk about empathy as a feeling of relatability or like-ness with another person or group, but this is not true empathy. Empathy must consist of a willingness to hear and see what may be uncomfortable emotional experiences, which includes hearing or seeing injustice (Segal 2011). This is not to say we all must share the same emotional responses to injustice. However, if we can openly receive and seek to understand the emotions of the marginalized, we are then able to humanize and have concern for that person or group. This is sometimes referred to as "empathic concern" in literature, a feeling of concern for an individual affected by adversity, which causes someone to focus on the situation the affected individual is experiencing (Cassels et al. 2010).

The answer to infra-humanization—the act of unconsciously denying that an outgroup experiences "uniquely human emotions" and believing thusly that the outgroup is less human (Castano and Giner-Sorolla 2006)—is not to assume that ingroup and outgroup emotional processes are the same. In other words, it is not enough to project feelings onto marginalized people in order to humanize them, for while we may all share certain basic emotions (e.g., anger, sadness, fear), the ways in which we perceive, process, and express these emotions can vary dramatically depending on cultural norms, individual experiences, and even the language used to describe an emotional experience within a particular community.

Higher levels of empathy are predictors of a higher "valuation" of others' welfare and well-being. They may also lead to prosocial behavior, such as altruism and helping to alleviate the other person's negative emotions (Cassels et al. 2010). Contrastingly, low levels of empathy may contribute to fundamental attribution error; that is, attributing minority stress and environmental circumstances to the shortcomings of a marginalized person's character. An example of this would be moralizing the homeless, such as assuming they came to live on the street after spending all their money on substance abuse, thus self-imposing poverty. This is a false attribution—the biggest factor influencing homelessness is a systemic issue, not a personal one. According to the 2016 U.S. Conference of Mayors *Hunger and Homelessness Survey*, the number one cause of homelessness in the United States is a lack of affordable housing. The second biggest is unemployment (Cornett et al. 2016). Considering the perspective of devalued groups is important for understanding them effectively, though adequate knowledge of their circumstances and disparities they face is also key.

Empathy is a vital precursor and part of social justice, which requires that there is a cohesion and understanding among cultural groups to facilitate a joint goal toward exposing systemic barriers and establishing a more equitable and just society for marginalized communities (Segal 2011). It is also a precursor of allyship (Louis et al. 2019). Without it, humanization is impossible and so is the dismantling of oppressive systems. This is a critical point to understand about humanization and the mobilization toward change. Racial justice is also gender justice. Queer justice is also disability justice. We must include an intersectional lens, else risk falling into the trap of disempowering people not only within our communities but also people whose experiences may appear on the surface distinct but are in actuality linked to us through oppressive reality. Other marginalized groups need to be elevated so we can all be elevated.

THE SECOND STEP TO DE-VILIFICATION IS TO RECENTER INTERSECTIONAL STORIES

Recentering projects are powerful because they bring to life stories that absolutely did exist, but simply were never told. Enby Spoken Histories is one such project—a preservation of queer and trans storytelling that ranges from ancestral voices being told anew to queer, trans, and nonbinary narratives saved to the archives to be passed to future generations. It is a community which revives and protects storytelling traditions, inspired Peruvian American trans twink/dyke artist Ángel Labarthe del Solar's and mixed Korean and Yurok trans Two-Spirit artist Coyote Park's deeply held beliefs that storytelling and art have the power to affect change (del Solar 2021). Writing about the connection of these stories to the livelihoods of the communities who share them, the creators state on their project website (2021):

> It is lifesaving to offer space for real conversations, stories that incorporate joy and resilience, questioning and discovery. It can also be lifesaving for listeners seeking human resonance with someone who may or may not be like them. Enby Spoken Histories interrupts previous narratives of what we can become, and who will remember us. Storytelling is essential for both starting and continuing conversations for change.

The power in these narratives is not, then, just that they are told, but that those who listen to them feel seen, heard, and that they are part of a bigger community. Through this interchange is also the power to save lives, particularly the lives of queer and trans youth of color, particularly Two-Spirit youth, who have high rates of suicide and depression, often reporting a sense of isolation as part of their lived experience (Ferlatte et al. 2019). These are methods of relating to one another that truly arose as an intersectional approach to reclamation and hope.

Media production and representations expose the constant identity constructions and contestations occurring in society. As Jamaican British theorist and sociologist Stuart Hall (1989) reminds us, identities are born and maintained "within, not outside, representations" (69). It is these representations that shape how we come to see ourselves and others. That is, media productions not only present reality but create it. A network television show which chooses to center a white, straight cast—or marginalize a QBIPOC one—is actively commenting, not just on the lives that already exist, but those which should exist, and by what standards they should live and be understood. And, due to the influence that screens have on shaping what narratives are heard, providers of this content have direct control of exposure and representation, regardless of the actual demographic share in the United States (Fursich 2010).

Intersectional (Mis)representation in Media

The exact magnitude of the effect invisibility and Othering representation has on the audience —or the evolution of QBIPOC stigma in society as whole— is unclear. However, it is safe to say that QBIPOC watching on the other side of the screen are implicitly taking note, to detrimental ends. One queer scholar, Richard Dyer, went so far as to say that cinematic representation for "oppressed groups was, and by and large still is, a relentless parade of insults" (Dyer 1993, 1). If we grow up without seeing our core identities reflected on screen, we grow up thinking the ceiling for our accomplishments and overall success in a social system are extremely limited, and that the models for our hopes, goals, and behaviors should be based on people who don't look like us. The more we see ourselves mocked, beaten, or erased on-screen, the more we slowly, inevitably come to believe that erasure and violence are what the world expects of us, and perhaps we should even expect it of ourselves.

The lack of representation, misrepresentation, or blatant marginalization for Intersectional Others in films and television is at least partially due to the lack of representation at the highest levels of the media industry. In a 2018 study by the Directors Guild of America (DGA), researchers found that, behind the scenes, directors of feature films in were overwhelming white cis men (90% and 88%, respectively). Another study on media inequality reported that, of the top 100 films, 81 had no LGBTQIA2S+ representation, and, of the 31 characters that were present, only 32.3% were BIPOC.

The study did not measure the intersection of queerness and race behind the scenes, but they did report that only one woman of color—yes, you heard me correctly—worked as a director of a top-grossing film. It is likely that the number of QBIPOC in director roles was zero (Smith et al. 2018). At the time of the report, guild president Thomas Schlamme said the results revealed that "discriminatory practices are still rampant across every corner of the feature film business." He added that improved diversity in indie filmmaking is a "misconception" (DGA 2018).

These patterns are also replicated in identities of the cast. Research from the University of Southern California (USC) Annenberg Inclusion Initiative (Smith 2020), which examined the racial and sexual identities of leads and speaking characters across the 1,300 top-grossing films, found that Asian Americans and Pacific Islanders—grouped together in this study—were scarcely represented in visual media between 2007 and 2019. They identified just 44 films featuring an Asian American or Pacific Islander lead, 14 of which were Dwayne "The Rock" Johnson. Only six of those identified were women, and none were queer or trans. From 2014 to 2019, researchers identified only 15 characters who were also gay, lesbian, or bisexual. None were trans. One may think that the Oscar wins of Chloe Zhao (*Nomadland*) and Bong Joon-ho (*Parasite*) changed the tide for these groups. However, it is not enough.

Villainous Sissies and Treacherous Dykes

Shifting media representation for Intersectional Others may shed more light on the history of vilification, as well as possibilities for de-vilfication. Media visibility, or lack thereof, is often a mirror of social attitudes toward specific groups of people. And for most of the 20th century, mainstream media routinely ignored LGBTQIA2S+ people, focusing on white gay and lesbian representation when shown at all. Even these roles were sensationalized to the point of ridicule. In 1930, the Hays' Motion Picture Producers and Distributors of America created the Motion Picture Production Code, which literally banned "inference of sex perversion" (i.e., queerness). There were few objections, though, when queer characters appeared as villainous sissies or treacherous dykes (White 1999).

When they weren't sensationalized villains, queer and trans characters on screen were subject to death and brutality. Studies show that, in the ten years between 1961 and 1971, there were 32 films featuring gay and lesbian characters. Of those, 13 committed suicide and 18 were murdered (Gross 2001). Aside from brutalization, common contemporary narratives include the "militant queer," and the "assimilationist" (Rodriguez 2018). These inaccurate or absent representations make it very apparent that stigma is still a real barrier to community power. Today, the film industry is moving beyond these older stereotypes for Intersectional Others, with films like *The Half of It* (2020) and shows like *Pose* (2019–2021), but representation still has a lot of catching up to do if it ever intends to come close to heterogeneity we often see in films with white straight leads.

Heroes of Our Own Stories

When creating a compelling character for a story narrative, writers seek to give that character layers and complexity—a character with which the audience can relate, placed within a world that they can immerse themselves in fully. This means that a character must have flaws, insecurities, habits, aspirations, and, importantly, a backstory. We're all familiar with movies that fail to give the protagonist their own psychology and backstory. Whether due to low budget, time constraints, or plain-old bad writing, these movies simply will never capture our attention in the same way. More often than not, marginalized characters suffer from these woes—that is, they lack backstories and complexity in all of these ways. And at the intersections, Intersectional Others are often left without these things altogether.

Have you heard of Michaela Coel's *I May Destroy You*? Perhaps not, and not because it's not an amazing series with groundbreaking casting and provocative content, but rather because it flew under mainstream radar and was snubbed by the 2020 Golden Globes award committee, which chose to instead nominate shows like *Emily in Paris*—twice. If you don't believe white supremacy is real, I challenge you to watch the former and the latter side-by-side and judge the quality of their content. A damning exposé by the *LA Times* revealed that members of the Hollywood Foreign Press Association—the institution responsible for doling out Golden Globes each year—were flown out to the set of *Emily in Paris* and provided extravagant hotel accommodations on Paramount Network's dime prior to receiving their nominations (Perman 2021). Dehumanization of QBIPOC begins with the occlusion of their lived experiences, which are almost always occluded by the romanticized stories of the privileged, like white tourist/social media influencer/marketer Emily in *Emily in Paris*.

If audiences look more microscopically at *I May Destroy You*, they will find a powerful tale of sexual trauma, but, perhaps even more importantly, they will also find a heartfelt, genuine story of Blackness, queerness, and community, the likes of which rarely makes its way onto a mainstream television network. It takes its time to naturally deliver conversations on thought-provoking and important issues like consent, identity, control, and the nature of morality. Part of this realness is the Black queer director Michaela Coel's own realness, who stated in a few interviews that she, like the characters in the show, struggled with sexual assault in her own history. It is precisely through this type of visual bravery that we can begin de-vilifying the lives and voices of QBIPOC, who deserve to have their stories told. There is a power in storytelling and communicating authentic experiences.

#OscarsSoWhite

De-vilification can only come when Intersectional Others can be the heroes of their own stories. One overwhelming barrier to this is the prevalence of white- and straight-washing in American media. It is offensive to imply that Intersectional Others need white straight heroes to be their saviors, or that they should be relegated to side characters ad infinitum. The Twitter campaigns #OscarsSoWhite and #WhitewashedOut in 2016, started by bi Asian American actress and comedian Margaret Cho, pointed out the ludicrosity of this white-centered colonial tradition. When Cho was asked how she felt about *The Great Wall* (2016), which featured Matt Damon as white savior, she tweeted, "We have to stop perpetuating the racist myth that only a white man can save the world."

The 2021 Golden Globes ceremony was historical in some ways. We can look at shows like *Schitt's Creek* (2015–2020), which normalize and celebrate queer identity in all its forms—but not colors. In his acceptance speech for 2020 *Best Comedy Television Series*, coproducer Dan Levy, who starred as David in the show, commented on the lack of inclusivity in the industry when he said:

> Inclusion can bring about growth and love to a community. In the spirit of inclusion, I hope this time next year this ceremony reflects the true breadth and diversity of the film and television being made today, because there is so much more to be celebrated.

Levy's coded language couldn't be more felt by Intersectional Others, who are, and have been all along, very aware of the lack of positive visibility in media, as well as award ceremonies, specifically.

Schitt's Creek won nine Golden Globes in 2020, and that absolutely counts as a historic sweep for LGBTQIA2S+ communities at large. However, we've always known that white queers are the "good gays," and lauding the success of this show can easily mask the marginalization of other queer people if we get complacent. There are more important stories to tell which have never been told on the big screen. Whiteness, even in the context of queer whiteness, has always been afforded the privilege of multiplicity—of stories with nuance and characters with their own opinions, desires, and personalities—where BIPOC are monolithic Others. White queer narratives are thus valorized in relative position to Black and Brown queerness.

THE THIRD STEP TO DE-VILIFICATION IS
TO RECENTER THROUGH REFLECTION
AND SOCIAL CONSCIOUSNESS

Recentering is not intended to sound easy—it is not easy. The United States' history of Othering runs deep, making the reversal of its damage akin to the extraction of venom from a festering wound, one which has affected the very heart of the nation. However, self-reflection and the gathering of awareness of our positions and influence in society are the first steps toward extraction as they cause those in dominant social positions to make space for Others who would be dominated, pushed to the margins, and forgotten.

It is not just white straight men who must reflect on their privilege, although this is certainly true. All of us must do work to affect change through introspection and critical examination of our participation, benefiting, use of privilege at the expense of others inside and outside our communities. This includes BIPOC and white queer folks as well, who harbor their own privileged identities within the plethora we all hold, constantly intersecting, at any given time. We, Intersectional Others, too, harbor privilege within the nuances of our selfhoods, as some sexual identities are less stigmatized or more easily able to "pass" than others. Some have class privilege, some able-bodied privilege. We all carry within us both the voices of society's oppressors and its oppressed, and it is our responsibility to lay claim to both and reflect on their effects. Black queer scholar bell hooks, in *Talking Back, Thinking Feminist, Thinking Black* (1989), wrote:

> It is necessary to remember, as we think critically about domination, that we all have the capacity to act in ways that oppress, dominate, wound (whether or not that power is institutionalized). It is necessary to remember that it is first the potential oppressor within that we must resist—the potential victim within that we must rescue—otherwise we cannot hope for an end to domination, for liberation. (25)

Our Internal Oppressors

One way in which scholars and activists have attempted to recenter the issues of the oppressed is, somewhat ironically, through the critical examination of whiteness, a niche within the broader scope of critical race theory. Whiteness has historically been used as the metric by which all other marginalized people are measured, making it all the more important to interrogate our positionality and bias with regards to it, in addition to its validity as a measuring stick to start. The field of whiteness studies emerged in the mid-1990s, and the number of courses and texts offered on this topic have proliferated since then.

Some scholars, such as mixed Arab-British author Layla Saad, have even created anti-racist personal discovery materials, which enable those with white privilege to better understand their contributions and gains from white supremacy. In her book *Me and White Supremacy*, for instance, Layla Saad (2020) discussed the importance of bringing that which may be unconscious or "just below the surface" to conscious awareness through regular reflective exercises. To this end, she wrote, "You cannot dismantle what you cannot see. You cannot challenge what you do not understand" (Saad 2020, ix). Indeed, it is not only reflection that is needed, but an active stance toward challenging one's own internalized oppression, and, as Brazilian educator Paulo Freire felt one's internal oppressor (Freire 1968).

However, education on decentering whiteness and recentering marginalized voices is not without risks—there are several potential roadblocks. Professors in whiteness studies often find themselves to be the target of accusations or harassment, including the insinuation that, by recentering feminist, queer, and non-white voices, they are somehow furthering "their own agenda" (Matias and Mackey 2016; Sueyoshi 2013). Those who claim this forget that no education is neutral, and every curriculum is in fact centered on an institutional, individual, or system-based goal. Most often, these goals reinforce problematic norms whereby whiteness and straightness are privileged.

Queer Asian American historian and Dean of the College of Ethnic Studies at San Francisco State University, Amy Sueyoshi, wrote about these challenges saying:

> From offensive anonymous e-mails to the more aggressive filing of sexual harassment suits, these nightmare incidents have rendered whiteness studies classrooms a warzone in which combative students come to embody the very whiteness that the curriculum works to undo. (Sueyoshi 2013, 375)

Importantly, Sueyoshi also places these issues in their historical context. Systems and academic institutions in the United States have commonly delegitimized the importance of Ethnic Studies—cutting departments, reducing funding, or lacking courses altogether (Sueyoshi 2013, 377). An interesting paradox thus develops for whiteness studies as a field of interest. That is, by intentionally causing uncomfortable reflection on the status quo and privileges associated with maintaining it, the resulting discomfort can cause some students to further perpetuate the cycle of oppression through aggression and defensive denial of their biases. Even educators must work through their own biases and strategies to address the paradox they help create.

Critical Consciousness Theory

Brazilian educator Paulo Freire's critical consciousness pedagogy, a part of his larger work *Pedagogy of the Oppressed* (1968), has long been hailed as fundamental to the conversation around oppression, liberation, and education. Freire asserted that only through true awareness of one's oppression and positionality in society could an oppressed person affect change. He was opposed to the notion that the oppressed were marginalized—what he labeled "marginals"—but argued they always existed within the same systems as the oppressors. Thus, the aim should not be to integrate oppressed people but to transform structures so they could become "beings for themselves" (Freire 2018, 161). However, this would be against the interests of society's oppressors, as they are more invested in changing the oppressed person's mind than their circumstances. Indeed, leading an oppressed person to adapt their thinking, rather than change their circumstances, allows the oppressors to achieve domination more easily, as well as maintain the status quo.

Critical consciousness theory emphasizes the need for critical reflection and dialogical education as a vehicle for liberation (Freire 1986), something I also argue in this book. However, because many oppressors create educational systems which promote rote and receptive learning—what Freire referred to as the "banking model" of education—rather than critical engagement, it may be that students in the U.S. school system accept the oppressive ideology more easily, rarely contesting it at all as they are taught to receive, not question, information. Here, I posit that education should not be seen as the ultimate tool through which change must occur for the Othered, however. It is the perspective of the privileged to consider the U.S. educational system to be an equitable one. Arguably Intersectional Others should and do often develop their own tools to achieve liberation and social consciousness. When an individual is used to existing at the margins of society, they may find it easier to think critically about their oppressors than someone accustomed to being an integrated part of an oppressive system (hooks 1989).

Studies have pointed to significant disparities for BIPOC in access to financial resources for education, graduate rates, expulsion rates, special education placement, and enrollment in higher education. Let's take high school graduate rates, for example. These rates are substantially lower for Black and Latino/a/x Americans (68% and 76%, respectively) than they are for white Americans (85%) (National Center for Education Statistics [NCES] 2015). So, what does this mean about the pursuit of the American Dream? It means that these students will not only have lower rates of job placement after high school, but also lower acceptance into higher education programs. Ultimately, it will lead to significant income inequality and quality of life differences for marginalized students as they continue on their journeys toward their future lives. For queer students of color, these inequalities may be compounded by factors like low family acceptance of queer identity (Ryan et al. 2010), higher rates of depression and suicide (Flanders et al. 2019), and higher rates of bullying and harassment in academic settings (Pritchard 2013).

Critical examination, while a vehicle for attaining power, cannot happen solely on an individual basis—it must also happen collectively within our communities, as well as societally. One person's ability to reflect is not enough, although it is still an important piece of social consciousness. Without this critical examination, we cannot hope to move forward toward meaningful change, because we will continue to perpetuate harm toward those who do not benefit from our privileges.

Decentering Whiteness and Straightness

It is essential, if we expect to ever associate goodness with Otherness, that we decenter what is currently the center of society's conversation on goodness—whiteness and straightness. Much closer to Crenshaw's 1989 notion of "demarginalization," recentering is the act not only of making space for folks on the margins but also uplifting their voices, their work, their histories, and their identities so that they may be brought into the light, rather than be forgotten. Perhaps the biggest devastation to QBIPOC communities is the fact that stories and histories are forgotten, retold from the wrong lens, or destroyed through the epistemic violence inherent in colonization (Kingston 2015).

When the white straight mainstream and social elite can actively reflect on their privileges and act on those reflections, there is the potential for a transfer of power to take place, and the chance to recenter those less privileged. One example of this self-reflection is the body of literature written by white gay historian and activist Allan Bérubé, who was deeply thoughtful about his presence and responsibilities as a white, gay person in the world. He said,

> I want to find an antidote to the ways that whiteness numbs me, makes me not see what is right in front of me, takes away my intelligence, divides me from people I care about. . . . I want to become less invested in whiteness while staying white myself—always remembering that I can't just decide to stand outside of whiteness or exempt myself from its unearned privileges. I want to be careful not to avoid its responsibilities by fleeing into narratives of how I have been oppressed as a gay man. (Riemer and Brown 2019, 33)

Reinjecting intersectional voices into the white- and straight-washed histories of our country's past brings to visibility what was previously invisible.

There is great power in bringing collective awareness to issues that cause discomfort for the mainstream United States, because the comfortable avoidance of others' pain becomes impossible. If dehumanization is invisibilizing and delegitimizing intersectional stories, then de-vilification is possible if we allow ourselves to face the traumas and rawness of the stories they themselves tell. The discomfort felt when hearing and seeing these stories told is, often, actually the discomfort of realizing that the (Black queer) protagonists are real human beings, and that their traumas are perpetuated by those of us privileged enough to sit on the other side of the screen.

The Harm of White Progressive Guilt and Performative Activism

When self-reflection does not occur, phenomena like "performative activism" are more likely to emerge, whereby those in privileged positions may offer the pretense of centering marginalized voices, but instead tout their own contributions loudly, overwhelming the potential good that may have come from those contributions. This often happens when white progressives in the mainstream U.S. national body feel compelled to "prove" their allyship and increase their social capital. Some journalists have noted increased usage of the term "performative activism" since the killing of George Floyd, when social media activism became quite prevalent (Tiong 2020).

Today, Intersectional Others listen, tired, as white progressives discuss and perform "wokeness" and allyship, ideas they have self-determined will be helpful without consulting the communities they are attempting to be woke about in the first place. This process of self-determining can only be seen as an attempt to assuage guilt (Iyer, Leach, and Crosby 2003), just as much as it is to prove they are "doing their part" and furthering the trajectory of justice. The problem with this perspective is that real, meaningful action is never taken. Instead, actions are performative in nature and done for social attention. And the reason action isn't taken is simple—it benefits the privileged in society to keep their privilege. The privileged are invested in racial and sexual inequality, perhaps subconsciously, because it helps them stay in power and retain leadership and capital. That is, you cannot be, or have, the best of everything if everyone has everything (Carroll 2020).

The Safety Pin, the Pussy Hat, and the Black Box

There are three widely publicized moments of performative activism that immediately come to mind, all in recent history, although performances occur frequently and at various scales, of course. The first is the "safety pin movement" started by self-proclaimed "white allies," which erupted after former president Donald trump was elected in November 2016. The election had effectively emboldened white supremacists and led to a surge in hate crimes against BIPOC, LGBTQIA2S+ people and immigrants, primarily. Originating in the United Kingdom at the time of the Brexit vote in June 2016, safety pins as ally accessories were meant to symbolize "I am safe and here for you" to marginalized people everywhere (Abad-Santos 2016). The funny thing was, when you talked to the marginalized people who were supposedly benefiting from this service, few knew what the safety pin even meant, few endorsed it, and most perceived it, at best, to be an empty gesture laden with white guilt. At worst, it was a self-indulgent and outrageous attempt for "allies" to act as saviors by means of armchair politics, without ever engaging in meaningful action at all.

The second comes to mind because it's so blatantly an act of performative white cis feminism. What I'm referring to is the Pink Pussy Hat Project, to some considered the symbol of the U.S. Women's March on Washington in 2017 (Black 2017). Pussy hats arose in response to the leaking of Donald Trump's *Access Hollywood* tape. On the tape, the president infamously states:

> You know I'm automatically attracted to beautiful—I just start kissing them. It's like a magnet. Just kiss. I don't even wait. And when you're a star, they let you do it. You can do anything. Grab 'em by the pussy. You can do anything. (Loofbourow 2020)

Queer and trans women of color could be heard shouting "Not all women have pussies. Not all pussies are pink" throughout the four years (Mandler 2019), decrying the exclusionary nature of the symbol, which emphasized a very specific type of U.S. womanhood, rather than being trans- and racially inclusive. Since the initial march, Women's March organizers attempted to add LGBTQIA2S+ women and women of color to its leadership, but the pussy hat remained, a reminder that "inclusive" progressive movements, even when receiving feedback that their actions are harmful, are slow to change (Gökarıksel and Smith 2017). Many women remained unswayed by this conflict and continued to wear the hats through the last march in 2020.

Then, in June 2020, one month after George Floyd was killed, instagrammers found their social media feeds curiously filled with black boxes, all with the hashtags #BlackLivesMatter or #BlackoutTuesday. The initiating parties of the original movement, #TheShowMustBePaused, two Black feminists and music executives, Jamila Thomas and Brianna Agyemang, started the trend reportedly to "disrupt the work week" and garner support for the Black community, while also drawing attention to racial inequities in the music industry (Kaufman 2020).

Their original hashtag and intention were lost in the shuffle, however, as white progressives shared the box, theoretically to support their cause. What many organizers, including Black Lives Matter cofounder Alicia

Garza, noticed was that the viral spread of the #BlackLivesMatter squares was counterproductive—it made sharing information, news, and garnering attention for the actual movement impossible. Not only this, but no context was offered for the squares in most cases, creating a vague message at best (Heilweil 2020). Instead, the hashtag was flooded by a black wall of performative gesturing. In sum, intention matters, consultation with communities about what they need matters, and investing in a symbol is not enough—there must be follow-through.

Chapter 7

Voices for Change

To reclaim our personal and community power is to expose the wellness and power already harnessed by Intersectional Others who lived before us and live today. It is in storytelling that we can see this power most—not in academia or privileged groups—but in the words and actions of grassroots individuals and groups from whom power was attempted to be taken. In *The Way Forward with a Broken Heart*, queer Black author-activist Alice Walker (2012) asserted, "Healing begins where the wound was made." I take this to mean that the most marginalized of our society are closest to its ailments, and thus closest to knowing how to heal them.

Make no mistake. Changemakers on the ground are special. They have the flexibility to move much more quickly, challenge norms through innovative means—social media, word-of-mouth, community building, and original printed works, to name a few—leaning less heavily on institutional bureaucracy and larger systems. These are the people through which we first learn about empowering queer Black, Indigenous, and People of Color (QBIPOC) because these are the people who confront, resist, and reject disempowerment every day. It is hubris to assume that just because a movement is not mainstream means it is not important or powerful. Intersectional Others have been organizing from the margins and shouting rallying cries since the inceptions of their Otherness.

One of the highlights of this book is the effort to uplift and center the voices of QBIPOC within or without "normal" structures within the United States—not celebrities, but real people acting as changemakers in their communities. As we discussed previously on humanization, recentering QBIPOC voices enacts change, as it is a refusal, and ultimately a restructuring, of the hegemonic discourse we absorb through media, research, and organizations which reinforce the notion that white straight dominance is an accepted reality in the United States. Importantly, this book hopes to make visible the work of those who have previously been invisibilized, but whose work should and must be recognized and uplifted. In this way, collective memory and this book can preserve the voices of QBIPOC for years to come. It is not a small undertaking.

COLLECTING THE DATA

I intentionally sought to interview six QBIPOC with varying identities, histories, professions, and aspirations in order to gain a better understanding of the types of change that are occurring and the ways in which power may manifest which are unique to the lenses outside the scope of mainstream systems in this country. Regarding the idea of "queer sexuality," I broadly included any participant who identified as non-straight and on the LGBTQIA2S+ spectrum. Similarly, for race, I welcomed anyone that identified as BIPOC, and non-white, including those who identified as mixed race. Because this book is invested in unearthing racial and sexual histories and memories, it felt of the utmost importance to ensure I was not contributing to the gatekeeping tendencies already embedded in both majority and minority cultures in the United States. There are already rampant attempts in our country to define who is "queer enough" or "Brown enough." Therefore, anyone identifying as an Intersectional Other was "enough" for inclusion in this book.

For the purposes of the interviews that were completed, it felt important that the six participants were given complete control over their own identity descriptions and any potential exposure to public searches or opinions as a product of this work. For instance, two interviewees wished to use pseudonyms, and one wished to keep their sexuality undisclosed. Space for this variation in disclosure was intentional as we are all in our own unique stage of identity development, as well as our own stage of disclosure within our communities and with the public. The questions were open-ended and focused on the examination of power, change, and liberation. The chapter at hand will discuss themes that arose across the interviews, as well as any specific points of interest within a single interview. The quotations being used for this chapter are excerpts of the full interviews, as they were too long to add in their complete forms.

INTRODUCING THE PARTICIPANTS

The participant stories written here are truly the gems of the book. The stories, albeit incompletely as stories are wont to do, capture the complex perspectives of real people actively negotiating with, rejecting, and rework-ing hegemonic reality in the United States. Importantly, the stories also hold within them dualities that can be observed by the readers—they are beautiful, and at the same time raw and rough-around-the-edges; joyful, and at the same time painful to read and bring awareness to; with community, and at the same time without it. They sum up quite wonderfully the history of power we have woven up to this point, but with an air of introspection and real humanity. This is the humanization which has historically been stripped from us. It is the recentering of our emotional complexities without constraints. It is our chance for de-vilifying and reclaiming our power.

I wanted to take the time to introduce the people chosen for this book, so the readers might begin to understand why they feel and say what they do, and why their words matter. As mentioned earlier, each participant has a unique set of positionalities, and they were allowed to define how little and how much of these positionalities should be revealed to the readers. I will list them in order of appearance in the interview here. First is Loa Niumeitolu (she/they), a queer Takataapui Tongan/Pacific Islander person. Second is Dawn Surratt (she/her), a Black lesbian working class (with "enough credit to PRETEND to be 'middle class'") "temporarily able-bodied" nurse practitio-ner. Third is Dylan Medina (he/they), a 30-year-old Filipino American queer cis immigrant and researcher. Fourth is Nora Bashar (she/her), a 32-year-old bi half-Palestinian cis woman. Fifth is Stevie Nystrom (she/her), a 32-year-old mixed Mexican/white able-bodied cis lesbian who works as a senior scientist at a biotechnology company. And the sixth and final participant is Somya Pandey (she/her), a 19-year-old South Asian American engineering student.

THE INTERVIEW

The first question of the interview was deceivingly simple. It gave a general definition for "social power," and then asked participants, "How do you define power in the context of your own life?" Understandably, each of the six participants defined power differently based on their individual experi-ences within their communities. Even so, there was a notable conviction in the responses. One person defined power as remembrance, which they felt was a personal defiance of colonization, which, as we discussed in early in chapter 4, often acts as a force of cultural genocide and erasure. Part of this erasure is the traumatic destruction of individual and collective memory, which makes restoring and maintaining memory a powerful act of resistance, for all of us, but especially for Indigenous peoples. In this case, memory allowed the participant to access selfhood, their connection to Creator, and appreciation of their identity as a Takataapui queer person. Loa Niumeitolu said:

> As an indigenous Takataapui, queer person, I define my self-determination as power to remember, although colonization tries each day to erase my memory, that being queer is a sacred gift from Creator to pulsate the fullness of life into the world. To access my self-determination, I follow a spiritual path of sobriety and serenity, which includes disconnecting from harmful cultural practices I grew up with and letting go of relationships with biological family members that don't allow me to grow.

Dawn Surratt defined power more broadly, commenting on the potential for power to be a positive force in the world, one which she hoped to manifest in her own life and work as a medical provider. It was a sentiment shared by a couple participants:

> It is not coincidental that this question is being asked as last week I just started reading "The Purpose of Power: How We Come Together When We Fall Apart" by Alicia Garza: "Power is the ability to impact and affect the conditions of your own life and the lives of others" (p.57). I would edit that statement by saying POSITIVELY impact & IMPROVE conditions etc. At least the kind of power that I am interested in manifesting and enacting—since power can be used in many ways and towards different ends.

A few folks were immediately triggered to think about powerlessness, with one discussing the "futility and disconnect" that has come with the COVID-19 pandemic, certainly a feeling many of us have experienced, particularly as QBIPOC who may have been aware of existing social inequities, many of which have only been amplified by the pandemic. Dylan Medina discussed the importance of power in the context of liberties that were unavailable prior to gaining permanent residency status in the United States. He said:

> Power to me means having the freedom to make decisions for myself. As some-one who grew up in the U.S. navigating institutions as formerly undocumented and later with a precarious immigration status, I felt powerless at-times knowing how many hurdles I had to overcome to gain access to the most basic service. Having permanent residency now, I feel that I have the freedom and authority to finally make decisions for myself without worrying about additional barriers.

Another participant still focused on the tension between power and power-lessness through the lens of class, reflecting on the use of power on them from authority, such as employers. Nora Bashar wrote:

I often think about the oppression that results from institutional power and privilege, where an official authority can decide who will have access to certain resources and one group benefits at the expense of another. Within the context of my own life, I think about my professional experiences and the dynamic between employers and workers. At times, I may fear rejection from my colleagues for having different world views and politics, but my employer has the power to end my employment at will, which impacts all other aspects of my life. Under capitalism, power comes predominantly from the ruling class which puts the accumulation of wealth above the well-being of people.

Often, the constructs of "strength" and "power" are conflated, but I did not want to make that mistake in this book, as strengths are traits which can give us power and advantages but may not be or feel powerful in and of themselves. In many ways, at the very heart of this book is the paradox of identifying and manifesting power from an Othered position. That is, is it possible to, while—whether by individuals, family, community, or society—for QBIPOC to be powerful prior to liberation occurring, or is this something that simply cannot exist? I posed this question to the participants, and it was difficult for them, just as it is challenging for me to answer, even after all my research and clinical work in this area. I asked, "From your point-of-view, are there any advantages to being 'Other' and existing in the margins?"

One participant, Dawn Surratt, was stumped by this, saying she didn't "want to respond to this question [with] the center or default position being white, male and/or highly privileged in terms of class. But that's what being an 'other' who occupies the margins is." A few participants were able to identify certain advantages but seemed less able to elaborate. Stevie Nystrom, a scientist, offered the interesting perspective that

> [b]eing "other" allows for differences in perspective, and without perspective it is hard for anything to grow or change. It is similar to evolution, those who were born "others" may have been advantageous in life and that became the new norm.

Dylan Medina discussed how Othering taught him to create out of survival and safety. I agree, and it was interesting he came from this perspective, and specifically noted that he held dear the identity of "immigrant." It caused me to wonder if his immigrant identity affected his perspective. He wrote:

> Being othered taught me to be innovative and find and strengthen communities where I feel safe and welcomed. Evidently, there's a lot of trauma that comes with being marginalized but it also provides you the skills to survive and be creative.

Nora Bashar discussed the empathy she developed as a part of being Othered:

> One advantage of being "othered" myself is that it has made me more aware of how others are marginalized and exploited as well. Being a woman of color who consistently experiences varying levels of bigotry, I hear stories from QTBIPOC about the oppression directed at them simply for existing and can't help but empathize.

Only one participant wrote an answer to this question that was just as extensive as their other answers. Loa Niumeitolu came from a completely different angle and felt that "living in the margins" gave her an understanding and appreciation of life and her own journey.

> Like bell hooks exclaimed, the margins, away from the center, away from the status quo, are sites of possibilities to create liberation and truthful love. I am queer in many ways, not only in my desire to intimately partner with a woman. I came to this world born into the margins of each community I've entered and it has offered me a deeper understanding about my life and how to relate to the world in a loving, forgiving, accepting, and open-hearted way. The margins have allowed me to appreciate and hone the multiple practices that sustain me, like being a poet and writer; farming; being a mother to my 22-year-old son; being an Aunti to younger people; being mentored by Elders; and ever imagining and working toward healing this world we share together.

It was a perspective that felt deeply rooted in intersectionality and the hopeful healing and beauty it brings to the world and to the self. I was mesmerized by this response as it was a feeling I attempted to get in touch during my tenure writing this book, yet one I had difficulty accepting at times, particularly when writing about the traumas of white, straight violence against marginalized people. Somehow, despite being exposed to cultural erasure, historical trauma, and even a professed lack of acceptance from family and from themselves at times, this participant tapped into gratitude, love, and a spiritual connection to their intersectional self. It was inspiring to witness.

While healing and appreciation are clearly possible even amid oppression, it is still a powerful force that often causes Intersectional Others to feel ineffective at enacting change. It may even feel like gaining power is impossible under certain circumstances. I wanted to know, on a micro-level, how these particular queer folks of color exercised power. I asked, "What are some personal ways in which you feel you exercise power in your life and the lives of those around you? Are there any ways in which you wish you could exercise power, but feel you can't?"

Interestingly, "education" was the most common response to this question, with three participants mentioning it immediately. And yet, two of those three noted how they did not actually see this as a way to exercise power, but rather a way to bring awareness to issues affecting marginalized communities. Stevie Nystrom, for instance, said:

> I don't know if I have ever felt like I exercised power. I have been a founding member of an OUT in Stem program in my graduate school, but I saw that as educating the grad community. I . . . speak up when homophobic things are said, but again I see that as educating the other party.

Dylan Medina's response was similar.

> Personally, I don't think I'm necessarily exercising power over others. However, I do use my academic training to shed light on issues facing vulnerable populations.

This may indicate either a discomfort with the idea of holding power, when it is often portrayed as a villainous construct (e.g., the proverbial saying of "Absolute power corrupts absolutely"), or it may speak to the perception that power is often out-of-reach for these QBIPOC. It may also be age-related as both people who felt this way were in their 30s, whereas the person who felt education indeed was a means of exercising power was not. Dawn Surratt said,

> When I turned 50 some years ago, I realized that I had more years behind me than in front of me. Since then I've thought about how I can use the power that comes with being in this age cohort in a . . . society obsessed with the commodification of youthfulness that is tainted by a capitalist, heteronormative & ableist unattainable ideal. How can I use my experiences, mistakes, interests, and skills to positively impact the lives in my immediate sphere. . . . I would love to volunteer in a junior high school that is nearby. The students there are mostly Asian, Latino, Indigenous, and/or Black. They are poor and working class. I'd love to be a tutor, but again the limitations of the COVID-19 pandemic have put this on ice for now.

She also commented on a desire to exercise power by restoring ancestral memory and ensuring that the stories of Black elders were not forgotten.

> [T]here are some Black seniors who live on my street, mostly women that I've seen, who I'd like to interview about what it was like living during Jim Crow, moving to California and living through the early years after the Civil Rights

legislation was initially passed. . . . it's important to get these stories recorded first-hand by people of color, particularly other black people.

The other three participants, Loa Niumeitolu, Nora Bashar, and Stevie Nystrom, wrote on the power of self-expression and acceptance for exercising power in the midst of systemic oppression. Stevie Nystrom said:

> I accepted that I like my hair short and I wear flannel and vests which stereotypically codes me as a lesbian. I do it cause I like it and I feel more like me but I still worry about how others will perceive me. In that case, I have some power, enough to dress like I am, but not enough to not care about how others view me.

Loa Niumeitolu mentioned the risk they undertook to reach authenticity, saying:

> I have had to exercise great power to stay and accept my queer self. . . . My choice about who I love directly reflects how much I choose to trust myself and listen to my authentic, personal truths. . . . I have had to risk going against my parents, against my grandparents, against my culture, against Western culture, to find my true self, to find my own spiritual power to follow. The best way that I have been able to access my self-determination, my unique true power, is to break all the rules that the status quo instructs us to follow.

And Nora Bashar took the interesting perspective of leveraging expression to help others:

> I exercise my personal power by expressing myself, for example, through social media and fashion. Being a woman of color in the United States means that some people will treat me differently and that sometimes I will be treated as lesser than by those who hold power. I acknowledge that I personally have privilege by being cisgender and having a lighter complexion, and I try to use my privilege to lift the voices of other QTBIPOC, especially marginalized people who consistently experience oppression.

In writing this book, it was critical to not only address ways that Intersectional Others could own their power or see examples of power throughout U.S. history but also identify the barriers facing them as they attempted to create change for themselves and their communities. This was the next question I posed to the interviewees. I asked, "What do you believe to be the biggest barriers to you and your communities achieving power? Are those primarily within or outside of your communities, and how do you see this?" This question brought the most diverse array of responses of all interview questions. Somya Pandey, for instance, focused on the lack of representation and visibility for QBIPOC in the media. She said:

> Underrepresentation! Although this has been changing for the better in recent years, I often still don't see myself represented in the media or in the tapestry of American values. And even when I do, my communities are often represented as one bloc, not as the diverse and unique communities I'm familiar with. This causes a disconnect with how society perceives me and how I perceive myself, as folks who don't know me will often assume untrue things about me.

Two of the respondents focused on their racial/ethnic identities, rather than their queer identities. I do not believe it to be a coincidence that the two people who responded this way were Black and Indigenous, as these are two of the most marginalized groups in the country. Loa Niumeitolu wrote:

> I belong to an ethnic and racial community, Pacific Islanders, that is more hyper invisible, marginalized, and criminalized as indigenous immigrants than my SF Bay Area queer identity. I am able to organize and find visibility with Two-Spirit QTBIPOC in the SF Bay Area. . . . However, my own Pacific Islander community suffers greatly from invisibility and marginalization. The API or AAPI rubric incorrectly names us and keeps us invisible under an Asian umbrella. We are not Asians, we are Pacific Islanders . . . this kind of treatment leaves me discouraged, but I find support in the indigenous rights movements happening right now, particularly where I live with the Lisjan Ohlone in Berkeley. Indigenous people of California have been misnamed, rendered invisible through physical and cultural genocide and yet they're still here fighting for their sacred sites and waking up each morning on this land to live out their dreams.

Dawn Surratt, on the other hand, said:

> Misogynist violence within communities of color. State violence against communities of color. Police impunity and unaccountability. Struggling public schools—academically and financially. The historical and willful neglect (and definitely NOT benign) that redlining has caused. And as redlining gives way perversely to gentrification in parts of Oakland and other cities, poor people have to move further and further away from companies in the cities that pay better wages, provide benefits, and have dignified working conditions. Distraction. Ennui. The COVID-19 pandemic. Historical trauma and grief. Extreme income inequality. The interaction of these macro and micro level forces combine to cause feelings of overwhelm, apathy, and entrapment.

Yet another focused on lack of support and policing within the larger queer community. Stevie Nystrom wrote:

> I think one of the biggest barriers is that within the community we do not support each other. We ask to be accepted by the "norm" in society with the same respect and opportunities. At the same time, [we] police ourselves within the community. Those who fully believe in heteronormaltivity [*sic*] see how the LGBT+ community treats the trans and bisexual community and think that it is ok. I think this perpetuates biases that are continuously spread and hinders the ability for us to be truly accepted.

Nora Bashar felt two barriers were inseparable and equally important. She said:

> White supremacy and capitalism, which are inextricably linked and originate from outside of my communities, are the barriers predominantly responsible for normalizing and encouraging the abuse and exploitation of QTBIPOC. Capitalism was constructed within a white supremacist society, which means that its outcomes uphold white supremacy and that dismantling capitalism is at the core of challenging white supremacy.

Given the fact that these very real constraints on power for Intersectional Others exist, I wanted to see if the participants saw societal change and liberation as potential realities. Beyond the micro-level of their own lives, I wanted to know if they predicted a liberatory future for Intersectional Others. This question was partially to differentiate notions of "power" and "change" from those of "liberation." To some, the three are very much similar and overlapping, even. To others, liberation becomes a utopian concept we can never quite reach. I asked, "Acknowledging there are very real constraints on power, do you feel it is possible to enact change, gain power, and/or achieve liberation? If so, how? And if not, why not?"

Their responses surprised me, given the fact that some did not feel they could exercise power, and others listed barrier after barrier to change being enacted. The biggest theme I can really comment on here is hope, which was a feeling that came across in every narrative, as well as the uniqueness of each voice as they called for this hope through their own experiences. Dylan Medina was an educator and commented on hope from younger generations:

> Witnessing continuous movements and seeing particularly the younger generation be more vocal and willing to dismantle oppressive systems has been giving me a lot of hope that change is possible. Indeed, looking back at QTBIPOC history, we have seen important changes take place. Moving forward, we need

to continue to uplift the voices and lived experiences of QTBIPOC individuals in various means to change policies and society.

Somya Pandey, who had strong roots in political activism, felt that change was possible with more intersectional leadership and policy shifts:

> Yes, absolutely. I think the best way to make real change is to put members of our community into powerful social and political positions. Though changing a society for the better starts with the individual, creating policy that supports QTBIPOC folks is equally as important. I believe voter registration and pushes to bring our community to the ballot box are some of the most important actions we can take right now.

Others recognized the steady, sometimes glacial pace at which change and liberation occurs, with one feeling that "true" liberation may never actually come. Dawn Surratt, for instance, wrote:

> Yes, enacting positive change and gaining power is possible, but it is a slow and steady undertaking. Achieving liberation won't happen in my lifetime: those with political and economic power on a local, national, and global scale are not going to go quietly into the good night. However, I am heartened & inspired by movements of people on the margins . . . work that cuts across so many borders and identities.

Stevie Nystrom said:

> I think it is possible to enact change, gain power, and achieve liberation but I don't think it will be at 100% . . . I see what happens with the African American community and know that full acceptance is not possible. As someone who grew up in a catholic home, there are "rules" that just can't change no matter how much society evolves. The change is happening but at a snail's pace. This makes sense because lasting change doesn't happen overnight. If we keep pushing the positive LGBT+ representation in media, I think that it could help immensely. Don't use LGBT+ as tokens, pedophiles . . . Don't kill us off every time we are happy. . . We are people too.

Nora Bashar saw liberation through a unified working-class revolution. She explained:

> Unifying our struggles as working class people from all backgrounds is, in my opinion, the key to achieving lasting liberation. It is possible to enact change when we come together to fight against state-sanctioned violence, patriarchal

oppression, bigotry, and capitalism. There is power in numbers and the more we unite the working class against a system that continues to exploit us, the better off we all are.

And lastly, Loa Niumeitolu wrote:

Yes, there are real ways to enact change and to bring liberation. The world is alive to create change that brings balance. I am an indigenous person and being queer to me is grounded in my being indigenous to land and engaging in reciprocity in all my relationships with all beings, even ones that are rendered non-conscious by Western cultures. Relationships are living, actively recipro- cal continuous interactions. Therefore, change is constantly happening and liberation, through relationships, are occurring every moment. I didn't begin life confidently saying I was queer. It took me all the way to only right now, as a 50 year old, to confidently say that I am attracted to women and that I choose to love women romantically.

After searching for themes in these interviews, I felt impressed by their breadth, thoughtfulness, and emotional connections to social justice. It was clear that all respondents cared deeply for not only the people in their imme- diate circles, but those in the world around them—I saw it in the Black elders that Dawn Surratt wanted to interview, the Two-Spirit QTBIPOC community that Loa Niumeitolu bonded and organized with when they came to the Bay Area, and Somya Pandey's desire to use power to affect positive change around her. I spied it in Nora Bashar's empathy for those oppressed, Stevie Nystrom's OUT in Stem program, and Dylan Media's hope for youth and future generations.

After each person listed numerous barriers to power and change, I was quite taken aback by the hope and vulnerability expressed as each person discussed their own vision of liberation. It told me that, despite our shared historical trauma, Intersectional Others are still dreaming of an equitable society and a revolution of norms. It reminded me of the powerful words of self-professed Chicana dyke-feminist author and activist Gloria E. Anzaldúa, who in 1987 proclaimed, "I will have my voice: Indian, Spanish, white. I will have my serpent's tongue—my woman's voice, my sexual voice, my poet's voice. I will overcome the tradition of silence" (81). Each person, in their own way, was working toward that liberatory future, whether through activ- ism, healthcare, science, or education, and those futures looked strikingly similar—a place where Intersectional Others could be safe, be welcome, and be seen.

Chapter 8

"I am Other"

Owning Our Innate Power

In September 2020, trans artist-activist iO Tillett Wright published *Self Evident Truths,* a strikingly beautiful monograph featuring the images of 10,000 queer and trans people in the United States, many of them Black, Indigenous, and Other People of Color (BIPOC). Much like the 2001 Hapa Project by Kip Fulbeck—which illustrated the heterogeneity and ubiquity of mixed Asian people in the States—it was a magnificent display of community power, one which celebrated all the uniqueness and beauty that Intersectional Others, in their multitudinous combinations, bring. The monograph featured a foreword by queer Black Lives Matter cofounder Patrisse Cullors, along with photographs of several public figures, such as Amok Manon and Cara DeLevigne.

What is perhaps most powerful of all is the intention behind the book. Conceived in 2010, it was an attempt to humanize and galvanize LGBTQIA2S+ people in the face of California's Proposition 8, a time when there was intense national debate over the basic humanity of queer and trans people, the validity of their love, and the ability for them to legally marry. Prop 8 has since been overturned (Rohrer 2014), ruled unconstitutional by the California Supreme Court in 2012. However, the art retains its activist origins, and the emotion and humanity depicted in the photographs sends an undeniably powerful message to those who would dehumanize Intersectional Others. Truly, as Wright stated in a 2020 interview with *them.*, it is a "10,000-person piece of proof that if you are other than straight or cis, you are not alone" (Kim 2020). Intersectional Others are everywhere.

There is a power in otherness that goes undiscussed—the unique power wielded by folks who carry marginalized identities, to create, organize and revolutionize beliefs, structures, and systems. To be sure, it does not benefit the systems and people in power to recognize such a thing, because to have marginalized peoples acknowledge their own power is to provide them with the perspective to overcome their oppressors. Yet, this power is real, and it is precisely what we witness in the Black Lives Matter movement, a movement that has quickly become the largest of its kind in decades (Garza 2020). Evident here is the power to direct attention and conversation toward a productive end—by this, we mean change produced by the movement, not productive for the oppressors—one which highlights the experiences of those who have previously been alienated, forgotten or condemned. If this power is strategically used, the Black Lives Matter movement, as an example, may fundamentally shift the way we talk about race, and by extension oppression.

OUR OWN EXAMPLE

Brazilian educator Paulo Freire (1968) once said about power and liberation, "The oppressed must be their own example in the struggle for their redemption" (54). Indeed, Intersectional Others cannot rely on their oppressors to aid them in gaining power, as oppressors not only benefit from an oppressive system, but they are not attuned to the problems of the oppressed. Instead, we must recall and rely on the fact that we have a power born from within. We are closest to the social problems which permeate our lives and communities, and thus the most knowledgeable about how to solve those problems. We know intimately the fear, rage, sadness, and exhaustion that accompany police brutality, racist remarks, homophobia, social rejection, and community trauma. We know what our communities need and are missing. We also know what brings us pride. Being an Other carries with it its own power, its own significance. It allows us to inform real systemic change. What does it mean, then, to "own" our Otherness? How do we become satisfied with, or even proud of, the marginalized label that has been placed on us by society?

When we consider the full power of being Othered, we must first examine the true meaning of marginalization. Is, for instance, existing in the margins more than simply being a statistical outlier? bell hooks (1989) beautifully wrote of her positionality,

> When I left that concrete space in the margins, I kept alive in my heart ways of knowing reality which affirm continually not only the primacy of resistance but the necessity of a resistance that is sustained by remembrance of the past, which includes recollections of broken tongues giving us ways to speak that decolonise our minds, our very beings. (36)

Intersectional Others, practically by definition, have the capacity to create change in ways non-Othered individuals cannot—to revolutionize by playing outside the sociopolitical rules; to create and innovate by thinking beyond current scientific paradigms. Is it possible, then, that Intersectional Others hold power simply by working outside the confines of normal expectations, as Gloria Anzaldúa (1987) implied, with the ability to cross boundaries and understand alternate perspectives more fluidly than those without intersecting identities?

More and more, there have been calls to action from community leaders and organizers to come into our power as marginalized people (Garza 2020). Being in touch with core identities is a precursor to enacting change and finding liberation. Because it is the aim of oppressors and the social elite to minimize and dilute the plight of the marginalized through assimilation and false allyship, it becomes all the more important to scream aloud our Otherness. Otherness is not something to be ashamed or afraid of, but something to be radically owned. If the U.S. social elite tells us to lower our voices, because silence aids their causes, we must be louder. If they tell us to be like them— look like them, act like them, achieve like them—we must have our own way of moving through the world. Roxane Gay, Black queer author of *Bad Feminist* (2014), wrote about exclusionary feminism and history:

> Queerness helped me understand feminism better, and the importance of feminism. When you look at the history of feminism, queer women have been left out. It was the concerns of heterosexual white women that feminism was [interested in]. I was reading these writers who were outsiders for various reasons—not only from society as a whole, but also queerness—and they helped me begin to be okay with being on the outside looking in, and with life being messy. Sometimes it is just better on the outside. (112)

Being attuned to our differences *is* what makes us powerful. Attunement is precisely what allows us to interrogate systems, and ask, "Why am I being subjected to this?" or, "Why are we being treated differently?" We recognize that we don't quite fit in the systems at large, so we ask, "Why does the leadership in this country not look like me?" Indeed, we can ask numerous questions to this effect. Why are corporations considering only the perspectives of a select few? Why is it this way and how can I change it to make it better for LGBTQIA2S+ people and BIPOC around me? And if it can't be made better, why should I participate in this system at all? Why shouldn't I make my own system?

POWER AS A THREAT TO THE OPPRESSOR

It is important to recognize that, when a marginalized person defies the expectations of elite society and steps into their own power, there is intense pressure to "come into the fold." It is inherently threatening to an oppressive system for oppressed persons to be successful independently, and not through the scaffolding of the elite, which makes them much more easily controlled. It's not hard to find examples of the destruction that might ensue when someone refuses to submit to respectability politics and instead turns toward resistance. Often, it takes the form of suppression to the point of invisibility, incarceration, or death.

The Black Panthers and the "Threat" of Black Liberation

We can look at the ways in which creators of history textbooks often choose to paint the figures of the Black Power movement (e.g., Angela Davis, Malcolm X, Stokely Carmichael) of the 1960s and 1970s as "extremists," rather than recognizing them as multidimensional people working toward liberation (Burgess 1968). That is, U.S. mainstream history in the 1960s, 1970s, and beyond often rejected the notion that the movement was composed of people who wished to claim power in their own right and for the betterment of their communities (Carmichael, Ture, and Hamilton 1992).

Indeed, if we look at the Ten Point Program outlined by Black Panther Party leadership after their founding in 1966, we see what was often portrayed as "aggressive" or "unreasonable" demands were just requests for liberation—mirrored, by no accident—in many of Black Lives Matter movement requests (Taylor 2016). The requests included an end to police brutality, which came at the heels of Malcolm X's assassination, and the loss of countless other Black lives before him. They also called for basic rights, like fair employment, equitable housing, and equal treatment in the justice system (Carmichael, Ture, and Hamilton 1992).

In 1969, the Black Panthers started several social programs, including anti-hunger campaigns like the Free Breakfast for Children Program and educational initiatives like Oakland Community School, which fed over 10,000 children across the United States and provided education for 150 children, respectively. For some of the children, enrollment in Free Breakfast for Children marked the first time eating breakfast, ever. It's hard to argue that these social programs provided significant community—and, theoretically, national—benefits. In fact, there are recoverable reports from teachers at the time, who reported a staggering improvement in the childrens' attentional capacities in class, as well as less tearfulness and emotional ability. We cannot claim to know the exact source of this improvement, but we can guess studying through hunger was an obstacle prior to enrollment (Heynan 2009).

We now know that the Black Panther Party was an active target of the Federal Bureau of Investigation (FBI) counterintelligence program (i.e.,

COINTELPRO) and that the group was declared an enemy of the U.S. government by FBI director J. Edgar Hoover because of their "communist ideas" in 1969. At the time, he called them the nation's "greatest threat to internal security" (Thevenin 2004). This was part of the social climate which led to Black queer activist Angela Davis's placement on the FBI's "Ten Most Wanted Fugitives" list, her arrest, and her imprisonment in 1970. Despite Hoover's attempts to eradicate the Black Panther Party's influence, Davis' incarceration became a symbol of intersectional power and recentered attention on Black vilification, state violence, and the prison-industrial complex, issues still very relevant today (Davis 2016).

Evidence now points to the fact that the state and federal governments used aggressive measures to limit Black power in the interest of white supremacy (Carmichael, Ture, and Hamilton 1992), and that the accusations of extremity would have been better directed inward. There is documented evidence, for instance, that the FBI exploited rivalries in Black community groups and targeted gay and lesbian activists within the Black Power movement to sow division. More often than not, the FBI strategically employed COINTELPRO to issue "poison-pen letters"—sending letters containing malicious information about queer Black activists—and the targeted outing of queers to other activists and reporters in order to discredit them (Leighton 2016).

They also dismantled the Free Breakfast for Children program, but prior to doing so, went around trying to bungle the success of the program wherever they could (Meister 2017). There are several accounts of government sabotage across the country, including Oakland and Baltimore police raids on breakfast sites where children were harassed and photographed against their consent, rumors spread by the police in San Francisco that the food carried venereal diseases, and even one report of Chicago police breaking into a church just to destroy and urinate on the food (Heynan 2005). And it was the FBI who—in a public display of state-sanctioned violence on December 6, 1969, and in collaboration with the Chicago Police Department—executed a pre-dawn raid and gunned down Black Panther Party members Fred Hampton and Mark Clark in their own beds. In January 1970, the coroner's jury ruled it "justifiable homicide" after police reports alleged that Hampton and Clark engaged in a "fierce gun battle" which forced them to shoot approximately 100 bullets they did that day. Ballistics experts later determined that only one bullet was shot by the Black Panthers, while the other 99 were shot by the police (Bennett 2010). This is the potential penalty for coming into power, and one we see reflected in reactions to Black Lives Matter protests, as well as other instances of resistance across U.S. history.

RETHINKING AND REDEFINING POWER

For the purposes of this book, I submit that, in the process of rethinking and redefining power, the first thing we must do is come to know it fully, and then deconstruct it. Power in the United States has traditionally been defined through the lens of white straight patriarchal dominance. Therefore, when we are asked to think of "power," many of us conjure up mental imagery reflective of this hierarchy—Mark Zuckerberg, Jeff Bezos, President Biden, and those like them. In the imaginings of these figures, we can extrapolate that power in the United States means immense wealth and class privilege, as well as political and social positionality. We can also extrapolate that power is a racialized, gendered, and sexualized construct.

Scholarly commentaries on power are similarly problematic. German sociologist Max Weber (1922), often cited by Western scholarship, defined "power" as a person's ability to exercise their will over another, despite resistance. More recent definitions have included three main categories informed by Weber's work—power as *influence* (e.g., Dahl 1957; Simon 1957), power as *potential influence* (e.g., French and Raven 1959), and power as *resource or outcome control* (Dépret and Fiske 1993). All of these, however, are built on a premise that power is a dominating, controlling force, perhaps even coercive by nature. While this is one way in which we can contextualize power, we must also ask, "Is it the only way?"

There are two assumptions we must make to deconstruct the notion of power in the United States. The first is that the mainstream understanding of power as a dominating-subjugating force is at its core colonial, meaning that non-Western traditions of thought and manners of power are concomitantly inferiorized. In Chapter 4, we discussed this using the term "coloniality of power" (Mignolo 2007), which accompanies the notions that our way of hierarchizing the world, our ways of being, and our knowledge is according to a Western assumption of normalcy.

The second is that we must reject this limited view of power, thereby expanding it beyond its racist, heterosexist, patriarchal assumptions, and meaning. As such, we recognize power as a construct with possibility outside Western coloniality. If we are able to do this, naturally, a flexible definition of power emerges, with a multitude of sources, mechanisms, and trajectories. French philosopher Michel Foucault, who interrogated strict definitions of power and critiqued the Western view that power is in the hands of a select few, said:

> One must rather conduct an ascending analysis of power, starting, that is, from its infinitesimal mechanisms, which each have their own history, their own trajectory, their own techniques and tactics, and then see how these mechanisms of

power have been—and continue to be—invested, colonised, utilised, involuted, transformed, displaced, extended etc., by ever more general mechanisms and by forms of global domination. (Foucault 1980, 99)

By expanding our definition of power, and perhaps not seeking to define it at all, we are able to better see how it manifests and is felt deeply by Intersectional Others. We assert that power can be seen in the smallest of expressions and in the widest range of circumstances, resistant to the hierarchies and constraints imposed by white heteronormative society. Herein, we include a vast array of manifestations, including the power of revolutionary action and self; the power of body reclamation, pleasure, and self-love; the power to break barriers; the power to bridge communities; and the power to use creation as radical transformation.

POWER OF REVOLUTIONARY ACTION AND SELF

French author Albert Camus said in his 1951 book *The Rebel*, "The only way to deal with an unfree world is to become so absolutely free that your very existence is an act of rebellion." The act of pursuing liberation is one of the most rebellious things we can do in an oppressive system. In doing so, we embody the very thing our oppressors attempt to remove in order to maintain power, the spirit of revolution. We discussed earlier the importance of recentering intersectional voices in the process of humanization—it is just as important in the process of revolution.

A Shift in Social Justice Pedagogy

Part of this change is the redefinition of social justice pedagogy and the dialogue on oppression itself. Prior to 2010, oppression was often discussed in reference to binary constructs like "racist" and "non-racist or "homophobe" and "non-homophobe." This simple division in identity politics became a justification for inaction and passivity in the face of violence. Intersectional Others are dramatically changing national conversations on race and sexuality. For one, silence is no longer a socially acceptable response to witnessing oppression. It does not represent a desire to be apolitical or an easy solution as it did prior to 2010, but rather signals complicity and an ignorance of responsibility toward social justice for humanity (Applebaum 2010).

One example of this changing rhetoric can be found in bystander intervention efforts by community organizations, such as Hollaback, which have sought to address street harassment and hate crimes in the United States with online and public training mechanisms (Dimond et al. 2013). A reaction to the well-known sociological phenomenon, the "bystander effect" (Darley and Latané 1968)—whereby individual bystanders are less likely to intervene in an emergency if they are with a group of people due to a diffusion of responsibility, allowing the emergency to continue—Bystander Intervention Training has actively adapted as an enterprise to recent surges in hate crimes since the election of former president Donald Trump (Edwards and Rushins 2018) by working with Asian Americans Advancing Justice (AAAJ) to develop training specific to anti-Asian hate in the COVID-19 pandemic. Bystander interventions have been found to be highly effective at reducing the likelihood of both anti-Asian (Cheng, Kim, Tsong, and Wong 2021) and anti-LGBTQIA2S+ (Potter, Fountain and Stapleton 2012) hate crimes occurring.

Indeed, to take an active stance on oppression, rather than succumbing to this diffusion, we must not seek to be "non-racist," but "anti-racist." Ibram Kendi (2019), author of *How to Be an Antiracist*, explains the difference between these two:

> The opposite of racist isn't "not racist." It is "anti-racist." What's the difference? One endorses either the idea of a racial hierarchy as a racist, or racial equality as an anti-racist. One either believes problems are rooted in groups of people, as a racist, or locates the roots of problems in power and policies, as an anti-racist. One either allows racial inequities to persevere, as a racist, or confronts racial inequities, as an anti-racist. There is no in-between safe space of "not racist." (9)

Kendi is not alone in feeling this way but riding off a wave of empowering rhetoric that continues to shape the social justice landscape. It is a decidedly powerful stance against inequity.

Galvanizing Intersectional Others

The notion of "identity politics" within the context of social movements often becomes, in and of itself, a paradox. This is often due to the misconception that galvanization or solidarity within the community can only occur when there is a singular focus for the energy of the movement, allowing its participants to concentrate efforts more efficiently. Examples of this would be choosing to rally around gay identity or Asian American identity, but not both (Powell 1999). Mirroring society, social movements often operate with binary logic in an effort to empower the rights of a single community. However, in doing so they alienate those on the margins or within the spectrum of the binary (Kumashiro 2001).

The rhetoric around this is beginning to shift as Intersectional Others are taking highly visible positions on the forefront of social change. It has become clear, for example, that galvanization can absolutely occur within an intersectional framework. The Black Lives Matter movement, as an example, has taken a decidedly queer, Black, and feminist stance on oppression, police brutality, and systemic injustice—it is a movement led by three Black women, two of whom, Alicia Garza and Patrisse Cullors, identify as queer (Garza, Tometi, and Cullors 2014). While it may be tempting to downplay the significance of this as "just one movement," the magnitude of Black Lives Matter's effect on the national and global sociopolitical landscape is enormous—and those are just the effects we can *see* in the present. To date, it has generated the largest number of protests since the end of the Civil War era (Garza 2020), making it profoundly impactful, and, arguably, the *most* impactful movement of our generation. As we examine the power of queer Black, Indigenous, and People of Color (QBIPOC) in the context of cultural and social revolutions in U.S. history, it is important to acknowledge that queer justice and racial justice have always been integral to each other. Their revolutions have similarly been intertwined.

On April 20, 2021, Derek Chauvin was found guilty of the murder of George Floyd, and convicted with second- and third-degree murder, as well as second-degree manslaughter. He faces up to 75 years in prison. It was a sentencing that allowed the country to breathe a sigh of relief, at least temporarily, as many social justice advocates continue to call for extensive reforms in policing and the criminal justice system. It is easy to forget with this win that Derek Chauvin was never originally arrested, and the Minneapolis Police Department may not have *ever* decided to do so if not for Black Lives Matter and demands for justice. Since the murder of George Floyd, many have contested the efficacy of rioting and other resistances for producing change. In particular, contestations have been raised by conservatives, as well as disillusioned BIPOC who had become accustomed to perpetrators averting accountability and justice. However, it is precisely *because* of the power manifested and exercised by organizers, and supporters of the movement, that we see the justice we do.

Cumulative Realities

Marsha P. Johnson, Black trans activist, drag queen, and a tireless worker for queer liberation, is quoted as saying, "History isn't something you look back at and say it was inevitable, it happens because people make decisions that are sometimes very impulsive and of the moment, but those moments are cumulative realities" (n.p.). The truth of this statement is a painful reality for those who are Othered, but it is importantly also a statement of hope and resistance. Larger revolutionary events feel like a wildfire. They burn bright, reach far, and then that moment is extinguished; however, the impact of the wildfire is long-lasting for the communities it reaches. Those are the events, like the nationwide Black Lives Matter protests and Stonewall uprising, that steal the spotlight.

Small moments of resistance can feel more like a candle, arguably a miniscule impact compared to the wildfire when first ignited. However, the candle holds in it a flame that has the power to affect change, emotion, and ideology in others. These are the moments that are often undocumented and invisible because they are overwritten by the mainstream but encoded in the memories of those who were there. And those moments matter just as much, if not more, because as Johnson pointed out, when that candle becomes a vigil, a sea of flames that are no longer miniscule at all, it has the power to unify and create a collective, cumulative reality for all of us.

Compton's Cafeteria

Queer youth of color have always been a driving force of radical social justice movements, fresh eyes on social injustices at play. Many of them were part of Vanguard in 1965, a queer liberation organization geared toward helping San Francisco Tenderloin youth, who were "attempting to get a sense of dignity and responsibility too long denied" (Vanguard 1966). As we discussed before in chapter 2, the Tenderloin District, back then referred to as the "gay ghetto," was a part of San Francisco heavily populated by QBIPOC, who were often subjected to especially high levels of police brutality (Levine 1979).

Tensions were high due to continual police raids, and one night in August 1966, they swelled bigger than ever. The diner, which had historically been a meeting spot for Vanguard and a queer and trans community space (Vanguard 1966), instituted a service charge for customers meeting at the diner beyond their mealtimes, making these groups easily identifiable for the other patrons and management. When San Francisco police arrived at the scene, a "screaming queen" reportedly threw a glass of water in one cop's face (Silverman and Stryker 2005). What is now known as the Compton's Cafeteria Riot ensued, the first documented uprising of trans and queer people as a united front in U.S. history (Levin 2019).

The incident was only mentioned in local queer—and not mainstream—media at the time. This caused the riot to be obscured until research by trans activist and professor of Gender and Women's Studies at the University of Arizona Susan Stryker unearthed the 1966 news headline, "Drag queens protest police harassment at Compton's Cafeteria." Stryker felt compelled to interview residents who knew of, or participated in, the riot, as the local archives showed no further record of the incident (Silverman and Stryker 2005). According to her source, activist Raymond Broshears, drag queens, and trans women led the resistance that day. Broshears reported,

When the police grabbed the arm of one of the transvestites, he threw his cup of coffee in the cop's face. . . . Gays began breaking out every window in the place . . . the police tried to grab them and throw them in the paddy wagon, but they found this no easy task for Gays began hitting them "below the belt" and drag queens [started] smashing them in the face with extremely heavy purses. A police car had every window broken, a newspaper shack outside the cafeteria was burned to the ground and general havoc [was] raised that night in the Tenderloin. The next day drag queens, hair fairies, conservative Gays, and hustlers joined in a picket of the cafeteria. (Stryker 1998, 356)

Donna Persona—a Latina American trans activist and board member for the San Francisco Trans March Committee who had frequented Compton's Cafeteria as a teen—said in a 2019 interview with *The Guardian* that the drag queens at the diner that day "took bullets for us . . . everyone in the [LGBTQIA2S+] community stands on their shoulders" (Levin 2019).

In a powerful move to immortalize the moment of trans resistance, three Black trans women came together and, in 2017, founded Compton's Transgender Cultural District, eight blocks of the Tenderloin District which encompassed Compton's Cafeteria. It is the world's first legally recognized urban area devoted to the preservation and celebration of the trans community. And it's not just a reclamation of power in name alone—which would have been legendary in and of itself—but a substantial change to the infrastructure of the area, with year-round interventions to help trans folks of color in San Francisco, including an affordable housing project, COVID-19 testing, empowerment workshops, and programming to help aspiring trans entrepreneurs.

Cofounder of the Transgender Cultural District and Black queer and trans activist Honey Mahoganey stated in an interview with *ABC News*, "We realized that if we didn't do something, the Tenderloin was quickly going to become gentrified and our history was going to be completely erased" (Bollini 2021). Her other cofounder, Aria Sa'id, posed the question:

What does it look like to honor the legacy and the culture we've inherited as trans people—a culture of joy and resilience, in spite of our disparities and marginalization? We can create a world where we are economically and culturally and socially empowered. (Levin 2019)

Compton's Cafeteria Riot remains a symbol of the many instances intersectional resistances were likely buried or unacknowledged, despite their important impact on our liberatory futures.

"Stonewall Was a Riot!"

On the 50th anniversary of Stonewall in 2019, a new slogan was created out of anger and exasperation, and then was printed on T-shirts and posters across the country: "Stonewall was a riot!" The first Pride in 1970, then called Christopher Street Liberation Day, was a march not only against police brutality but also for a liberatory future (McMahon 2010). Liberation was a lifesaving endeavor, a rallying cry needed if only for the sole purpose that there were real targets on the backs of poor Black and Brown queer and trans people. Yet, these same people were the ones fighting the hardest for queer liberation. "They are always on the front line," said trans scholar Susan Stryker in an interview with the *New York Times*. "They are the ones who are being who they are, no matter what. They are catching all the homophobia, all the transphobia that are being directed at queer folks" (*New York Times* 2019). Indeed, Intersectional Others are all too familiar with the daily toll of police brutality and oppression, along with the sometimes-fatal cost of resistance.

Pride as an organized event in modern times, however, has become a symbol of rainbow capitalism (Falco and Gandhi 2019). It is a time when individuals who benefit from the privileges of being white and straight are suddenly fine with donning rainbow tanks and glitter to party at Pride, divorced from its perilous history. Abled bodies, pale-skinned bodies, and bodies with economic and sociopolitical capital can receive applause for *performing* Otherness, without feeling its long-term costs. Corporations come out with their newest line of Pride products and apparel, hoping to attract consumers (Abad-Santos 2018). Meanwhile, mainstream media continues to project queerness in ways that do not center the experiences of poor communities of color. Just as activists Sylvia Rivera and Marsha P. Johnson in the 1960s and 1970s were denigrated called "liabilities" for larger queer liberation due to their "Third World looks," and shoved aside when the camera crews came (Bell 1971, 46), modern Pride celebrations benefit from the work of those who are invisible and reap the rewards of progression.

"Gay liberation" as a movement and unifying concept emerged in the late 1960s and became fully visible as a banner for the LGBTQIA2S+ community by 1970, but there were deep divisions within. Queer scholars Karla Jay and Allen Young's 1992 anthology *Out of the Closets* captured the social mood and circumstances before the Stonewall rebellion, saying, "[G]ay men oppress gay women, white gays oppress Black gays, and straight-looking gays oppress transvestites" (ixi). Despite these rifts, the concept of "gay liberation" represented an early attempt at queer and trans solidarity against oppression (Cohen 2007), integrating ideologies from the civil rights, Black Power, women's rights, and New Left movements (Armstrong 2002; Kissack 1995; Valocchi 2001, 445–467).

On the eve of June 28, 1969, the Stonewall uprising in Greenwich Village became a major catalyst for progress in the gay liberation movement. In many ways, Stonewall was nothing special. It didn't mark the beginning of gay liberation, nor was it the first time queers fought back against police or organized politically (Stryker 2002), although it is certainly an attractive and convenient legend to repeat. Nevertheless, the rebellion that night, and a few nights after, have been cemented in the collective memory of the queer and trans folk who were there, as well as those who heard of the event, due to New York activist efforts, media coverage, and commemorative events after-the-fact (Armstrong and Crage 2006, 724–751).

Reports state that the incident began when a "butch dyke"—who many eyewitnesses believed to have been Stormé DeLarverie, a Black lesbian activist and drag king—resisted arrest and punched a police officer during a bar raid, fed up with the incessant police harassment around that time (Yardley 2014). Puerto Rican trans activist Victoria Cruz, who was reportedly there when the fight began, said in an interview with the City University of New York (CUNY) Brooklyn:

> Judy Garland had just been laid to rest. The hot and sticky weather had made us even more irritable. The atmosphere in the Village was uncharacteristically gloomy. Then, when the police showed up and started attacking us—attacking, particularly, lesbian and transgender women of color—we said: "No, honey. Not today!" (Jones 2019)

The fight triggered a rain of coins, bricks, and molotov cocktails by the crowd gathered there. The story goes that a line of street queens, nicknamed the "Stonewall Girls," then taunted the police force, forcing them down the local streets. Among the Stonewall Girls is said to be Puerto Rican, trans activist Sylvia Rivera, 17 at the time, who, according to a 2001 interview threw the *second* molotov cocktail that day (Carter 2004), as well as Marsha P. Johnson, Black trans activist, who had at one point climbed a lamppost, and proceeded to drop a brick or other heavy object onto a police car (Riemer and Brown 2019). Both activists were instrumental in the fight for queer and trans liberation that night and moving forward.

Due to the fact that there is little photographic or video footage from the uprising itself, Stonewall is commonly portrayed as a violent, spontaneous, singular event centering gayness, rather than the culmination of resistances it actually was. Records show, however, that protest activity in the United States had already grown more militant (Gitlin 1987)—with community antiwar efforts, the Compton's Cafeteria Riot, the Black Cat Raid, the Montgomery bus boycott, and the March on Washington for Gay Rights, all leading up to Stonewall. Queer and trans activists from both coasts attended the Democratic Convention in Chicago in August 1968, and they returned home inspired to radicalize their own movements (Carter 2004, 111). New York queer activists, for instance, founded a radical group in Greenwich

Village in early 1969 and discussed the steps for increasing "gay power" in print media (Carter 2004, 122). Los Angeles and San Francisco, by that Spring, were also hubs for gay liberation activity (Armstrong and Crage 2006).

First-hand accounts recall Stonewall as the uprising which publicly denounced police brutality, the criminalization of sexuality, and the blatant queerphobia structurally built into state policing in thousands of moments and raids just like Stonewall, but that were never recollected as famously. One thing Stonewall did *not* do was mark the end of queer oppression, and many people have pointed out that it was largely hailed as a success for white gays and lesbians, rather than for the QBIPOC who threw the first punches and bricks. Sylvia Rivera, in particular, vocally challenged white gay and lesbian middle-class activism, calling out its lack of intersectionality and regard for trans people. During the 1973 Christopher Street Liberation Day celebration three years after Stonewall, she was caught on camera pushing her way onto the stage, visibly distressed, saying, to sounds of jeering from the crowd:

> I have been beaten. I have had my nose broken. I have been thrown in jail. I have lost my job. I have lost my apartment for gay liberation and you all treat me this way? . . . The people are trying to do something for all of us, and not men and women that belong to a white middle class white club. (Carter 2004, 154)

Activist Lee Brewster, cofounder of Queens Liberation Front, was quoted as once saying that Sylvia Rivera, in many ways, *"was* gay liberation" (Riemer and Brown 2019, 111). Rivera strongly advocated for the inclusion of trans rights, BIPOC, the homeless, and the incarcerated in the larger fight for liberation. Among many organizing efforts, she was a founding member of the Street Transvestite Action Revolutionaries (STAR), along with Marsha P. Johnson (Shephard 2013). She was also part of the Gay Liberation Front (GLF), the Gay Activists' Alliance (GAA), and the Puerto Rican activist group, the Young Lords, as she often hoped that Latino/a/x communities would recognize that gay and trans issues were *also* Latino/a/x issues (Riemer and Brown 2019).

As nervous marchers walked up Sixth Avenue for the first Pride March, which ran for approximately 60 blocks, historical records state that you could hear Sylvia Rivera's "imperious" shout: "Gimme a G! . . . Gimme an A! . . . Gimme a Y!" as if she drove the march forward through pure will. Approximately 5,000 marchers eventually joined in, resulting in a sense of solidarity. One marcher reportedly called it a

> family reunion . . . in which we all, under the beneficent sun, lived, touched, smiled and—not tolerated, but welcomed—one another's differences not as a

lessening of our own particular selves, but as endless complements of that spark of self which is the sum of one soul. (Reimer and Brown 2019, 143)

THE POWER OF BODY RECLAMATION, SELF-LOVE, AND COLLECTIVE HEALING

Alok Vaid-Menon, South Asian queer and gender nonconforming creative, once wrote, "One of life's paradoxes is that we are encouraged to 'be ourselves,' but are often punished when we do" (Vaid-Menon 2020). Indeed, when someone utters that cliché, it is rarely to affirm the identities or expressions of someone who deviates significantly from societal norms. Vaid-Menon (2020) went on to say that we "learn from an early age that beauty is often about power. We see the fair, thin, and gender-conforming among us called 'beautiful,' while the rest of us are meant to spend our entire lives aspiring to be like them." This is why one the most profound manifestations of intersectional power is the reclamation of the body, of beauty, and of self-love—to recognize the impossibility of current beauty and healing paradigms so we may redefine them for ourselves. We, too, need healing. Even the healers among us need healing.

Self-Love As Resistance

Consider the powerful words of queer Black author and activist Sonya Renee Taylor, "Radical self-love demands that we see ourselves and others in the fullness of our complexities and intersections and that we work to create space for those intersections" (2021, 9). In these words, we hear Taylor exclaim that our intersections deserve to be seen, to be loved, and to be given space to thrive. As Intersectional Others, we have been told, time and time again, that our bodies are ugly, our skin too brown, our hair too wild or coarse. And, perhaps most toxic of all is the insinuation by society that we should be ashamed of these things, rather than consider them a source of beauty or joy.

Internalizing negative social views can easily lead to self-hatred and attempts to change who we are on a fundamental level, until we're no longer in touch with our true selves, but instead the version others tell us we should be. Unsurprisingly, studies suggest that perceived discrimination and internalized queerphobia are associated with body shame and discomfort for queer women (Brewster et al. 2014; Watson et al. 2015). This pressure is not inconsequential, and, as you might imagine, there is mounting evidence that eating concerns are linked to these constructs as well (Bayer 2014).

When we consider the effects of internalized oppression on bodily behavior—that is, policing of language, tone, attire, and even the most intimate of feelings and performances—it is easy to see why the pressure mounts. We begin to feel that we should apologize for our deepest desires and nuanced sexual experiences. Apologize for being *different*. Of these apologies, Taylor (2021) wrote:

> Living in a female body, a Black body, an aging body, a fat body, a body with mental illness is to awaken daily to a planet that expects a certain set of apologies to already live on our tongues. There is a level of 'not enough' or 'too much' sewn into these strands of difference. (13)

Knowing that we fight against the tide of internalized hatred from white heteronormative culture, we can resist by advocating for self-love. Total self-love is a reclaiming, revolutionary act. Black queer feminist Audre Lorde wrote, "Caring for myself is not self-indulgence, it is self-preservation, and that is an act of political warfare" (2017, 130). In a world where we are told our existence is worthless or less human, care for our personhood is a bold act of empowerment.

The Dangers and Powers of Pleasure and Sexual Joy

The notion of loving whomever we love has always been fraught in the United States. As a civil liberty, it has been contested through miscegenation law—legislation which has been upheld by 38 states across the nation's history (Pascoe 2009)—and contestation over same-sex marriage, such as the legacy of the Defense of Marriage Act (DoMA), not overturned until the 2015 U.S. Supreme Court *Obergefell v. Hodges* decision (Karpinski and Collins 2020). In 2021, a time when reproductive and marriage rights hang in the balance under a decidedly more conservative U.S. Supreme Court, it is powerful to reclaim pleasure and sexuality as a right for ourselves.

We are, as a society, encouraged to build our gender and sexual identities in relation to binary constructs—man-woman, top-bottom, and gay-straight—and this encouragement is rooted in a social system where binaries are seen as the default norms. It is easy to see pleasure as a purely sexual endeavor, but we can also see it as an expression of joy, of love, and a confrontation of society's denial of these for Intersectional Others historically. Black queer author James Baldwin (2014) said in his last interview:

> Loving anybody and being loved by anybody is a tremendous danger, a tremendous responsibility. Loving of children, raising of children. The terrors homosexuals go through in this society would not be so great if the society itself did

not go through so many terrors which it doesn't want to admit. The discovery of one's sexual preference doesn't have to be a trauma. It's a trauma because it's such a traumatized society. (63)

Faced with our traumatization, reclaiming pleasure is an act of resistance. It means redefining our relationship with our bodies, identities, and desires on our own terms.

In her book *Pleasure Activism: The Politics of Feeling Good*, Black queer feminist author adrienne marie brown (2019) discussed the ways in which pleasure and joy can be intertwined with social justice. She asserted that "one of the major ways we collaborate in our own oppression and suffering is by buying into the lie that we don't all deserve access to pleasure." One of the first things we lose when oppressed and traumatized is our capacity for thriving—we are focused instead on surviving. It follows that, as part of internalized oppression, Intersectional Others often deny access to our joyfulness, not just our pleasure. To reclaim power, we must allow ourselves access to that joy once again.

Black queer author Audre Lorde (1993) agreed that the erotic held power but was also used as to source of vilification and suppression. She said:

We have been taught to suspect this resource, vilified, abused, and devalued within western society. On the one hand, the superficially erotic has been encouraged as a sign of female inferiority; on the other hand, women have been made to suffer and to feel both contemptible and suspect by virtue of its existence. It is a short step from there to the false belief that only by the suppression of the erotic within our lives and consciousness can women be truly strong. But that strength is illusory, for it is fashioned within the context of male models of power. (340)

Intersectional Others—and, in particular, as Lorde pointed out, queer women of color and nonbinary femmes of color—have been taught that we should not experience satisfaction, and instead seek to suppress our desires in favor of submission and virtue, else be perceived as dangerous and hypersexual (Vance 1984). This message from white heteropatriarchal society serves to subjugate and deter us from gaining the power that pleasure and joy can bring into our lives. Ultimately, it creates a bind for us whereby to be "virtuous," we must also disempower ourselves. The construction of "virtuosity," while seemingly positive, becomes a sexualized and gendered force for control.

"Who Says We Don't Talk about Sex?"

Building off the bravery of queer ancestors, more recent creators are radically transforming not just our notions of racial, sexual, and gender equality, but exploring the very *meaning* of queer identity and experience. Part of this, as we discussed earlier, is acknowledging that Intersectional Others need not only experience pain but also deserve the humanities inherent in emotions like joy, love, and pleasure. This is a direct subversion of the dehumanizations we are subjected to, which tell us that we are less capable of these complex emotions. When we reclaim things like *love*, we yell to the world that we are *human*.

I find it revolutionary to focus on queer Asian American faces when discussions of erotic content and love arise. Not because they are the only groundbreaking content in existence—clearly, Audre Lorde's 1993 work *The Use of the Erotic* has been fundamental to the development of intersectional eroticism—but more because, as we have discussed previously, Asian American sexualities in this homonationalist state have been shaped as binaries of exoticization or emasculation. Therefore, it becomes a stance of revolution to reject these binaries and assert with realness the complexities of Asian intersectionality. Many scholars, such as queer Asian American scholar Richard Fung (2005) in *Looking for my Penis: The Eroticized Asian in Gay Video Porn*, have commented on the lack of Asian queer visibility in erotic media, among a larger issue of invisibility in U.S. media overall. In particular, Orientalism and sexual racism have led to an absence of Asian masculine presence in porn, due to perceptions that Asian masculinity is undesirable (Bader 2017).

When we investigate the personal and social barriers which hurt our hearts, we may empower ourselves by resisting them. Queer trans Chinese American artist Kit Yan explored immigration, family, love, rejection, and joy in his 2016 award-winning slam poetry show *Queer Heartache.* Yan (2021) wrote of the show on his website that

> *Queer Heartache* is a testament to the resilience of queer love in all its forms—
> between cis and trans siblings, lovers, pride parade attendees, and many more—
> in the face of heartbreaking barriers everywhere from the dating pool to the
> medical establishment.

The show boasted an emotional rawness that could be palpably felt in the theater, with high levels of relatability for queer people across the Asian diaspora.

Posing the question to the world, "Who says we don't talk about sex?" Chinese American lesbian activist and author Kitty Tsui addressed the Horizons Lesbian Conference in Chicago, Illinois, in April 1990 (Tsui 1992). Instrumental in the birth of the Asian American queer movement in San Francisco in the 1970s (Eng 1998), Tsui's bodybuilding, writing, and activism have always focused on pleasure and the expansion of queer Asian imagination, while simultaneous rejecting white colonial ideology on Asian queerness. In 1983, she published *Words of a Woman Who Breathes Fire*, the very first novel written by a Chinese American lesbian. Her other work, *Sparks Fly* (1997), expelled notions of Asian erotic submissiveness by centering her experiences with leather. In fact, *Sparks Fly* was penned by Eric Norton, her alterego, a gay leatherman. Despite criticism, she boldly moved into more and more public spaces over the course of her career and became the first Asian American woman featured on the cover of the queer porn magazine *On Our Backs*. As a performer, activist, and prolific author, Kitty Tsui truly defied gender and sexual expectations across her lifetime.

Rest as Cultural Preservation

Resting is a powerful act of reclaiming one's body, energy, and, above all, humanity. Importantly, it takes courage to rest from the weariness that oppression has lain on us. Without rest, we cannot sustainably continue the fight against oppression for ourselves and our communities. Community and individual trauma are known to greatly impact the nervous system due to the chronic stressors traumatized people endure when interacting with stigma and discrimination. Research has shown that getting "dorsal rest" is an effective response to dorsal vagal activation due to traumatization (Rosenberg 2017). This is because our nervous systems often reach a state of "freeze," or dissociation, when we are triggered, leading to bodily and mental exhaustion (Scaer 2001). Other symptoms related to trauma, such as compassion fatigue, burnout, and chronic anxiety are consequences of systems that have historically been built to benefit from the labor and dehumanization of marginalized people.

Blache Marie, cofounder of For Brown Bleeders, a collective of Black and Brown healers and artists, beautifully said about this:

> Self-care is rest and listening internally. Self-care is decolonizing, unwrapping ourselves from the structures that bind us. Resting toward freedom, asking: How can I support my wholeness? How can I ask others to support me in being whole? Self-care is study and connecting, with oneself, with ancestors, with source. (Chatterjee 2018)

Decolonized wellness may look like the rejection of dictation of body norms and destigmatizing sexual expressions defined through a colonial health lens, a lens which has created disordered eating and body shame.

Community spaces, such as Rest for Resistance and its parent organization QTPoC Mental Health, provide a reprieve for Intersectional Others as they contend with the traumatization of otherness and push for resistance.

According to the editor-in-chief, mixed desi queer nonbinary community organizer Dom Chatterjee, Rest for Resistance "strives to uplift marginalized communities, those who rarely get access to adequate health care or social support" and seeks "to create healing space for LGBTQIA2S+ individuals, namely trans & queer people of color, as well as other stigmatized groups such as sex workers, immigrants, persons with physical and/or mental disabilities, and those living at the intersections" (Rest for Resistance 2021).

Decolonizing Wellness and Prioritizing Collective Healing

Intersectional Others are revolutionizing self-care by rejecting mainstream models of care that may be more accessible but actively harm us. Beyond white colonized notions of self-care—which prioritize commercialized options like vacations and spas—QBIPOC have access to the methods of care gathered multi-generationally across the diaspora (Katoa-Taholo 2019). When our understanding of our personal history or culture has been damaged by colonial enterprises, engaging in "self-care" necessitates the rediscovering of what "support" or "well-being" means fundamentally.

We have discussed the U.S. healthcare system in the context of oppression for the broader QBIPOC community, but importantly, current treatment models in the United States are *also* products of colonialism. Therefore, decolonizing wellness also necessitates the *indigenization* of wellness—that is, the recentering of Indigenous and non-Western knowledge and histories in treatment, as well as the recognition that many health paradigms have used and appropriated Indigenous knowledge to further white-centric agendas of health over time. A couple examples of this include Erik Erikson's use of Lakota and Yurok knowledge in the development of his most famous theory, the eight stages of psychosocial development (Moin and Fish 2018), as well as the use of Siksiká (Blackfoot) knowledge to inform the development of Maslow's Hierarchy of Needs (Coope 2020).

We can revolutionize the way we care and heal by creating environments that commit to unpacking power and dismantling violence while offering models of collective care where we see ourselves as an integral part of our communities. Intersectional healing networks like the National Queer and Trans Therapists of Color Network (NQTTCN) and Inclusive Therapists allow QBIPOC to connect with mental health providers who match their identities and share their community experiences. This community care model rejects the top-down and white-dominated system of Othering by exposing the health inequities perpetrated by Psychology and Medicine.

The Multicultural and Social Justice Counseling Competencies

Proponents of decolonizing therapy, often BIPOC and queer health providers, have noted that traditional counseling theories must be critically examined, as most were developed within a predominantly white and Western framework. If not contextualized, these frameworks will reproduce colonial ideologies and perpetuate the invisibilizing of Indigenous approaches to healing (Tuck and Yang 2012). The Multicultural and Social Justice Counseling Competencies (MSJCC; Ratts, Singh, Nassar-McMillan, Butler, and McCullough 2016), which superseded the racially oriented framework of the Multicultural Counseling Competencies (Sue, Arrendondo and McDavis 1992), was built on the premise that "effectively balancing individual counseling with social justice advocacy is key to addressing the problems that individuals from marginalized populations bring to counseling" (34), and asked counselors to apply social justice paradigms to their work, such as those in relational-cultural theory (Miller 1976), critical race theory (Bell 1995), intersectionality theory (Crenshaw 1989), and liberation psychology (Martín-Baró 1994).

Such frameworks, which encourage the awareness of both provider and client of their unique positions of marginalization and privilege within the therapeutic context, are helpful for combating the implicit biases that often accompany being embedded in a profession that has historically dehumanized Intersectional Others. However, it is critical to not only follow a progression of competency guidelines based out of the mental health field's current trajectory, but also to actively humanize and recenter QBIPOC methods of healing. Our focus must be on de-vilification, not simply demarginalization (Crenshaw 1989). It must also be on humility, not only competency (Tervalon and Murray-Garcia 1998), which encourages a much more open, collaborative, deferential approach to education and treatment.

The Power of Kapwa for Psychological Healing

Often considered a "father of Sikolohiyang Pilipino (Indigenous Filipino/a/x psychology)" Virgilio Enriquez advocated throughout his life to indigenize psychology and expand Westernized views of social sciences to include Indigenous perspectives. Upon immigration to the United States, Enriquez discussed the ways in which it, and the world, might decolonize and heal from colonial trauma. One way to do this, he argued, was with "kapwa," a core tenet of Indigenous Filipino/a/x psychology, which he defined as the "recognition of shared identity, an inner self shared with others" (Enriquez 2004, 5). However, merely being together in a space does not mean that we are "in kapwa" with one another, he wrote. While kapwa is a concept of collective identity, it is also about the way interpersonal relationships function and are maintained within this collective.

"Pakikipagkapwa" (or, in English, "Critical Kapwa"), Enriquez (2004) felt, was a pedagogy that could be harnessed to heal individually and collectively, and offered a revolution in ideology, epistemology, and spirituality. Enriquez said:

> Pakikipagkapwa is much deeper and profound in its implications. It also means accepting and dealing with the other person as an equal. The company president and the office clerk may not have an equivalent role, status, or income but the Filipino way demands and implements the idea that they treat one another as fellow human beings (Kapwatao). This means a regard for the dignity and being of others. (Enriquez 2004, 47)

Thus, part of pakikipagkapwa is intentionally humanizing another person or group, which requires the awareness and use of non-Western social systems and structures to destroy the false binaries and hierarchies which perpetuate oppression in this country. Humanization through kapwa aims to reinforce an understanding of human interactions through multiple lenses—in essence, it asks us to analyze the ways in which we are all affected by oppressive systems. This humanization, along with a spiritual connection to the self and others, called "diwa" is critical to decolonizing both our senses of self and our healing processes (Desai 2016).

POWER TO BREAK BARRIERS: FROM PRISONS TO POLITICS

Fluidity may be one of the most powerful qualities of intersectionality, and one which is necessary to fully conceive not just the social politic surrounding it but also the identities themselves (Fieldman 2019). In her work *Borderlands/La Frontera* Gloria Anzaldua (1987) commented on the parallels between Mexico-U.S. diasporic queerness and Chicano queerness by situating both as transgressive "borderlands." Transgressive people, spaces, and ideology hold great power, as they are, in and of themselves, groundbreaking. In transgressing or "queering," we open ourselves up to new possibilities and futurities (Muñoz 2009), and those futurities necessarily include systemic change for Intersectional Others.

Coming Out of the Concrete Closet

Intersectional Others are disproportionately targeted and imprisoned. But we have evidence that their imprisonment was also the source of great power and resistance for the queer liberation movement. One interesting site of this resistance sat in Greenwich Village. The Women's House of Detention, or "The House of D" as it was called by its occupants and Village residents, was an 11-story art deco stone structure that towered over the city rooftops. Pictures of its interiors show brick walls and barred windows, and many depicted in the photographs were lesbian and nonbinary BIPOC (Thistlewaite 2019).

Billed when it opened in 1932 as a "school for citizenship" with hospital wards and vocational training, it no longer made this claim by the 1960s (Thistlewaite 2019, 2). Lesbians caught up in bar raids, charged with prostitution or drug use, or cornered by the mob or the police well understood that entrance to the House of D meant repeated cavity searches, filthy conditions, overcrowding, and countless humiliations. Women and nonbinary people were held for violations unavoidable in 1960s New York queer life—simply standing in a gay bar or on a street corner could land you in jail. So could the lack of gender-conforming clothing, of which each person had to wear at least three pieces to prove their straightness (Thistlewaite 2019).

We might assume a prison to be a place of despair, but perhaps it can sometimes be a place of hope. Black queer activist Audre Lorde as well as other historians have pointed to the Women's House of Detention as the epicenter of queer life in Greenwich Village from the mid-1950s into the 1960s, a place where queer women were often heard conversing openly with one another in Manhattan, even before the gay liberation movement had fully taken hold. Lorde (1982) wrote of it:

> Information and endearments flew up and down, the conversants apparently oblivious to the ears of the passersby as they discussed the availability of lawyers, the length of stay, family, conditions, and the undying quality of true love. The Women's House of Detention, right smack in the middle of the Village, always felt like one up for our side—a defiant pocket of female resistance, everpresent as a reminder of possibility, as well as punishment. (206)

It was a spectacle of open queerness that often bled into the streets below, as prisoners checked in with their loved ones who peered up at them from the sidewalk. Prisoners and their visitors dominated the streets with their voices, their gestures, and their shouted intimacies. Affections flew back and forth in a courageous, unapologetic performance. Stolen privacy led to a public, flaunted queerness that required bold defense in hostile territory outside (Nestle 2008). During the Stonewall uprising, lesbians may not have been roaming the Village streets in the numbers their gay and trans comrades were, but there were hundreds of dykes in the House of Detention during the uprising. And whenever lesbians were arrested, they were put in the House of D, meaning they still participated in the resistance from up-high—yelling, throwing things, and contributing their presence to the movement (Thistlewaite 2019).

Freedom Is a Constant Struggle

Mass incarceration, prison abolition, and prisoner justice have been some of the biggest concerns for QBIPOC activists over the last several decades. It is neither a sign that community violence has run amok, nor a sign that certain people are prone to violence naturally (Mogul, Ritchie and Whitlock 2011). Rather, it is a sign that our society still manifests racial and sexual oppression in the criminal justice system. In 2009, Henry Louis Gates Jr., a Black professor at Harvard University, was arrested for allegedly attempting to "break in" to his *own* home. Since that ludicrous incident, there have been many others which have prompted national recognition of the biases inherent in policing and the criminal justice system (Mogul, Ritchie and Whitlock 2011).

Due to conversations brought on by the Black Lives Matter movement, there is much greater social awareness that Black and Brown queer and trans folks are severely impacted by mass incarceration, police bias, and police brutality (Garza 2020). Studies suggest that approximately 25% of LGBTQIA2S+ people who have had encounters with police have experienced misconduct or discrimination, and this number goes up for QBIPOC, who suffer from multiple sources of discrimination (Garza 2020; Lambda Legal 2014). For instance, according to a report by community organization BreakOUT! and the National Council of Crime and Delinquency (2014), 87% of queer and trans youth of color have been approached by police in their lifetimes, compared to just 33% of white queer and trans youth. And in an 2016 analysis of complaints made between 2010 and 2015 to the New York City Civilian Complaint Review Board from LGBTQIA2S+ people, researchers found that Black and Latino/a/x queer and trans victims were significantly overrepresented. Studies indicate there is also a bias in court proceedings, including sentencing and jail time (Center for American Progress 2016).

While one in three adults in the United States, and 3.8% of adults in the United States, identify as BIPOC and LGBTQIA2S+ respectively, these numbers increase drastically when we look inside the prison system, with two in three prisoners identifying as BIPOC and 7.9% identifying as LGBTQIA2S+ (Center for American Progress 2016). Once in the prison system, queer and trans prisoners suffer from abuse and excessive punishment from guards and other prisoners as well. From 2011 to 2012, for instance, the U.S. Department of Justice reported that 5.4% of queer prisoners and 15.2% of trans prisoners had been sexually abused by prison staff, compared to 2.4% of the prison population overall (Black and Pink 2015).

Due to the social invisibility faced by QBIPOC prisoners, it can be hard to address human rights concerns that take place, which range from sexual violence to the denial of legal rights and arbitration (Davis and Shaylor 2001). In her 1998 essay *Masked Racism: Reflections on the Prison-Industrial Complex*, queer Black activist and former political prisoner Angela Davis wrote about the "disappearing" of problems in the prison-industrial complex:

> Imprisonment has become the response of first resort to far too many of the social problems that burden people who are ensconced in poverty. . . . Homelessness, unemployment, drug addiction, mental illness, and illiteracy are only a few of the problems that disappear from public view when the human beings contending with them are relegated to cages. Prisons thus perform a feat of magic. . . . But prisons do not disappear problems, they disappear human beings. (4)

A report by Black and Pink (2015), a national LGBTQIA2S+ abolitionist network dedicated to advocating for queer and trans prisoners, found that, of LGBTQIA2S+ prisoners across the United States, Black and Latino/a/x prisoners were more likely to have their first arrest occur when they were under 18 compared to white respondents (66% versus 51%). The frequency of incarceration varied in the report, but Black, Latino/a/x, and mixed-race prisoners were also more likely to have experienced multiple incarcerations than their white counterparts. 85% of all LGBTQIA2S+ youth in juvenile incarceration facilities were also BIPOC.

The structural inequities which significantly impact the lives of Intersectional Others won't disappear on their own. While prison abolition is a primary goal for many aware of these disparities, social justice, and community organizations like Black and Pink are arguing for other measures to create concrete, meaningful change as well. One of these is the elimination of "stop-and-frisk" police practices, which studies have shown as based in anti-BIPOC and anti-LGBTQIA2S+ discrimination. Another is a call to pass the End Racial Profiling Act (ERPA), federal legislation which would prohibit racial, sexual and gender profiling, and provide police with anti-bias training (Black and Pink 2015). Significantly changing the ways in which the criminal justice system operates within the United States, and how QBIPOC people interact with the system, is not a simple task, but it is one that is absolutely necessary. As Angela Davis (2016) aptly put it, "Freedom is a constant struggle," and without freedom, there can be no justice.

Enacting Change from Within the System

We have discussed the woes of attempting to access power and liberation "using the master's tools" (Lorde 2012); however, there are several advantages to working within a system or larger institution, one of the biggest being an ability to infiltrate them, changing them from the inside. Stacey Abrams, Black lesbian activist and former Minority Leader of the Georgia House of Representatives, wrote in her book *Lead from the Outside* (2018), "Like most who are underestimated, I have learned to over-perform, and find soft, but key ways to take credit. Because, ultimately, leadership and power require the confidence to effectively wield both" (49). While she's not *wrong*, we each have our own ways of projecting our voices. Abrams was able to dual-wield grassroots organization and political insider rights with effective results. She is largely credited, for instance, as the organizer behind Georgia's "flip" to majority Democrat in the 2020 presidential election, what is considered one of the key victories securing President Joe Biden's title as president of the United States (Epstein 2021).

However, doing this comes with sacrifices. For instance, there may be community stigma around "selling out," sometimes referred to in scholarly literature as the "acting white phenomenon"—a cultural invalidation that involves the perception that a racialized Other, when succeeding in an activity, is behaving like a white person. The accusation that someone is "acting white" may be intentional or unintentional, but nevertheless discredits or undermines an individual's membership in a particular cultural group (Durkee et al. 2019). There are two implications to this type of gatekeeping. One is that we are *so* accustomed to seeing white people in power that we cannot even fathom the idea that BIPOC would be able to wield it. The other is that to be succeeding within a system is somehow negative. These cultural invalidations are harmful not just to the individual, but the community as a whole, as perpetuating the belief that only white or straight folks can achieve success ultimately keeps all marginalized people down and limits the potential for collective mobility.

While there are often contentious relationships between those who do grassroots advocacy work and those embedded in institutional frameworks, arguably both are critical when it comes to helping marginalized people gain societal power. Grassroots advocacy, for one, benefits from the flexibility of working outside a bureaucratic system. It harnesses the power of community interchange, idealism, and a deep understanding of community needs, requiring a bottom-up approach to power that is attuned to the wants and needs of the people. On the other hand, institutionally embedded Others have the power to change a system from the top-down, as they may be able to gain trust from other members of the institution, holding some leverage or influence in, or from, those relationships. They also benefit from the privilege of being—at least to some extent—visible in that environment, whether in the hallway, conference room, or in a leadership circle. They inject the voice of the Othered at a higher level than can be reached on the ground alone. Both of these are necessary to achieve true systemic change.

The QBIPOC Insiders

Queer activists of color have always made bold political moves, despite rampant queerphobia, racism, and the community erasure of QBIPOC experiences. Indeed, there are a multitude of QBIPOC "insiders" to whom I could give credit in this book, although they deserve more pages than I can allot in a dedication page.

Grande Mere. One such person was gay Latino activist and drag queen José Julio Sarria, also known as "Grande Mere" or "Empress José the First" to San Franciscans. In the 1950s, he worked at the infamous Black Cat Tavern as a cocktail server and was known for performing and encouraging resistance to police oppression at the bar. Other patrons reported that he would often grab and persuade them to sing *God Save the Nelly Queens* together before a night's end. Speaking of this regular occurrence in the documentary *Word Is Out*, gay journalist George Mendenhall said of Sarria:

> It sounds silly, but if you lived at that time and had the oppression coming down from the police department and from society, there was nowhere to turn . . . and to be able to put your arms around other gay men and to be able to stand up and sing "God Save Us Nelly Queens". . . we were really not saying "God Save Us Nelly Queens." We were saying "We have our rights, too." (Mariposa Film Group 1977)

Sarria ran for a seat on the San Francisco Board of Supervisors in 1962 and became the first openly gay candidate to run for public office, a fact often eclipsed in (white) mainstream media by the valorization of Harvey Milk (Gorman 2014). He almost won, but when the Board realized how close the vote was, they rushed 34 other candidates into the race. Even so, he won close to 6,000 votes in the election, forcing the city leaders to think twice before underestimating queer candidates (Shilts 1982). It was a monumental achievement and, in 1962, Sarria and other QBIPOC activists formed *The Tavern Guild*, the country's first gay business association, which was dedicated to demanding justice and providing bail for queers arrested in gay bar raids without cause (Bullough 2002). Sarria recognized his own power, and said of his groundbreaking work, "From that day on, nobody ran for anything in San Francisco without knocking on the door of the gay community" (Lockhart 2002, 36).

The Freedom Vote. The story of Black queer activist Aaron Henry, the Mississippi President of the National Association for the Advancement of Colored People (NAACP), is a narrative often lost in the larger struggle for queer liberation. Henry was arrested on sodomy charges and disorderly conduct at least four recorded times, likely to get himself thrown out of office. Yet, through tenacity, he managed to get reelected 33 times and remained in his post from 1960 to 1993. The sodomy charges came at a time that, in Henry's words,

marked an interesting point in the history of intimidation of civil rights workers. No longer were bigoted officials satisfied with trying to brand us as communist, a charge that was "getting old." So they picked a new charge—one detested equally by whites and Negroes—homosexuality. (Howard 2001, 161)Henry was the Chair of the Mississippi Democratic Freedom Party and actively challenged the overwhelming whiteness prevalent in the state's democratic network. After his friend and fellow NAACP board member Medger Evers was shot in Jackson in 1963, he became one of the state's most vocal activists for racial equity (Williams 2013). He ran for governor the year of his friend's murder, under what he called the "freedom vote." It was a mock election as Black candidates couldn't run in gubernatorial races at the time. Eighty thousand Black voters turned up to cast their ballots anyhow, and it was a smart, strategic play for visibility and community power.

In 1964, Henry ran for U.S. Senate, and, due to a surge of support from Black voters and grassroots campaign efforts, completely outdid his opponent, 61,004 to 139 votes. It is safe to say he would have won, had it not been for the compounded oppressions of racism, heterosexism, and voter suppression. The state's election commission declared him ineligible to run as some of his petitioners had not paid the poll tax (Marshall 2013), an unconstitutional tax frequently imposed on voting to prevent marginalized people from gaining entry to powerful positions (Ackerman and Nou 2009). Ultimately, these races demonstrated the power of the Black vote and paved the way for the Voting Rights Act of 1965, improving the rights and futures for not just Black people, but Intersectional Others who saw Aaron Henry as a symbol of what was possible.

A New Wave of QBIPOC Political Power

In 2021, several state legislatures saw their first queer members of color, and the U.S. Congress welcomed its first queer Black members, shattering their respective rainbow ceilings, and bringing powerful, fresh voices to the forefront of political change. Kim Jackson, an Episcopal church leader in Atlanta, for instance, made history as the first Black lesbian elected to the Georgian Senate. She did so with 80 percent of the vote, representing the wave of change rippling through much of the more conservative areas of the United States (Burress 2021). Jackson was one of at least 40 Intersectional Others who won elections in state legislatures in 2021 and one of at least 16 nonincumbents. In New York, for instance, Ritchie Torres and Mondaire Jones won their House races and became the first two Black gay candidates elected to Congress. Torres, a Bronx native who identified as Afro-Latino, was also the first queer congressperson from New York City (Avery 2020).

At the beginning of his term, President Joe Biden also appointed several "firsts" to positions in the Biden-Harris administration. Among the public appointments were two lesbians of color, Vice President Kamala Harris's Chief-of-Staff Karine Jean-Pierre and White House Communications Director Pili Tobar (Johnson 2020). In a 2020 interview with *NBC News*, Annise Parker, president of the LGBTQ Victory Fund, which supports queer and trans candidates in their runs for public office, said, "As our nation grapples with racism, police brutality and a pandemic that disproportionately affects people of color and LGBTQ people, these are the voices that can pull us from the brink and toward a more united and fair society" (Avery 2020).

Then there is U.S. Representative Sharice Davids, the first Native lesbian congressmember, elected in 2018 to represent Kansas's third congressional district, thereby replacing white straight incumbent Kevin Yoder, who, prior to her election, had represented his district for 15 years. In her 2021 children's book *Sharice's Big Voice: A Native Kid Becomes A Congresswoman*, she reflected on her unique path to office, and the staggering lack of representation for Native youth in literature. Davids said in an interview about the book:

> I know that especially our LGBTQ+ youth often hear messages that are not affirming or validating of their experience. One of the things that I hope that people can get from this book . . . is that you are important, your voice deserves to be heard. (Sosin 2021)

THE POWER TO BRIDGE COMMUNITIES AND LIVELIHOODS

While Black Lives Matter has certainly shone in the spotlight, garnering strong intercommunity support in the fight against police brutality and the loss of Black lives, it is worth noting that queer activists and activists of color have fought many times, as well as plenty at the intersections, side by side. In his essay *Slicing Silence: Asian Progressives Coming Out* (2001), Chinese American queer activist Daniel Tsang wrote, "We may have been invisible, but many of us were active in the Civil Rights Movement and in the antiwar movement as well as the emerging women's and gay liberation movements" (220).

Despite oppressive hierarchies structured by the white straight U.S. elite and mainstream to pit marginalized people against each other (Kim 1999), Intersectional Others have long fought together in struggles across racial, gender, sexual, and other intersectional lines, and these intercommunity struggles have been well-documented photographically, even when not easily accessible through writings. The LGBT Community Center National History Archives, San Jose State University Special Collections and Archives, and the USC Libraries, for instance, have snapshots of early Christopher Street Liberation Day parades (1970 and 1972) and Pride festivals across the country—New York City, Santa Ana, San Francisco, and more—where queer Native, Latino/a/x, Black, and white youth are front and center, marching collaboratively to support liberation for their contingencies and all (Riemer and Brown 2019).

In 2014, queer Black Kenyan artist Jim ChuChu sparked conversation by creating a multicolored visual art piece entitled *All Oppression is Connected*, which illustrated the multitude of intersecting ways in which global communities are affected by the same prejudices (figure 8.1).

Figure 8.1 "All Oppression Is Connected." Mural by Jim Chuchu. Inspired by the poetry of Staceyann Chin. ©2006–2021, Jim Chuchu.

Intersectional Others, with ever-mixing identities, have the greatest power to bridge people and systems, as we represent a million communities in and of ourselves. It's important to remember that race and sexuality are only two pieces of the larger intersectional puzzle. We all carry a host of identities and exist somewhere on the continuum of privilege and Otherness as each of these identities plays a role in how we move throughout the world, and how others perceive us. At the intersections, we have the power to touch those in the communities we inhabit. We have the power to bring justice to those communities, or remain silent in those communities, thereby harming them through complicity.

Building Coalitions across Difference

In 1993, Black and Chicana feminist scholars Angela Davis and Elizabeth Martinez met at the University of California, San Diego, to discuss BIPOC coalition-building. Davis said during that discussion:

> This is not the first period during which we have confronted the difficult problem of using difference as a way of bringing people together, rather than as incontrovertible evidence of separation. There are more options than sameness, opposition, or hierarchical relations. One of the basic challenges confronting women of color today, as Audre Lorde has pointed out, is to think about and act upon notions of equality across difference. There are so many ways in which we can conceptualize coalitions, alliances, and networks that we would be doing ourselves a disservice to argue that there is only one way to construct relations across racial and ethnic boundaries. (1)

In other words, it is a mistake to assume we cannot forge connections and build coalitions due to differences in history, identity, and opinion. To the contrary, all marginalized people share a connectedness through their experiences of racism, queerphobia, ableism, sexism, and oppression across the diaspora. Although our oppression often causes us to feel small and disparate, our intersections have the power to humanize, unite, and mobilize us.

The gay liberation struggle of the late 1960s and 1970s was increasingly mindful of intersectional voices, and several attempted the create coalitions with revolutionary groups of all types to expand the reach and power of its movement. The New York chapter of the GLF, for instance, marched with the Black Panthers in antiwar demonstrations, stating that "homosexual liberation cannot develop in a vacuum" and thus cross-group alliances needed to be forged (Riemer and Brown 2019, 122). The first Washington D.C. Pride March attempted to forge an alliance between the National Organization for Women and the National Coalition of Black Lesbians and Gays (Sueyoshi

2019), representing a change in identity discourse as well. Civil rights movements were no longer segregated struggles, but shared struggles against oppression, and more powerful together. In the words of Audre Lorde (1982), "There is no such thing as a single-issue struggle, because we do not live single-issue lives" (138).

Asian American queer activists—such as Gil Mangaoang, Daniel Tsang, and Merle Woo—all spoke openly and fervently about the need for community-based political activism as a precursor to power and liberation, which helped national coalitions to more fluidly form between Asian American LGBTQIA2S+ people and other queer groups in the 1980s (Tsang 2001). Of these coalitions, queer Malaysian American activist Siong-Huat Chua, cofounder in 1979 of Boston Asian Gay Men and Lesbians (BAGMAL)—the oldest Asian queer organization in the United States—said, "A distinctive feature of the North American gay Asian movement is its international perspective . . . the political and cultural exchanges that have developed have enriched the movements on both sides of the Pacific" (45), indicating that it was not only interracial alliances that needed to be formed but also *international* alliances to properly combat colonial influences of oppression and colonialism.

Black gay politician Melvin Boozer, the president of the Washington D.C. GAA in 1979, and the first openly gay man nominated for vice president of the United States, declined the nomination at the Democratic Convention in 1980, and said in his convention speech:

> Would you ask me how I dare to compare the civil rights struggle with the struggle for lesbian and gay rights? I can compare them and I do compare them, because I know what it means to be called a 'nigger' and I know what it means to be called a 'faggot,' and I understand the differences in the marrow of my bones. And I can sum up that difference in one word: *none*. (Rutledge 1992, 156)

While this is an oversimplified proclamation of shared struggles—because to claim racial and sexual oppressions occludes the unique issues each carries—it is nonetheless a bold, radical statement on the systemic issues that plague all who are oppressed, one which very few leaders publicly expressed at the time.

The National Third World Lesbian and Gay Conference

In the late 1970s and through the 1980s, intercommunity networks flourished through regional and national conferences, as well as solidarity marches. In October 1979, for instance, the very first National Third World Lesbian and

Gay Conference at Howard University in Washington D.C., hosted by the National Coalition of Black Gays, drew Intersectional Others from all over the country. The conference was groundbreaking in so many ways, and naturally garnered national and global attention from groups like the Sandinistas in Nicaragua and socialist Compañeros in Mexico, and even drew the praise of the Consul General of Nicaragua in San Francisco, which issued the following statement: "May from your conference be born a movement that identifies, that unites and struggles with the liberation movements of all oppressed people" (Tsang 2001).

The keynote address *When Will the Ignorance End* was delivered by Black queer activist Audre Lorde and published in the 1979 Summer issue of the *Gay Insurgent*, a local newsletter. It must have set an inspiring, yet sobering, tone for the conference. Outside of the poorly printed summer issue, the speech is hard to locate in the literature, despite many Audre Lorde scholars attempting to find it in print. It is therefore painstakingly copied word-for-word for my readers, and preserved for posterity, here.

> So I stand here as a 46 year old Black Lesbian Feminist warrior poet come to do my work . . . the tasks of joyfulness, of struggle, of community, and the work of redefining our joint power and goals, so that our younger people need never suffer in the isolation that so many of us have known. And while we are here, I ask that each of you remember the ghosts that came before us. . . . Some of our sisters and brothers are not here because they did not survive our holocausts, nor live to see the day when there finally was a National Conference of Third World Lesbians and Gays. (12)

The 1979 conference happily coincided with the First National Lesbian and Gay March on Washington. Gay Chinese American activist Daniel Tsang wrote of the protest that "the early morning march through the Black neighborhood and through Chinatown was the first time Black and Asian lesbians and gay men had paraded through their own neighborhoods" (Tsang 1980, 84-85). Japanese American lesbian poet and activist Michiyo Fukaya, the representative of the Lesbian and Gay Asian Collective, echoed that sentiment, proclaiming it was the "first time in the history of the American hemisphere that Asian American gays and lesbians joined to form a network of support" (Sueyoshi 2019, 131). The Asian contingent of the march alone was composed of several ethnic groups, including Chinese, Japanese, Indonesian, Filipino, Indian, and Malaysian diasporic people, as well as several global regions, including North America, Asia, and the Caribbean (Leong 2014).

The time marked an explosion of creativity and authorship from queer feminists of color, who often sought to publish works with established feminist presses, such as the Women's Press Collective, but also started their own publishing groups, such that created in 1980 by Black lesbians Barbara Smith and Audre Lorde, Kitchen Table: Women of Color Press. These grassroots efforts in the 1980s liberation movements are often forgotten but nonetheless critical to the development of strong regional and national bonds for all Intersectional Others.

Barriers to Intercommunity Solidarity

Intersectional Others have the power to bridge our communities together, but often can't do it alone. Black queer activist Alicia Garza, in her book *The Purpose of Power: How We Come Together When We Fall Apart* (2021), wrote:

> We can't be afraid to establish a base that is larger than the people we feel comfortable with. Movements and bases cannot be cliques of people who already know each other. We have to reach beyond the choir and take seriously the task of organizing the unorganized—the people who don't already speak the same language, the people who don't eat, sleep and breathe social justice, the people who have everything at stake and are looking to be less isolated and more connected and who want to win changes in their lives and the lives of the people they love. (52)

There are numerous advantages to intercommunity solidarity, yet it is exceedingly easy to succumb to division imposed by mainstream society. We have all heard, for instance, the myth of Asian American "model minority" status, which originated in the 1960s—the belief that Asian Americans are somehow superior to Black and Brown folk in the United States due to unparalleled academic success and work ethic, which "set them apart" from other marginalized groups. This one-note portrayal not only serves to reduce and homogenize Asian American experiences, but importantly also pits them against other marginalized communities.

When the white mainstream valorizes Asian Americans for their individualism and self-reliance, it simultaneously devalues other BIPOC, implying they are dependent and deficient, a process called "racial triangulation" (Kim 1999). We can see racial triangulation at work when we consider the cultural narrative of the "welfare queen," a stereotype developed during the Reagan administration meant to vilify Black women who were deemed "degenerate" and "reliant" on the U.S. welfare system. It was a racialized and gendered stereotype which ultimately enabled public disgust and racist discourse to flourish (Hancock 2003).

Racial triangulation has negatively impacted interracial solidarity over time, evidenced by anti-Black sentiments that are often prevalent in the Asian

American communities, and vice versa, something younger generations have actively worked to combat (Yi and Todd 2021). We can see the results of these efforts in the Black Lives Matter protests after George Floyd's death in May 2020, which saw a significant rise in Asian American support. Then, after the March 2021 spa shootings in Georgia, in which six Asian American women were killed, we similarly saw Black social justice advocates, entertainers, athletes, and even former president Barack Obama take a stand against anti-Asian hate (Chang 2021). The landscape of racial conversation is changing as constructs like racial triangulation are brought into public awareness, allowing for them to be dismantled slowly over time.

Chinese American activist Grace Lee Boggs said in a 2010 interview with *Democracy Now* on modern activism and community solidarity that "the only way to survive is by taking care of each other" (Boggs 2010). It does not, as Boggs suggested, serve Asian Americans to buy into the model minority myth, nor does it serve Intersectional Others in the United States, who are also suffering from the effects of oppression. It does, however, serve those who hold wealth and power—white straight men—who are then able to avoid responsibility for creating the racial triangulation in the first place. The result of racial triangulation is that we are so focused on intercommunity hatred that we are unable to mobilize ourselves communally against our actual oppressors. How much power would we have, if instead of directing our anger toward each other, we joined together in solidarity and directed it where it belonged?

Contemporary Solidarity Efforts

Many Intersectional Others—the Black Youth Project 100 (BYP100), Black LGBTQ+ Activists for Change (BLAC), and Intersectional Voices Collective, to name a few—are, right now, actively integrating the intersectional lens into their social justice work, drawing inspiration from a long history of activist efforts (Clement 2020; Salahieh 2020). They benefited from the experiences of people like queer mixed Chinese American Stuart Gaffney, key plaintiff in the landmark 2008 California Supreme Court case overturning the ban on same-sex marriage Proposition 8, who used his parents' experiences with anti-miscegenation law to argue Prop 8's unconstitutionality in court (Marriage Equality USA 2017), as well as queer Latino/a/x activist groups, like San Francisco's Ellas en Acción, New York's Las Buenas Amigas, and Puerto Rico's Colectivo de Concientización Gay, all of which fought for intersectional rights. Some of these were not recognized outside of their locales until recently when books like *Queer Brown Voices* acknowledged and amplified their efforts (Quesada, Gomez and Vidal-Ortiz 2015).

Certainly the most visible, and likely also the biggest, organizing efforts of our time have been those of the Black Lives Matter movement, cofounded by Black queer organizers Alicia Garza and Patrice Cullors, as well as Black straight organizer Opal Tometi. A movement which grew even more rapidly after the Ferguson uprising in 2014, Black Lives Matter has truly been a symbol of intersectional power. In *The Purpose of Power*, Alicia Garza (2020) wrote that the

> rallying cry of Black Lives Matter recognized that a new kind of leadership was needed . . . it challenged those in power to reckon with the deep racism that continues to be dismissed and ignored. But it was also a challenge to all of us: to harness and organize our power in different and more effective ways, as Black people and all people who want justice. (x)

She went on to say that power itself wasn't enough. It needed to be "power with purpose. It is the power we need to keep building and using to transform society" (x). In the face of profound loss and oppression, Black Lives Matter was a message which conveyed the necessity of transformation and an end to Othering violence.

Building a sense of expansion, that intersecting identities were part and parcel of the struggle, was also critical to the movement's power. Garza felt that "Black Lives Matter, working alongside the activists and organizers who emerged from the Ferguson uprising, created political and cultural space for a more expansive version of Blackness to emerge" (134). Blackness was not just about being respectable to whiteness; it was not even about defending middle-class America. It was about uplifting *all,* but *especially* those who existed at the most marginalized intersections of Blackness. As she pointed out, however, progress wasn't without contestation. At Ferguson, for instance, queer Black organizers reported they were often called "dykes" while protesting and told they would be "fucked straight." Garza confessed that she also felt a class struggle ensued over her choice of dress during the protests, as some locals insinuated she would not be accepted for "doing her hair" and wearing a dress (Garza 2020, 134)—all of these are symbolic fights over what it means to be an Intersectional Other in activist circles.

It is important to center the voices of QBIPOC, but not because we are solely racially or sexually Othered. Our representations of queerness are only as powerful as our manifestations of solidarity, and the same is true for our Blackness or Asianness or Indigenous roots. No movement can survive without solidarity within and outside of the community context; support is the air that allows the flame of resistance to flourish and grow. When we can carry one another—in our struggle and our joy, in our frustrations and our contradictions—we make more room in the world for healing justice, and we find community and peace beyond our grief as Others in this country. We reject perpetuating the harm we have endured.

CREATION AS RADICAL TRANSFORMATION

Art has always served as some form of resistance. Black queer author Toni Cade Bambera is quoted as saying:

> As a cultural worker who belongs to an oppressed people my job is to make revolution irresistible. One of the ways I attempt to do that is by celebrating those victories within the Black community. And I think the mere fact that we're still breathing is a cause for celebration. (Bambera 2012, 35)

Art is not so much about reactive expression as it is intentional presence. It is our un-Othering. We do not create because we have the answers. We create because we are possessed by our questions. It is how we convey the ideas of those who have been silenced. It is how we heal from the wounds cut by oppressive systems. Meaningful creation serves and expands our consciousness as a people.

Black queer poet, Phillip Williams, in a 2021 interview with them, said that he often asks himself, "What can I bring into this work so that it is as expansive as I am? Heteronormativity is too small" (Ajani 2021). Intersectionality—in its essence, in its complexities—is expansive. It is world-making. It is a direct contradiction of society's present assumptions of heteronormativity and white normativity—instead, it preaches hybridity and fluidity. Intersectional Others, by virtue of living in resistance to these assumptions, may enact or perform a potential futurity which rejects them entirely (Muñoz 2009). Cuban American queer theorist Jose Esteban Muñoz said of this:

> We may never touch queerness, but we can feel it as the warm illumination of a horizon imbued with potentiality. We have never been queer, yet queerness exists for us as an ideality that can be distilled from the past and used to imagine a future. The future is queerness's domain. (Muñoz 2009, 1)

Intersectional Others, different as we are, can imagine a whole host of possibilities for the future that those caught within dominant paradigms cannot.

White heteronormative society is inherently threatened by difference, because difference provides us with the ability to challenge it. So, it tells us that difference is something to be shunned, and thus something of which we should feel shame. Something to be feared, and thus something of which all should be afraid. However, the *most* transformative moments in history have come from minds who saw the world differently, and thus saw an opportunity to grow beyond the boundaries of society and its disciplines. Referring to his acceptance of the MacArthur Genius Grant, a prestigious award given to innovators who have demonstrated great promise in their respective fields, queer Vietnamese American poet Ocean Phuong said, "Be prepared to be unfathomable to the rest of the world" (Cochran 2019). Testing the limits of art, science, and move, intersectional visionaries have not been appreciated in their lifetimes for their revolutionary ideas, yet their work nonetheless had a profound impact on the world posthumously, such as the creative transformations of author Zora Neale Hurston.

In September 2020, National Public Radio's *Throughline* cohost Gene Demby made an interesting remark about what he called "taking the bribe" by the white mainstream, in an episode addressing James Baldwin's legacy. As BIPOC, he said, "we are constantly faced with 'taking the bribe.' The bribe is silence. It's 'just pursue your craft and make your money.' The bribe is to adjust yourself to injustice." When Intersectional Others "take the bribe," we allow ourselves to internalize dominant ideology, which then stifles our voices and power. When we allow our creative and cultural productions to be diminished by the mainstream, we jeopardize our abilities to imagine a future outside of what is already accepted and known. This leads to a deformation of attention to issues necessary for queer people of color to thrive (Demby 2020). And ultimately, when we start producing work that no longer captures the public eye or revolutionizes our mediums, we become a part of the hegemonic system that rejects us. When we think about visionaries, we rarely think of those who succumb to society's constraints of normalcy—we think of those who are the furthest away from common.

"As Gay As It Was Black"

Black scholar and director of the Hutchins Center for African and African American Research at Harvard University, Henry Louis Gates Jr., wrote in his essay *The Black Man's Burden* (1993) that the Harlem Renaissance was "surely as gay as it was black, not that it was exclusively either of these" (133). The 1920s Harlem—which is well-known for producing a flowering of art, music, and writing—was indisputably gay and being "in the life" was part its landscape. Queer historian Eric Garber (1989) wrote about this cultural moment:

> At the beginning of the twentieth century, a homosexual subculture, uniquely Afro-American in substance, began to take shape in New York's Harlem. Throughout the so- called Harlem Renaissance period, roughly 1920 to 1935, black lesbians and gay men were meeting each other [on] street corners,

socializing in cabarets and rent parties, and worshiping in church on Sundays, creating a language, a social structure, and a complex network of institutions. (1)

While the Harlem Renaissance is often seen as a racialized period in U.S. history, the fact is, it was also a powerhouse of racial-sexual interchange. Without the contributions of Black queer creatives like Langston Hughes, Ethel Waters, and Alain Locke, the Renaissance would have likely never gained the same momentum (Gates 1993). In a segregated America, they spearheaded the definitions of not only Black creativity but also Black identity. Although Intersectional Others in many ways existed in legal and societal limbo, the Harlem Renaissance celebrated sexuality with a total level of tolerance remarkable for that era (Harris 2008). Queer artists of the Harlem Renaissance were determined to use their art to promote pride in both their race and their sexualities.

The "New Negro" Versus the "Perfumed Orchid"

Alain LeRoy Locke, who many consider the architect and scholarly mind behind the cultural and creative movement, hoped to use the notion of the "New Negro" to transform negative associations with Black identity in mainstream U.S. society. But Locke's mission to shine a positive light on this group came at a cost. It inadvertently embraced the views and sociopolitical systems that denounced both Black and queer people in the United States. Henry Louis Gates Jr. (2020) explained, "If the New Negroes of the Harlem Renaissance sought to erase their received racist image in the Western imagination, they also erased their racial selves" (321).

Unlike many of his Renaissance peers, Locke believed that artistry and the Great Migration, not political activism, were the keys to Black liberation. Black queer folk would only forge new and authentic senses of self, he argued, by pursuing artistic excellence and insisting on social mobility as a result. His writing conveyed a firm belief that self-determination would eventually transcend racial oppression and yield respectability for Black queers (McKee 2016). As Locke wrote, "The question is no longer what whites think of the Negro but of what the Negro wants to do and what price he is willing to pay to do it" (Stewart 2018, 448).

Locke was discreet about his queerness, but it was a public secret among those who knew him (Harris 2001). In his essay *'Outing' Alain L. Locke*, biographer Leonard Harris (2001) accused some scholars of misleading the public about—and indeed completely obscuring in some cases—Locke's gayness, leading to the false assumption that "Locke's sexuality was irrelevant to his intellectual and personal history" (321). Due to this common obfuscation of the time, the 1989 release of the critically acclaimed film *Looking for Langston*, which portrayed the intimate relationship between Hughes and Locke, caused quite a stir, resulting in tremendous efforts by the Langston Hughes estate to shut it down in order to "protect" Hughes's legacy (Villarosa 2011).

University of California, Santa Barbara (UCSB) professor of Black Studies Jeffrey Stewart (2018) wrote in *The New Negro: The Life of Alain Locke* that Locke believed that "the function of literature, art, the theater and so on was to complete the process of self-integration" and "produce a black subjectivity that could become the agent of a cultural and social revolution in America" (728). Locke turned his beliefs into action during the Renaissance, when he developed his theory of the "New Negro," which became popular among Black thought leaders. Aside from Zora Neale Hurston, who was a student of Franz Boas at Columbia University, he was one of the first among his peers to take Boas' work to its logical conclusions and declare racial essentialism illegitimate, pointing out that racial categories were based in nationality and social grouping rather than biology (Stewart 2018, 265).

Richard Bruce Nugent, on the other hand, the "perfumed orchid of the New Negro Movement," did not hide his sexuality like Locke or Hughes. In a 1926 issue of the radical literary magazine *Fire!!*, he is known to have written about the Renaissance unabashedly, "You did what you wanted to. Nobody was in the closet. There wasn't any closet" (Stokes 2003, 912). His words were not entirely true, as some performers and creatives did choose to stay closeted (McKee 2016). However, those who did often imbued their work with coded references to their sexuality (Katz 1989).

> According to author Langston Hughes, *Fire!!*'s mission was to symbolically burn up a lot of the old, dead conventional Negro-white ideas of the past . . . into a realization of the existence of the younger Negro writers and artists and provide us with an outlet for publication not available in the limited pages of the small Negro magazines then existing. (Samuels 2000, 14)

Ironically, the magazine headquarters burned down soon after its first, and last, issue was published in 1926. While its tenure was short, the magazine covered numerous topics considered radical for the time, including prostitution, homosexuality, bisexuality, and interracial relationships. Contributions included the works of renowned Black queer creatives such as Zora Neale Hurston, Richard Bruce Nugent, Wallace Thurman, and Countee Cullen (Hutchinson 2007).

Nugent's writing in *Fire!!* was theoretically momentous, being the first time an explicitly queer piece was published by a Black author. However, it was precisely these types of overt, un-coded exclamations that caused Nugent to be outcast by several of his Renaissance peers, whose motivations were mainly working toward "respectability," such as scholar Alain Locke. Queer theorist Michael Cobb (2000), who extensively researched the "impolite queers" of the Harlem Renaissance, stated:

> Whether this is true or not, his [Nugent's] early crossing into the taboo territory of same-sex sexuality has cast him into the role of race traitor, and, as a consequence, he provides a fruitful place to begin asking more detailed questions about race and queerness in the Harlem Renaissance's literature. Significantly, Nugent becomes a re-occurring and rich icon of the queer in Harlem, and his penchant for insolence, as we shall see, is certainly an issue. (329)

As Cobb (2000) ascertained, if Nugent was truly the first Black author to publish a piece on queerness in U.S. history, that achievement in and of itself should be noteworthy. However, Nugent's work was largely eclipsed by other Black queer creatives from the era, potentially due to this "impoliteness," which Cobb goes so far as to label "race traitor" material. Regarding the publication, Cobb (2000) stated, "Nugent, as we know, wrote the homosexual piece that would help shock a different kind of African-American literary recognition; he wrote the kind of piece that was intended to get the journal 'banned in Boston'" (330). The fact that Nugent's prose was published in *Fire!!* at all speaks to the distinct camps that formed within QBIPOC circles regarding assimilatory strategies of liberation.

Blues and Queer Sexualities

In her book *Blues Legacies and Black Feminism* (2011), Black queer activist Angela Davis wrote that "[t]he blues woman openly challenged the gender politics implicit in traditional cultural representations of marriage and heterosexual love" (27). Gertrude "Ma" Rainey's 1928 song *Prove It On Me* was specifically cited by Davis as a precursor to the lesbian movement of the 1970s, the lyrics of which candidly addressed Rainey's sexuality, as well as its stigma in public. The song's print advertisement made this quite evident, for instance. On it was pictured Rainey in a tailored suit jacket, tie, and vest talking to two people in femme-of-center drag, a police officer scrutinizing their every move. The ad's text coyly asked, "What's all this? Scandal? Maybe so, but you wouldn't have thought it of 'Ma' Rainey. But look at that cop watching her! What does it all mean? But 'Ma' just sings 'Prove It on Me'" (Katz 1989, 48–49).

Rainey challenged the sexual and gendered assumptions made about women at the peak of her popularity. In her 1924 hit song *Shave 'Em Dry*, Rainey sang in coded lyrics, "Here's one thing I don't understand/ Why a good-looking woman likes a workin' man/ hey, hey, hey, daddy, let me shave 'em dry." Later in the song, she sang, "Goin' downtown to spread the news/ State Street women wearin' brogan shoes." At the time, brogan shoes were indicative of queerness or gender nonconformity, as they were not considered "feminine enough" for cis straight women. Through these lyrics, we can hear that performers during the Renaissance were aware of the limitations of expression, and the potential consequences of being outed during the early 20th century (Rowden 2007). They were a subtle resistance, a flexing of sexual and gender norms for Black women and nonbinary people. A musical expression of the complex breadth of humanity commonly denied Black queers, the complexity of homonormative lives.

Creative Divergence from (White) Mainstream Feminism

White liberal cis feminism, in particular, such as that which undergirded the 2017–2020 Women's March on Washington, has been subject to longstanding critique by queer and trans activists of color for performative gestures which ultimately harm the larger feminist movement in the United States by excluding intersectional perspectives. They have historically created a "historical myopia" which obscures the needs of those who do not benefit from the privileges that straightness, cisness, or paler skin brings. This historical myopia is not the fault of feminists as a whole, many of whom have definitively expanded and revolutionized feminist praxis (e.g., Audre Lorde, bell hooks, Gloria Anzaldúa). Rather, this historical myopia is created by white liberal feminists within the larger movement who endorse dangerous liberal and imperialist politics and seek patriarchal approval and power to assimilate or shape the language of feminism. As bell hooks notes, the "patriarchal-dominated mass media is far more interested in promoting the views of women who want both to claim feminism and repudiate it at the same time . . . and who openly accept patriarchal sexuality" (hooks 2006, 96–97).

Whereas "first-wave feminism" focused mainly on suffrage (for white women) and overturning legal obstacles to gender equality (e.g., property rights), second-wave feminism broadened the debate to include a wider range of issues, such as sexuality, the workplace, reproductive rights, and social inequities (Freedman 2003). However, the second wave's focus on these issues furthered marginalization for Intersectional Others. In the 1960s and 1970s, figures like Lorraine Hansberry, Roxanne Gay, Willyce Kim, Angela Davis, and Audre Lorde propelled QBIPOC feminism into creative spaces, allowing for more nuanced conversations on power to take place. Black lesbian poet Cheryl Clarke (2005) wrote in her book *"After Mecca": Women Poets and the Black Arts Movement*:

During the sixties, we spent quite a lot of air time critiquing the "New Negro Renaissance" as bourgeois; however, we used some of its tactics to once again build a movement of new writing . . . the Black Arts Movement was not the first time black people "reinvented themselves 'new.'" So—we, i.e., lesbian-feminists—black lesbian feminists, black gay feminists, as well as the gay liberation movement used the "voice" strategy to inspire changes of attitude, to teach, and to critique. (62)

As "third-wave" feminism took hold in the United States in the 1980s and 1990s, a division within the larger feminist movement naturally emerged between white cis feminists—such as Katie Roiphe, Rene Denfeld, Camille Paglia, and Naomi Wolf, whose monolithic politics revealed their privileged status—and LGBTQIA2S+ feminists and feminists of color, such as Black queer feminist bell hooks and Native feminist Carolyn Sorisio, who criticized the former for "soft-selling" feminism (hooks 2006, 97) and neglecting to generate "substantive" contributions to the feminist agenda (Sorisio 1997, 143). By assuming all women were equally oppressed, white cis feminists created a "half-historicized" feminist doctrine, which was relegated to the status of "fact" due to their privileges, and thus passed on as fact to consecutive generations of U.S. feminists (Weatherby 2005).

Studies on the intentional coming together and movement-building of queer feminists of color have demonstrated the ways in which they can create unique spaces for vision and solidarity across difference (Nixon 2020). Functioning out of different lenses, bodies, and lived experiences, queer feminists of color have always critically engaged with the mainstream feminist movements of the United States, completely aware of the ways in which it departed from their realities. A new space and vision needed to be created, which put Intersectional Others at the forefront of gender and sexual politics. Not only was a new societal space necessary for QBIPOC feminists, but a space which truly *saw* its inhabitants without relying on hierarchies of oppression. Of this, Afro-Caribbean lesbian scholar and activist M. Jacqui Alexander (2013) wrote beautifully in the feminist anthology *This Bridge We Call Home: Radical Visions for Transformation,*

We are not born women of color. We become women of color. In order to become women of color, we would need to become fluent in each others' histories, to resist and unlearn an impulse to claim first oppression, most-devastating oppression, one-of-a-kind oppression, defying comparison oppression. We would have to unlearn an impulse that allows mythologies about each other to replace knowing about one another. (91)

Alexander's words demonstrated the rising social consciousness of QBIPOC feminists, as her transnational prose joined the proses of Gloria Anzaldúa and

AnaLouise Keating, QBIPOC feminists regarded for their visionary creativity and transgressive ideology in the United States and beyond.

Disrupting Linearity and Space through Art and Performance

Creation has historically allowed thinkers to stretch social boundaries. Queer creation, in particular, exists in a special limbo between reality and fantasy. All performances, for instance, hold dual states of being. In one the "performer"—that is, the creator or actor—produces a subject for either themselves to enjoy, or others to consume through witnessing. In doing so, that performer is able to interact with their performance without *being* the performance. Black Studies scholar Jesse Goldberg (2020), for instance, discussed the concept of "die-ins" in performance, whereby protests are performed on stage theatrically, ending in death. In a very literal way, "die-ins" allow creation to stretch boundaries between reality and fantasy, suspending the subject between life and death, and allowing the performer to walk away unscathed after their show of resistance. Dual outcomes are thus permitted to coexist. It is a "resurrection" of sorts, as Goldberg wrote.

Aloha Is a Performance

Kānaka Maoli (Native Hawaiian) scholar and queer theorist Stephanie Nohelani Teves (2018) problematized the global commercialization and performance of "aloha" in her work *Defiant Indigeneity: The Politics of Hawaiian Performance*. She wrote:

> [A]loha is a performance, negotiated at the intersections of ancestral knowledge and outsider expectations, manifest in the daily contradictions and complexities of Kānaka Maoli indigeneity. Usually conferred through the sharing of a lei, a kiss on the cheek, or perhaps a smile, aloha is supposed to transfer a feeling of overall welcome and warmth. This imagined performance affirms in the global imagination the existence of something that is real, that represents Hawai'i, that comes from Hawaiians, but that is now a gift given to the world. (2)

While colonization has altered the global perception of "aloha," giving the illusion that Indigenous peoples are docile, happy, and acquiescent to U.S. imperialism, Teves argued that Hawaiian performance has the power to resist colonial heteropatriarchal norms. Native queer and Two-Spirit performances, such as Indigenous drag, can allow Kānaka Maoli (Native Hawaiians) to defy and resist colonially imposed notions of aloha, in effect revitalizing Indigenous identity as a whole. This "defiant indigeneity" had the power to alter expectations established through settler colonialism.

Self-Portrait on the Border

We may also consider the work of Chicana queer disabled artist Frida Kahlo, whose creativity operated at the intersections of several identities, effectively queering the binaries through which differences are normatively mapped. She celebrated her differences, including her mestiza identity, her socialist politic, as well as her connections to the diaspora. In a radical act of alignment, Kahlo is known to have altered her birth date on record to match the date of the 1910 Mexican People's Revolution (Haynes 2006). In very literal ways, Kahlo disrupted linear temporality, adapting her age to her artistic vision and honoring her transgressive capabilities racially, spatially, and sexually (Anzaldúa 1987). Among her portraitures while living in the United States was the *Self-Portrait on the Border of Mexico and the United States* (1932), further illustrating her deep connection with the metaphorical and actual borderlands. Condescendingly, she gave an interview to the *Detroit News* on her art around the time of the aforementioned painting, which resulted in an article published with the title, "Wife of the Master Mural Painter Gleefully Dabbles in Works of Art," referring to her partner Diego Rivera (Herrera 2002), as if she wasn't prolific and iconic in her own right.

Of her powerful revolutionary spirit, Mexican author Carlos Fuentes wrote, "born with the Revolution, Frida Kahlo both mirrors and transcends the central event of twentieth-century Mexico . . . mak[ing] her fantastically, unavoidably, dangerously symbolic—or is it symptomatic?—of Mexico" (Fuentes and Lowe 1995, 10). Due to diasporic racial hierarchies, Kahlo was abstractly placed "in between" cultures, as the cultural location of mixed people, or "mestizos," in Latin America—like "criollos" in the Caribbean and "mulattos" in the Southern United States—is complex. Racially neither Black nor white, nor a simple combination of the two, "mestizos" are caught in a battleground between assumptions of "Blackness" and "whiteness." When called a surrealist in the 1950s, Frida Kahlo responded, "I never painted dreams. I paint my own reality" (Kahlo, 1953, n.p.).

Disidentificatory Performances

In his work *Disidentifications: Queers of Color and the Performance of Politics*, Cuban American queer theorist José Estéban Muñoz (1999) argued that performance art by queers of color is intrinsically political. This is because dominant ideology, which fundamentally rejects the lives of Intersectional Others, still exists. In so arguing, Muñoz reconceptualized political identity and processes as constructs which could interact with performance art and queer aesthetics (Muñoz 1999). He called these interactions "disidentificatory performances," or performances through which Intersectional Others might transgress or create in order to articulate a truth about cultural hegemony

(Muñoz 1999). Performances by **QBIPOC** powerfully resist that hegemony and have the potential to create a new future for their communities and selves. Of this, he said:

> Often we can glimpse the worlds proposed and promised by queerness in the realm of the aesthetic. The aesthetic, especially the queer aesthetic, frequently contains blueprints and schemata of a forward-dawning futurity. . . . Queerness is also a performative because it is not simply a being but a doing for and toward the future. Queerness is essentially about the rejection of a here and now and an insistence on potentiality or concrete possibility for another world. (Muñoz 2009, 1)

There are many Intersectional Others whose performances and artistries exemplify "disidentification," the process by which someone outside the racial and sexual mainstream negotiates majority culture—not by aligning themselves with or against exclusionary works, but rather by transforming these works for their own cultural purposes (Muñoz 1999). One such person is South Asian American gender nonconforming artist and activist Alok Vaid-Menon, who defies binaries and uses their art and aesthetic to trans-form—and bring humanity—to the music, fashion, and art industries. Their 2019 Instagram campaign, #DegenderFashion, an attempt to strip the fashion industry of its rigid binary assumptions, demonstrated the power of leverag-ing the reciprocal relationship between art and activism. In an interview with *Huffington Post*, Vaid-Menon reportedly said:

> [I]t's not that nonbinary people are new. It's that gender-variant people, every century, have templated forms of living, loving and looking that were so revo-lutionary, so glamorous, with such splendor, that they had to be forcibly annihi-lated and extinguished because of their potentiality. The gift of transness is one of potentiality and metamorphosis. We actually show the world that transforma-tion is not only possible, but that it is happening all around you. (Tanaïs 2021)

It is in this "metamorphosis" that we can see potential power and liberation for Intersectional Others, not only now, but in the past and future as well. As beings growing in awareness of our Otherness, we have the capabilities to change the narratives told about our histories, as well as the capabilities to destroy and remake dominant paradigms for the better.

Conclusion

As I write this, in 2021, we are still in the COVID-19 pandemic. I have officially written the entirety of this book during a global disaster. It has deeply changed my connection to the work, as the catastrophic consequences of multiple marginalization have become more and more obvious as time has gone on. Intersectional Others continue to be evicted, face unemployment, and feel food insecure at high rates. They are also facing higher rates of COVID-19 infection, depression, and traumatic stress due to the pandemic (Sears, Conron, and Flores 2021). It has left many of us in a state of existential dread for over a year now.

But amid these dark moments, I also saw the luminous beginnings develop. In September 2021, Confederate General Robert E. Lee's 12-ton statue was finally torn down in Richmond, Virginia. Due to court litigation, its removal was delayed by over a year—the original order was issued in June 2020 by Virginia governor Ralph Northam, following George Floyd's murder. Former president Trump reportedly "deplored" its removal, publicly claiming Lee would have won the war in Afghanistan had he served in the U.S. military today, presumably implying he would have been a better "commander-in-chief" than President Joe Biden (Brown 2021). In saying so, Trump, unbeknownst to him, reiterated the strong link between racism, nationalism, and imperialism.

Trump's words do not exist in a vacuum but are shared by many who hail General Lee a hero among heroes, a devout Christian with acclaimed military acumen and an ethic to "unite" the country during greater political division. Some even mistakenly believe Lee was an abolitionist, a belief fueled in large part by the misunderstanding of one heavily quoted letter he wrote in 1856, which called slavery a "moral & political evil." However, the quote does not stop there. He continued:

I think it however a greater evil to the white man than to the black race. . . .
The blacks are immeasurably better off here than in Africa, morally, socially
& physically. The painful discipline they are undergoing, is necessary for their
instruction as a race. (Serwer 2021)

But that's not all. Within the confines of the statue base is a time capsule
with 60 artifacts from 1887, some thought to be Confederate objects. In its
place, the governor commissioned a new time capsule to be built, complete
with modern-day artifacts including a Kente cloth worn at the 400th com-
memoration of 1619, a Black Lives Matter sticker, Stop Asian Hate fliers, a
Pride pin, and a vial of Pfizer's (expired) COVID-19 vaccine (Franklin 2021).
As if a metaphor for the foundation of the United States, the base for the
statue will be deconstructed, then reimagined and built anew. The new time
capsule will then be sealed and sent forth into the future, where it will remain
unopened perhaps for another 134 years, if the last one was any indication.
We won't know the thoughts of those future beholders on the commemora-
tion cloth, COVID-19 vial, or Black Lives Matter sticker. However, it is
likely the capsule will go through a similar cycle once opened, reimagined
once again.

QUEERNESS AND MARGINALITY
AS RADICAL REIMAGINING

This book endeavored not to necessarily heal the effects of oppression on
Intersectional Others but provide a space for the reader to reflect on, awaken
to, and reimagine their power from the margins. It endeavored to be a space
of powerful marginality. Not, as Black queer author bell hooks said, the

> marginality one wishes to lose—to give up or surrender as part of moving into
> the center—but rather as a site one stays in, clings to even, because it nourishes
> one's capacity to resist. It offers one the possibility of radical perspective from
> which to see and create, to imagine alternatives, new worlds. (150)

It seems natural, at this book's conclusion, to return a quote from bell hooks's
1989 essay *Choosing the Margins as a Space of Radical Openness*. Her work
was, after all, the source of inspiration for this book.

In more ways than one, this book was a space of radical openness and
world-building. It purposefully reconstructed historical memory for queer
Black, Indigenous, and People of Color (QBIPOC) whose stories and activism have traditionally been excluded or silenced through colonialism and systemic oppression. Cuban American queer theorist José Estéban Muñoz (2009)

said, "Queerness is a longing that propels us onward, beyond romances of the negative and toiling in the present. Queerness is a thing that lets us feel that this world is not enough, that indeed something is missing" (1). When we think of radical marginality and queerness, we can think of a collective struggling toward a better world—past, present, and future.

Every single person in this book—Sylvia Rivera, Gil Mangoalang, Gertrude "Ma" Rainey—deserved to have their lives valued and remembered, just as much, or even more so, than the Harvey Milks of the gay liberation movement, whose actions have always been held high as revolutionary, despite the fact that they fought with less to lose. The Riveras, Mangoalangs, and Raineys have always deserved to have their humanities de-vilified. This book was a chance for a QBIPOC author to write about QBIPOC histories and subvert traumatic patterns in which white straight historians write about lives they know little about to gain privileges they need even less. It is its own recentered storytelling. Quite literally, this book has plucked marginal subjects from obscurity and recentered them on its pages for all to see. We are taking up rightful space in the center of our own narrative.

We talked earlier of the metamorphosis that comes with awareness and disidentification (Muñoz 1999), with actively being aware of our various sexual and racial marginalizations and negotiating those with the dominant social paradigms, whatever those may be for us. In this book, readers—and me, as the author—also metamorphize through growing consciousness resulting from the digestion of material aimed at bringing awareness to the chains which have held us down systemically in the United States. Bringing awareness to the ways in which we have collectively fought against those chains over time. In investing in reflection and education, we also invested in the transformation of our consciousnesses. You may remember that this was the third step to de-vilification of the Other.

In some ways, this book also set out to act as a source of transformative justice, in the most basic sense. "Transformative justice," at its core, responds to harm by transforming the conditions that make that harm possible (Barrie 2020). And when we consider the ways in which we can put this knowledge into practice, transformative justice must be one of those ways. It is an important framework which acknowledges the impacts of oppression on the cycles of violence in this country. Too often, dehumanization inherent in oppression vilifies Intersectional Others, ultimately leading to the deeply embedded systemic problems we discuss in this book, like healthcare disparities, QBIPOC criminalization, and mass incarceration and injustice—all in the name of catching the criminal and bringing them to "justice" (Center for American Progress 2016).

But it's just not that simple. We live in a world where calling the police can be fatal for marginalized lives. Where bias is entrenched in the law.

Where dehumanization, before empathy, is standard for Intersectional Others. Transformative justice, therefore, and indeed, this book also, must be a conversation between the communities harmed by oppressive histories and the systems at work perpetuating that harm. This is importantly done, as mixed Sri Lankan queer disabled author and organizer Leah Lakshmi Piepzna-Samarasinha and Black queer organizer and political strategist Ejeris Dixon (2020) discussed in *Beyond Survival*, by reaching an equilibrium that includes community power, agency, and accountability.

We all have a responsibility to each other.

Bibliography

Abramowitz, Alan, and Jennifer McCoy. 2019. "United States: Racial resentment, negative partisanship, and polarization in Trump's America." *The ANNALS of the American Academy of Political and Social Science* 681, no. 1: 137–156.

Abrams, Stacy. 2019. *Lead from the Outside: How to Build Your Future and Make Real Change*. Picador: New York.

Ackerman, Bruce, and Jennifer Nou. 2009. "Canonizing the civil rights revolution: The people and the poll tax." *Northwestern University Law Review* 103: 63.

Ahmed, Tanveer. 2005. "The Muslim 'marginal man': understanding the psychological and sociological state of Western Muslims will help integrate society and avoid terrorism." *Policy: A Journal of Public Policy and Ideas* 21, no. 1: 35–41.

Ajani, Ashia. "*Mutiny* signals rebellion against the crushing reality of everyday life." *them.* September 9, 2021. https://www.them.us/story/phillip-b-williams-mutiny -poetry-collection-interview. Accessed September 10, 2021.

Alexander, E. 2021. Interview by Shereen Meraji. Payback's a B****. Code Switch NPR.

Alexander, M. Jaqui. 2006. *Pedagogies of Crossing*. Duke University Press.

Alfred, Taiaiake. 2005. *Wasase: Indigenous Pathways of Action and Freedom*. University of Toronto Press.

Alfred, Taiaiake. 2009. "Colonialism and state dependency." *Journal of Aboriginal Health* 5: 42–60.

Alfred, Taiaiake. 2015. "Cultural strength: Restoring the place of Indigenous knowledge in practice and policy." *Australian Aboriginal Studies* 1: 3–11.

Alfred, Taiaiake, and Jeff Corntassel. 2005. "Being indigenous: Resurgences against contemporary colonialism." *Government and Opposition* 40: 597–614.

Alimahomed, Sabrina. 2010. "Thinking outside the rainbow: Women of color redefining queer politics and identity." *Social Identities* 16, no. 2: 151–168.

American Civil Liberties Union [ACLU] 2021. "Why sodomy laws matter." *ACLU Website.* https://www.aclu.org/other/why-sodomy-laws-matter. Accessed September 1, 2021.

American Psychological Association 2021. "APA resolution on gender identity change efforts." *APA Website*. February 2021. Retrieved from: https://www.apa.org/about/policy/resolution-gender-identity-change-efforts.pdf.

Amodio, David M., and Patricia G. Devine. 2006. "Stereotyping and evaluation in implicit race bias: evidence for independent constructs and unique effects on behavior." *Journal of Personality and Social Psychology* 91, no. 4: 652.

Ansley, Frances Lee. 1989. "Stirring the Ashes: Race, class and the future of civil rights scholarship." *Cornell Law Review* 74: 993.

Anzaldúa, Gloria. 1987. *Borderlands/La Frontera: The New Mestiza*. Aunt Lute Books.

Apfelbaum, Evan P., Samuel R. Sommers, and Michael I. Norton. 2008. "Seeing race and seeming racist? Evaluating strategic colorblindness in social interaction." *Journal of Personality and Social Psychology* 95, no. 4: 918.

Applebaum, Barbara. 2010. *Being White, Being Good: White Complicity, White Moral Responsibility, and Social Justice Pedagogy*. Lexington Books.

Appleford, Katherine. 2016. "'This big bum thing has taken over the world': Considering black women's changing views on body image and the role of celebrity." *Critical Studies in Fashion and Beauty* 7, no. 2: 193–214.

Archer, Alfred, and Georgina Mills. 2019. "Anger, affective injustice, and emotion regulation." *Philosophical Topics* 47, no. 2: 75–94.

Arenas, Andrea-Teresa, and Eloisa Gómez. 2018. *Somos Latinas: Voices of Wisconsin Latina Activists*. Wisconsin Historical Society, i.

Armstrong, Elizabeth A., and Suzanna M. Crage. 2006. "Movements and memory: The making of the Stonewall myth." *American Sociological Review* 71, no. 5: 724–751.

Austin, Jill, Jennifer Brier, Jessica Herczeg-Konecny, and Anne Parsons. 2012. "When the erotic becomes illicit: Struggles over displaying queer history at a mainstream museum." *Radical History Review* 2012, no. 113: 187–197.

Avery, Dan. "Mondaire Jones joins Ritchie Torres as first gay Black men elected to Congress."

Avery, Dan. "Sodomy laws that labeled gay people sex offenders challenged in court." *NBC News*. April 7, 2021. Retrieved from: https://www.nbcnews.com/feature/nbc-out/sodomy-laws-labeled-gay-people-sex-offenders-challenged-court-n1263225.

Bader, Steven. 2017. "Asian Men as Targets of Sexual Racism in the Gay Community." *American Cultural Studies Capstone Research Papers* 8. https://cedar.wwu.edu/fairhaven_acscapstone/8.

Badgett, M., Holning Lau, Brad Sears, and Deborah Ho. 2007. "Bias in the workplace: Consistent evidence of sexual orientation and gender identity discrimination." *UCLA: The Williams Institute*. Retrieved from https://escholarship.org/uc/item/5h3731xr.

Bakare, Lanre. "Angela Davis: 'We knew that the role of the police was to protect white supremacy'" *The Guardian*. June 15, 2020. https://www.theguardian.com/us-news/2020/jun/15/angela-davis-on-george-floyd-as-long-as-the-violence-of-racism-remains-no-one-is-safe. Accessed August 20, 2021.

Baldwin, Bridgette. 2018. "Black, white, and blue: Bias, profiling, and policing in the age of Black Lives Matter." *Western New England Law Review* 40: 431.

Baldwin, James. 1984. *Notes of a Native Son*. Vol. 39. Beacon Press, 101.

Baldwin, James. 2013. *The Fire Next Time*. Vintage.

Baldwin, James. 2014. *James Baldwin: The last interview: And other conversations*. New York: Melville House.

Balsam, K. F., Molina, Y., Beadnell, B., Simoni, J., and Walters, K. 2011. "Measuring multiple minority stress: The LGBT people of color microaggressions scale." *Cultural Diversity and Ethnic Minority Psychology* 17, no. 2: 163.

Baltzell, Edward Digby. 1987. *The Protestant Establishment: Aristocracy and Caste in America*. Yale University Press.

Bambara, Toni Cade. 2012. "An interview with Toni Cade Bambara: Kay Bonetti." In *Conversations with Toni Cade Bambara*, edited by Thabiti Lewis. Jackson: University Press of Mississippi. 35.

Banks, Kira Hudson, Richard D. Harvey, Tanisha Thelemaque, and V. Anukem Onyinyechi. 2016. "The intersection of colorism and racial identity and the impact on mental health." *Meaning-Making, Internalized Racism, and African American Identity* 261.

Barnhardt, Carol. 2001. "A history of schooling for Alaska Native people." *Journal of American Indian Education* 40, no. 1: 1–30.

Barreyre, Nicolas. 2011. "The politics of economic crises: The panic of 1873, the end of reconstruction, and the realignment of American politics." *The Journal of the Gilded Age and Progressive Era* 10, no. 4: 403–423.

Barrie, Hannah. 2020. "No one is disposable: Towards feminist models of transformative justice." *Journal of Law and Social Policy* 33: 65.

Bar-Tal, Daniel. 2000 "From intractable conflict through conflict resolution to reconciliation: Psychological analysis." *Political Psychology* 21, no. 2: 351–365.

Baumard, Nicolas, and Dan Sperber. 2010. "Weird people, yes, but also weird experiments." *Behavioral and Brain Sciences* 33, no. 2–3: 84–85.

Beer, Tommy. "Report: Capitol mob came within 100 feet of pence." *Forbes*. January 15, 2021. https://www.forbes.com/sites/tommybeer/2021/01/15/report-capitol-mob -came-within-100-feet-of-pence/?sh=17b023ad18e6. Accessed March 20, 2021.

Beer, Tommy. "Trump called BLM protesters 'thugs' but capitol-storming supporters 'special.' *Forbes*. January 6, 2021. https://www.forbes.com/sites/tommybeer/2021 /01/06/trump-called-blm-protesters-thugs-but-capitol-storming-supporters-very -special/?sh=51c4a1cf3465. Accessed September 13, 2021.

Bell, Arthur. July 15, 1971. Village Voice 1: 46.

Bell, Derrick A. 1995. "Who's afraid of critical race theory." *University of Illinois Law Review* 1995, no. 4: 893.

Beltran, Veda Elizabeth. 2020. "The rise of white nationalist terrorism: A call for legislative action and reform." PhD diss., Johns Hopkins University.

Bennett, Hans. 2010. "The black panthers and the assassination of Fred Hampton." *Journal of Pan African Studies* 3, no. 6: 215–222.

Bennett, Judith M. 2000. " Lesbian-like" and the social history of lesbianisms." *Journal of the History of Sexuality* 9, no. 1/2: 1–24.

Berryman-Fink, Cynthia. 2006. "Reducing prejudice on campus: The role of inter-group contact in diversity education." *College Student Journal* 40, no. 3: 511–517.

Bérubé, Allan. 1990. *Coming Out Under Fire: The History of Gay Men and Women in World War II*. New York: Macmillan.

Bérubé, Allan. 2018. "How gay stays white and what kind of white it stays." In *Privilege*, edited by Michael Kimmel and Abby Ferber. London: Routledge. 180–208.

Bhatia, Sunil. 2002. "Orientalism in Euro-American and Indian psychology: Historical representations of" natives" in colonial and postcolonial contexts." *History of Psychology* 5, no. 4: 376.

Bieschke, Kathleen J., Jennifer A. Hardy, Ruth E. Fassinger, and James M. Croteau. 2008. "Intersecting identities of gender-transgressive sexual minorities." *Biennial Review of Counseling Psychology* 1: 177–207.

Black, Edwin. 2003. "Eugenics and the Nazis—the California connection." *San Francisco Chronicle*, November 9, 2003. https://www.sfgate.com/opinion/article/Eugenics-and-the-Nazis-the-California-2549771.php.

Black, Jason Edward. 2009. "Native resistive rhetoric and the decolonization of American Indian removal discourse." *Quarterly Journal of Speech* 95, no. 1: 66–88.

Black, Shannon. 2017. "KNIT+ RESIST: Placing the Pussyhat Project in the context of craft activism." *Gender, Place and Culture* 24, no. 5: 696–710.

Black Entertainment Television [BET]. "Listen: Charles Barkley's shocking statements about police brutality and Philando Castile." *BET News*. July 14, 2016. https://www.bet.com/news/sports/2016/070/14/listen—charles-barkley-s-shocking-statements-about-police-bruta.html Accessed August 1, 2021.

Black Lives Matter. 2021. "330 days to confirm what we already knew." *Facebook*, April 20, 2021. https://www.facebook.com/BlackLivesMatter.

Blackwood, Evelyn, and Saskia E. Wieringa, eds. 1999. *Female Desires: Same-sex Relations and Transgender Practices Across Cultures*. Columbia University Press.

Blattner, Sarah E. 2021. "Social and cultural inclusion of queered and racialized performance during Chicago's black pansy craze." *DePaul University College of Liberal Arts and Sciences Theses and Dissertations* 307: 2–6.

Boggs, Grace Lee. "Detroit activist, philosopher Grace Lee Boggs: 'The only way to survive is by taking care of one another.'" *Democracy Now*. April 02, 2010.

Bollini, Chris. 2021. "San Francisco celebrates 1st transgender district in the world." *ABC News*. March 25, 2021. Retrieved from:https://abc7news.com/comptons-transgender-cultural-district-cafeteria-riot-honey-mahogany-janette-johnson/10403834/.

Borda, Fals. 2013. "Action research in the convergence of disciplines." *International Journal of Action Research* 9, no. 2: 155.

Bordonaro, Louis. 2003. "The three percenters." *Ostomy Quarterly* 41, no. 1: 57–58.

Bost, Darius. 2015. "At the club: Locating early black gay AIDS activism in Washington, DC." *Special Issue on Race, Place and Scale*, Occasion 8.

Bostock, Bill. 2021. "Trump's first tweet about a 'Chinese virus' caused an increase of anti-Asian hashtags on Twitter, study finds." *Business Insider*. March 22, 2021.

Retrieved from: https://www.businessinsider.com/trump-chinese-virus-tweet -sparked-anti-asian-hashtags-spike-study-2021-3.

Bostwick, Wendy B., Carol J. Boyd, Tonda L. Hughes, Brady T. West, and Sean Esteban McCabe. 2014. "Discrimination and mental health among lesbian, gay, and bisexual adults in the United States." *American Journal of Orthopsychiatry* 84, no. 1: 35.

Brasher, Jordan. "The confederate battle flag, which rioters flew inside the US Capitol, has long been a symbol of white insurrection." *The Conversation.* January 14, 2021. https://theconversation.com/the-confederate-battle-flag-which-rioters -flew-inside-the-us-capitol-has-long-been-a-symbol-of-white-insurrection-153071 (Accessed February 13, 2021).

Braveheart-Jordan, M., and DeBruyn, L. 1995. "So she may walk in balance: Integrating the impact of historical trauma in the treatment of Native American Indian women." In J. Adleman and G. M. Enguídanos (Eds.), *Haworth Innovations in Feminist Studies. Racism in the Lives of Women: Testimony, Theory, and Guides to Antiracist Practice*, pp. 345–368. Harrington Park Press/ Haworth Press.

BreakOUT! and the National Council on Crime & Delinquency. 2014. "We deserve better: A report on policing in New Orleans by and for queer and trans youth of color." New Orleans: BreakOUT!: 1–12.

Brewer, Marilynn B., and Linnda R. Caporael. 2006. "An evolutionary perspective on social identity: Revisiting groups." *Evolution and Social Psychology* 143: 161.

Bridges, Sara K., Mary MD Selvidge, and Connie R. Matthews. 2003. "Lesbian women of color: Therapeutic issues and challenges." *Journal of Multicultural Counseling and Development* 31, no. 2: 113–130.

Broadwater, Luke and Matthew Rosenberg. "Republican Ties to Extremist Groups Are Under Scrutiny." *The New York Times.* January 29, 2021. https://www.nytimes.com /2021/01/29/us/republicans-trump-capitol-riot.html. Accessed March 1, 2021.

Brontsema, Robin. 2004. "A Queer Revolution: Reconceptualizing the Debate Over Linguistic Reclamation." *Colorado Research in Linguistics* 17: 1–5.

Brooks, Ronald, Mary Jane Rotheram-Borus, Eric G. Bing, George Ayala, and Charles L. Henry. 2003. "HIV and AIDS among men of color who have sex with men and men of color who have sex with men and women: An epidemiological profile." *AIDS Education and Prevention* 15, no. 1 Supplement: 1–6.

Brown, Adrienne Marie. 2019. *Pleasure Activism: The Politics of Feeling Good.* AK Press.

Brown, Jon. "Trump deplores removal of Richmond's Robert E. Lee statue." *FOX News.* September 9, 2021. https://www.foxnews.com/politics/trump-issues-state- ment-against-removing-robert-e-lee-statue. Accessed September 10, 2021.

Buenaventura, Steffi San. 1996 "Filipino folk spirituality and immigration: From mutual aid to religion." *Amerasia Journal* 22, no. 1: 1–30.

Bullough, Vern L. 2002. *Before Stonewall: Activists for Gay and Lesbian Rights in Historical Context.* New York: Haworth Press.

Burgess, Parke G. 1968. "The rhetoric of black power: A moral demand?" *Quarterly Journal of Speech* 54, no. 2: 122–133.

Burress, Jim. "Kim Jackson reflects on being Georgia's first openly gay state senator." *WABE News.* January 22, 2021. https://www.wabe.org/kim-jackson-reflects
-on-being-georgias-first-openly-gay-state-senator/. Accessed September 2, 2021.

Calabrese, Sarah K., Valerie A. Earnshaw, Douglas S. Krakower, Kristen Underhill,
Wilson Vincent, Manya Magnus, Nathan B. Hansen et al. 2018. "A closer look at
racism and heterosexism in medical students' clinical decision-making related to
HIV pre-exposure prophylaxis (PrEP): implications for PrEP education." *AIDS and
Behavior* 22, no. 4: 1122–1138.

Calabrese, Sarah K., Valerie A. Earnshaw, Kristen Underhill, Nathan B. Hansen, and
John F. Dovidio. 2014. "The impact of patient race on clinical decisions related to
prescribing HIV pre-exposure prophylaxis (PrEP): assumptions about sexual risk
compensation and implications for access." *AIDS and Behavior* 18, no. 2: 226–240.

Calavita, Kitty. 2000 "The paradoxes of race, class, identity, and "passing": Enforcing
the Chinese Exclusion Acts, 1882–1910." *Law and Social Inquiry* 25, no. 1: 1–40.

Calavita, Kitty. 2007. "Immigration law, race, and identity." *Annual Review of Law
and Social Science* 3: 1–20.

Caldwell, C., and Leighton, L. B. (Eds.). 2018. *Oppression and the Body: Roots,
Resistance, and Resolutions.* North Atlantic Books.

Caldwell, Travis. "Trump's 'We love you' to Capitol rioters is more of the same."
CNN News. January 7, 2021. https://www.cnn.com/2021/01/07/politics/trump-his-
tory-comments-trnd/index.html. Accessed March 2, 2021.

Camus, Albert. 2012. *The Rebel: An Essay on Man in Revolt.* Vintage.

Carmichael, Stokely, Kwame Ture, and Charles V. Hamilton. 1992. *Black Power:
The Politics of Liberation in America.* Vintage.

Carter, David. 2005. *Stonewall: The Riots that Sparked the Gay Revolution.* New
York: St. Martin's, pp. 111–188.

Carter, Stephen R. 1980. "Commitment amid complexity: Lorraine Hansberry's life
in action." *MELUS Autumn* 7, no. 3: 39–42.

Cass, Vivienne C. 1979. "Homosexual identity formation: A theoretical model."
Journal of Homosexuality 4, no. 3: 219–235.

Cassese, Erin C. 2021. "Partisan dehumanization in American politics." *Political
Behavior* 43, no. 1: 29–50.

Castallanos, Delina. "Geraldo Rivera: hoodie responsible for Trayvon Martin's
Death." *LA Times.* March 23, 2013. https://www.latimes.com/nation/la-xpm-2012
-mar-23-la-na-nn-geraldo-rivera-hoodie-trayvon-martin-20120323-story.html.
Accessed August 1, 2021.

Castano, Emanuele, and Roger Giner-Sorolla. 2006. "Not quite human:
Infrahumanization in response to collective responsibility for intergroup killing."
Journal of Personality and Social Psychology 90, no. 5: 804.

Cathay, Libby. 2021. "'Progress' flag to fly at state department for 1st time to mark
pride month." *ABC News.* June 25, 2021. https://abcnews.go.com/Politics/progress
-flag-fly-state-department-1st-time-mark/story?id=78473193. Accessed August 2,
2021.

Cave, Alfred A. 2003. "Abuse of power: Andrew Jackson and the Indian removal act
of 1830." *The Historian* 65, no. 6: 1330–1353.

Centers for Disease Control and Prevention [CDC]. 2020. "Diagnoses of HIV infection in the United States and dependent areas, 2018 (updated)." *HIV Surveillance Report* 2020. 31. Retrieved from: https://www.cdc.gov/hiv/group/racialethnic/africanamericans/index.html.

Center for American Progress. 2016. "Unjust: How the broken criminal justice system fails people of color." Retrieved at https://www.lgbtmap.org/file/lgbt-criminal-justice-poc.pdf. Accessed on September 2, 2021.

Center for the Study of Hate and Extremism. 2021. " Report to the nation: Anti-Asian prejudice & hate crime." *CSUSB Website*. Retrieved from: https://www.csusb.edu/sites/default/files/FACT%20SHEET-%20Anti-Asian%20Hate%202020%203.2.21.pdf.

Centers for Disease Control and Prevention [CDC] 2021. "Risk for COVID infection, hospitalization, and death by race/ethnicity." *CDC Website*. April 23, 2021. https://www.cdc.gov/coronavirus/2019-ncov/covid-data/investigations-discovery/hospitalization-death-by-race-ethnicity.html.

Chan, Sucheng. 1991. *Asian Americans: An Interpretive History*. Twayne Publishers.

Chandra, Amitabh, and Douglas O. Staiger. 2010. Identifying provider prejudice in healthcare. *National Bureau of Economic Research Working Papers* 16382: 16–19.

Chang, Ailsa. "The history of solidarity between Asian and black Americans." *NPR News*. April 2, 2021. https://www.npr.org/2021/04/02/983925014/the-history-of-solidarity-between-asian-and-black-americans. Accessed September 1, 2021.

Chang, Robert S. 1995. "Reverse racism: Affirmative Action, the family, and the dream that is America." *Hastings Constitutional Law Quarterly* 23: 1115.

Chang, Tiffany K., and Y. Barry Chung. 2015. "Transgender microaggressions: Complexity of the heterogeneity of transgender identities." *Journal of LGBT Issues in Counseling* 9, no. 3: 217–234.

Chappell, Bill, Vanessa Romo, and Jaclyn Diaz. "Official who said Atlanta shooting suspect was having a 'Bad Day' faces criticism." *National Public Radio*. March 18, 2021. https://www.npr.org/2021/03/17/978141138/atlanta-shooting-suspect-is-believed-to-have-visited-spas-he-targeted. Accessed April 1, 2021.

Chatterjee, Dom. "Making space for the QTPoC self in the self-care movement." *Colorbloq*. March 2018. https://www.colorbloq.org/article/making-space-for-the-qtpoc-self-in-the-self-care-movement. Accessed August 2, 2021.

Chauncey, George. 2008. *Gay New York: Gender, Urban Culture, and the Making of the Gay Male World, 1890-1940*. Hachette UK.

Chen, Emma. 2016. "Black face, queer space: The influence of black lesbian & transgender blues women of the Harlem renaissance on emerging queer communities." *Historical Perspectives: Santa Clara University Undergraduate Journal of History, Series II* 21, no. 1: 8.

Cheng, Hsiu-Lan, Helen Youngju Kim, Yuying Tsong, and Y. Joel Wong. 2021. "COVID-19 anti-Asian racism: A tripartite model of collective psychosocial resilience." *American Psychologist* 76, no. 4: 627.

Ching, Tamara (Trans Asian activist, Stanford University, Stanford, CA), in discussion with oral historian Jason Lin, August 5, 2018.

Choi, Kyung-Hee, Chong-suk Han, Jay Paul, and George Ayala. 2011. "Strategies for managing racism and homophobia among US ethnic and racial minority men who have sex with men." *AIDS Education and Prevention* 23, no. 2: 145–158.

Chou, Rosalind S. 2012. *Asian American Sexual Politics: The Construction of Race, Gender, and Sexuality*. Rowman & Littlefield Publishers.

Chua, Siong-huat. 1990. "Asian-Americans, Gay and Lesbian." In *Encyclopedia of Homosexuality*, edited by Wayne Dynes. Vol 1. New York: Garland. 84–85.

Cikara, Mina, Jay J. Van Bavel, Zachary A. Ingbretsen, and Tatiana Lau. 2017. "Decoding "us" and "them": Neural representations of generalized group concepts." *Journal of Experimental Psychology: General* 146, no. 5: 621.

Clement, Olivia. "LaChanze, Britton Smith, Mykal Kilgore, and more tapped for Juneteenth Jubilee." *PlayBill*. June 17, 2020. playbill.com/article/lachanze-britton-smith-mykal-kilgore-and-more-tapped-for-juneteenth-jubilee. Accessed September 1, 2021.

Cochran, Bryan N., Kimberly Balsam, Annesa Flentje, Carol A. Malte, and Tracy Simpson. 2013 "Mental health characteristics of sexual minority veterans." *Journal of Homosexuality* 60, no. 2–3: 419–435.

Cochran, Lisa. "MacArthur genius grant recipient Ocean Vuong talks Asian heritage and war." *Washington Square News*. October 4, 2019. https://nyunews.com/news/2019/10/03/ocean-vuong-recieves-genius-grant/ Accessed September 1, 2021.

Cohen, Cathy J. 1999. *The Boundaries of Blackness: AIDS and the Breakdown of Black Politics*. University of Chicago Press.

Cohen, Stephan. 2007. *The Gay Liberation Youth Movement in New York: 'An Army of Lovers Cannot Fail'*. Routledge.

Cole, E. R. 2009. "Intersectionality and research in psychology." *American Psychologist* 64, no. 3: 170.

Collective, Combahee River. 1977. *A Black Feminist Statement*.

Collins, P. H. 2002. *Black Feminist Thought: Knowledge, Consciousness, and the Politics of Empowerment*. Routledge.

Collins, P. H. 2004. *Black Sexual Politics: African Americans, Gender, and the New Racism*. Routledge.

Collins, P. H., and S. Bilge. 2016. *Intersectionality*. John Wiley & Sons.

Conron, Kerith J., Matthew J. Mimiaga, and Stewart J. Landers. 2010. "A population-based study of sexual orientation identity and gender differences in adult health." *American Journal of Public Health* 100, no. 10: 1953–1960.

Coope, Jonathan. 2020. "Indigenous knowledge and techno-scientific modernity: "Hierarchical integration" reconsidered." *Ecopsychology* 12, no. 2: 151–157.

Corbin, Caroline Mala. 2017. "Terrorists are always Muslim but never white: At the intersection of critical race theory and propaganda." *Fordham Law Review* 86: 455.

Cordova, Fred. 1973. The Filipino American: There's always an identity crisis. In S. Sue and N. Wagner (Eds.), *Asian Americans: Psychological perspectives*, pp. 136–139. Palo Alto, CA: Science and Behavior Books.

Córdova, Jeanne. 2011. *When We Were Outlaws: A Memoir of Love and Revolution*. Spinsters Ink.

Corntassel, Jeff. 2008. "Toward sustainable self-determination: Rethinking the contemporary Indigenous-rights discourse." *Alternatives* 33, no. 1: 105–132.

Corntassel, Jeff. 2012. "Re-envisioning resurgence: Indigenous pathways to decolonization and sustainable self-determination." *Decolonization: Indigeneity, Education & Society* 1, no. 1: 93–99.

Coulthard, G. 2007. "Subjects of empire: Indigenous peoples and the 'politics of recognition' in Canada." *Contemporary Political Theory* 3: 1–29.

Crawford, Mike J., Lavanya Thana, Lorna Farquharson, Lucy Palmer, Elizabeth Hancock, Paul Bassett, Jeremy Clarke, and Glenys D. Parry. 2016. "Patient experience of negative effects of psychological treatment: results of a national survey." *The British journal of psychiatry* 208, no. 3: 260–265.

Crenshaw, K. 1989. "Demarginalizing the intersection of race and sex: A black feminist critique of antidiscrimination doctrine, feminist theory and antiracist politics." *University of Chicago Legal Forum* 1989, no. 1: 139–140.

Crenshaw, K. 1991. "Mapping the margins: Identity politics, intersectionality, and violence against women." *Stanford Law Review* 43, no. 6: 1241–1299.

Cuellar, Norma G. 2017. "If you're not outraged, you're not paying attention." *Journal of Transcultural Nursing* 28, no. 6: 529–529.

Cyrus, Kali. 2017. "Multiple minorities as multiply marginalized: Applying the minority stress theory to LGBTQ people of color." *Journal of Gay and Lesbian Mental Health* 21, no. 3: 194–202.

D'Emilio, John. 1983. "Capitalism and gay identity." In *Powers of Desire*, edited by Anna Snitow, Christine Stansell, and Sharon Thompson. New York: Monthly Review Press. 100–113.

Dang, Alain Anh-Tuan, and Mandy Hu. 2005. *Asian Pacific American Lesbian, Gay, Bisexual, and Transgender People: A Community Portrait.* New York: National Gay and Lesbian Task Force Policy Institute.

Darley, John M., and Bibb Latané. 1968. "Bystander intervention in emergencies: diffusion of responsibility." *Journal of Personality and Social Psychology* 8, no. 4: 377.

das Nair, R., and C. Butler (Eds.). 2012. *Intersectionality, Sexuality and Psychological Therapies: Working with Lesbian, Gay and Bisexual Diversity.* John Wiley & Sons.

Dattel, Gene. 2009. *Cotton and Race in the Making of America: The Human Costs of Economic Power.* Government Institutes.

David, Eric John Ramos. 2008. "A colonial mentality model of depression for Filipino Americans." *Cultural Diversity and Ethnic Minority Psychology* 14, no. 2: 118.

Davis, Angela. 2000. "Masked racism: Reflections on the prison industrial complex." *Indigenous Law Bulletin* 4, no. 27: 4–7.

Davis, Angela. 2011. *Blues Legacies and Black Feminism: Gertrude Ma Rainey, Bessie Smith, and Billie Holiday.* New York: Knopf Doubleday Publishing Group.

Davis, Angela Y. 2016. *Freedom Is a Constant Struggle: Ferguson, Palestine, and the Foundations of a Movement.* Haymarket Books.

Davis, Angela Y. 2016. *If They Come in the Morning...: Voices of Resistance.* Verso Books.

Davis, Angela, and Elizabeth Martinez. 1994. "Coalition building among people of color." *Inscriptions* 7: 42–53.

Davis, Julie. 2001. "American Indian boarding school experiences: Recent studies from native perspectives." *OAH Magazine of History* 15, no. 2: 20–22.

De la Croix, Sukie. 2013. "Henry Gerber: Ahead of his time." *Washington Blade.* October 3, 2013. Retrieved from: https://washingtonblade.com/2013/10/03/henry -gerber-ahead-time/.

De Leon, F. M. "A heritage of well being: The connectivity of the Filipino." Presented at University of Saint Joseph Public Lecture and Book Donation Ceremony, Macau, China, September 2014.

DeBlaere, Cirleen, Melanie E. Brewster, Anthony Sarkees, and Bonnie Moradi. 2010. "Conducting research with LGB people of color: Methodological challenges and strategies." *The Counseling Psychologist* 38, no. 3: 331–362.

DeGagne, Alexa. 2018. "On Anger and Its Uses for Activism," In *Contemporary Inequalities and Social Justice*, edited by Janine Brody. Vol 1. Toronto: University of Toronto Press, 142–163.

DeLarver, Storme (Black lesbian activist, in discussion with Grace Chu). July 26, 2010. "From the Archives: An interview with lesbian Stonewall veteran Stormé DeLarverie." https://AfterEllen.com.

Delgado, Richard. 1984. "Imperial scholar: Reflections on a review of civil rights literature." *University of Pennsylvania Law Review* 132: 561.

Deliovsky, Kathy. 2008. *Normative White Femininity: Race, Gender and the Politics of Beauty*. Atlantis: Critical Studies in Gender, Culture and Social Justice 33, no. 1.

Demby, Gene. 2014. "The ugly, fascinating history of the word 'Racism'" *NPR.org*. January 6, 2014. Retrieved from: https://www.npr.org/sections/codeswitch/2014/01/05/260006815/the-ugly-fascinating-history-of-the-word-racism.

Denetdale, Jennifer Nez. 2006. "Chairmen, presidents, and princesses: The Navajo Nation, gender, and the politics of tradition." *Wicazo Sa Review* 21, no. 1: 9–28.

Desai, Maharaj. 2016. "Critical" Kapwa": Possibilities of collective healing from colonial trauma." *Educational Perspectives* 48: 34–40.

Desmond, Matthew. 2016. *Evicted: Poverty and Profit in the American City*. Crown.

Diamond, Lisa M. 2008. *Sexual Fluidity*. Harvard University Press.

Dimond, Jill P., Michaelanne Dye, Daphne LaRose, and Amy S. Bruckman. 2013. "Hollaback! The role of storytelling online in a social movement organization." In *Proceedings of the Conference on Computer Supported Cooperative Work*, pp. 477–490.

Dong, Arthur, dir. *The Question of Equality, Season 1, episode 1, "Outrage '69."* Aired October 1, 1995, on Channel Four Television. UK: Deep Focus Productions.

Dougherty, Keith L., and Jac C. Heckelman. 2008. "Voting on slavery at the Constitutional Convention." *Public Choice* 136, no. 3–4: 293.

Duran, Eduardo, and Bonnie Duran. 1995. *Native American postcolonial psychology*. New York: State University of New York Press.

Dyer, Richard. 1988. "White." *Screen* 29: 44.

Dyer, Richard. 1993. "Seen to be believed: Some problems in the representation of gay people as typical." In *The Matter of Images: Essays on Representation*, edited by Richard Dyer, Vol. 1. London: Routledge: 19–51.

Edwards, Griffin Sims, and Stephen Rushin. 2018. "The effect of President Trump's election on hate crimes." Available at SSRN 3102652.

Ekman, Paul, Wallace V. Friesen, Maureen O'sullivan, Anthony Chan, Irene Diacoyanni-Tarlatzis, Karl Heider, Rainer Krause et al. 1987. "Universals and cultural differences in the judgments of facial expressions of emotion." *Journal of Personality and Social Psychology* 53, no. 4: 712.

Ellingson, Laura, and Carolyn Ellis. 2008. "Autoethnography as constructionist project." In *Handbook of Constructionist Research*, edited by James Holstein and Jaber Gubrium. New York: Guilford Press. 445–465.

Elliot, Jane. 2003. "An unfinished crusade: An interview with Jane Elliot." Interview by Frontline/PBS. January 1, 2003. www.pbs.org.

Elliott, Aprele. 1996. "Ella Baker: Free agent in the civil rights movement." *Journal of Black Studies* 26, no. 5: 593–603.

Ellis, Carolyn. 2004. *The Ethnographic I: A Methodological Novel About Autoethnography.* Walnut Creek, CA: AltaMira.

Enriquez, Virgilio. 2004. *From Colonial to Liberation Psychology: The Philippine Experience.* Manila: De La Salle University Press, Inc.

Epstein, Reid and Astead Hernon. "The 10-year Stacey Abrams project to flip Georgia has come to fruition." *The New York Times.* January 6, 2021. https://www.nytimes.com/2021/01/06/us/politics/stacey-abrams-georgia.html. Accessed September 1 2021.

Erel, U., J. Haritaworn, E. G. Rodríguez, and C. Klesse. 2010. "On the depoliticisation of intersectionality talk: Conceptualising multiple oppressions in critical sexuality studies." In *Theorizing Intersectionality and Sexuality*, edited by Yvette Taylor, Sally Hines, and Mark Casey. London: Palgrave Macmillan. 56–77.

Erickson, Ingrid M. 2004. "Fighting fire with fire: Jane Elliott's antiracist pedagogy." *Counterpoints* 240: 145–157.

Espín, Oliva M. 2011. "The enduring popularity of Rosa de Lima, first saint of the Americas: Women, bodies, sainthood, and national identity." *CrossCurrents* 61, no. 1: 6–26.

Espiritu, Yen L. 1997. "Race, gender, class in the lives of Asian American." *Race, Gender and Class* 4, no. 3: 12–19.

Esses, Victoria M., John F. Dovidio, Lynne M. Jackson, and Tamara L. Armstrong. 2001. "The immigration dilemma: The role of perceived group competition, ethnic prejudice, and national identity." *Journal of Social Issues* 57, no. 3: 389–412.

Evans-Campbell, Teresa, Karina L. Walters, Cynthia R. Pearson, and Christopher D. Campbell. 2012. "Indian boarding school experience, substance use, and mental health among urban two-spirit American Indian/Alaska Natives." *The American Journal of Drug and Alcohol Abuse* 38, no. 5: 421–427.

Evans Dana. 2016. "Black lives matter's Opal Tometi explains how words can change human behavior." *The Cut.* March 22, 2016. https://www.thecut.com/2016/03/black-lives-matter-opal-tometi.html. Accessed August 2, 2021.

Falco, Aurea, and Sanjana Gandhi. 2019. "The rainbow business." *Eidos* 9, no. 1: 104–107.

Fanon, Frantz. 2007. *The Wretched of the Earth.* Grove/Atlantic, Inc.

Farrow, Anne, Joel Lang, and Jenifer Frank. 2006. *Complicity: How the North Promoted, Prolonged, and Profited from Slavery.* Random House Digital, Inc.

Fears, Darryl. "Hue and cry on whiteness studies." *The Washington Post.* June 20, 2003. https://www.washingtonpost.com/archive/politics/2003/06/20/hue-and-cry-on-whiteness-studies/4bd3161e-4a13-474b-977b-b3373f566e09/. Accessed on August 2, 2021.

Ferguson, R. A. 2007. "The relevance of race for the study of sexuality." In *A Companion to Lesbian, Gay, Bisexual, Transgender, and Queer Studies*, edited by G.E. Haggerty and M. McGarry. Oxford: Blackwell Publishing Ltd. 107–123.

Ferguson, Roderick (2018, March 28). *Queer of Color Critique*. Oxford Research Encyclopedia of Literature. Retrieved from http://oxfordre.com/literature/view/10.1093/ acrefore/9780190201098.001.0001/acrefore-9780190201098-e-33.

Ferguson, S. J. 2013. *Race, Gender, Sexuality, and Social Class: Dimensions of Inequality*. Sage.

Fields, Barbara Jeanne. 1990. "Slavery, race and ideology in the United States of America." *New Left Review* 181, no. 1: 95–118.

Fine, M.E., L.E. Weise, L.C. Powell, and L. Wong. 1997. *Off White: Readings on Race, Power, and Society*. Taylor and Francis.

Fitzgerald, Brian. 2006. *McCarthyism: The Red Scare*. Capstone.

Flanders, Corey E., Sarah A. Shuler, Sophie A. Desnoyers, and Nicole A. VanKim. 2019. "Relationships between social support, identity, anxiety, and depression among young bisexual people of color." *Journal of Bisexuality* 19, no. 2: 253–275.

Forrest, Brett. "What is QAnon? What we know about the conspiracy-theory group." *The Wall Street Journal*. February 4, 2021.https://www.wsj.com/articles/what-is-qanon-what-we-know-about-the-conspiracy-theory-11597694801. Accessed March 1, 2021.

Fotopoulou, A. 2012. "Intersectionality queer studies and hybridity: Methodological frameworks for social research." *Journal of International Women's Studies* 13, no. 2: 19–32.

Foucault, Michel. 1980. "Two lectures." In C. Gordon (Ed.), *Power/Knowledge: Selected Interviews and Other Writings 1972-1977*. Hemel Hempstead: Harvester Wheatsheaf.

Foucault, Michel. 2012. *The History of Sexuality, Vol. 2: The Use of Pleasure*. Vintage.

Freedman, Estelle B. 2003. *No Turning Back: The History of Feminism and the Future of Women*. New York: Ballantine Books.

Freire, P. 1968. *Pedagogy of the Oppressed*. New York: Herder.

Freire, P. 1985. *The Politics of Education: Culture, Power, and Liberation*. Greenwood Publishing Group.

Friedman, Elliot M., David R. Williams, Burton H. Singer, and Carol D. Ryff. 2009. "Chronic discrimination predicts higher circulating levels of E-selectin in a national sample: the MIDUS study." *Brain, behavior, and immunity* 23, no. 5: 684–692.

Fuentes, Carlos, and Sarah M. Lowe. 1995. *The Diary of Frida Kahlo: An Intimate Self-portrait*. Abrams.

Fung, Richard. 2005. "Looking for my penis: The eroticized Asian in gay video porn." In *A Companion to Asian American Studies*, Vol. 1, edited by Kent Ono: 235–253.

Funke, Teresa R. 2008. *The No-No Boys*. Bailiwick Press.

Gallo, Marcia M. 2006. "Different daughters." *OAH Magazine of History* 20, no. 2: 27–30.

Gallup, Andrew C., Janine Militello, Lexington Swartwood, and Serena Sackett. 2017. "Experimental evidence of contagious stretching and ingroup bias in budgerigars (Melopsittacus undulatus)." *Journal of Comparative Psychology* 131, no. 1: 69.

Ganna, Andrea, Karin J. H. Verweij, Michel G. Nivard, Robert Maier, Robbee Wedow, Alexander S. Busch, Abdel Abdellaoui et al. 2019. "Large-scale GWAS reveals insights into the genetic architecture of same-sex sexual behavior." *Science* 365, no. 6456: 1–8.

Garcia, Sandra. 2020. "Where did BIPOC come from?" *New York Times*, June 17, 2020. Retrieved from: https://www.nytimes.com/article/what-is-bipoc.html.

Garcia Coll, Cynthia, Flannery Patton, A. K. Marks, Radosveta Dimitrova, Hillary Yang, Gloria Suarez-Aviles, and Andrea Batchelor. 2012. "Understanding the immigrant paradox in youth: Developmental and contextual considerations." In *Capitalizing on migration: The potential of immigrant youth*, edited by AS Masten, K Liebkind & DJ Hernandez. New York: Cambridge University Press.

Garza, Alicia. 2020. *The Purpose of Power: How We Come Together When We Fall Apart*. One World.

Garza, Alicia. "A herstory of the #BlackLivesMatter movement." *The Feminist Wire*. October 7, 2014. https://thefeministwire.com/2014/10/blacklivesmatter-2/.

Gates, Henry Louis. 1993. "The black man's burden." In Michael Warner (Ed.), *Fear of a Queer Planet: Queer Politics and Social Theory*. Vol. 6. University of Minnesota Press.

Gates, Henry Louis. 1995. *Harlem on My Mind: Cultural Capital of Black America, 1900-1968*. New York: New Press; Dist. by W. W. Norton.

Gates, Henry Louis. 2020. "The Trope of a New Negro and the Reconstruction of the Image of the Black". In *The New American Studies*, edited by Philip Fisher, Berkeley: University of California Press. 319–345.

Gay, Roxane. 2019. *Love and Resistance: Out of the Closet into the Stonewall Era*. W. W. Norton & Company.

Gelso, Charles J., and Katri M. Kanninen. 2017. "Neutrality revisited: On the value of being neutral within an empathic atmosphere." *Journal of Psychotherapy Integration* 27, no. 3: 330.

Ginn, Wanda Y. 1995. "Jean Piaget-intellectual development." *Retrieved January* 4, no. 20: 10.

Goff, Phillip Atiba, Jennifer L. Eberhardt, Melissa J. Williams, and Matthew Christian Jackson. 2008 "Not yet human: implicit knowledge, historical dehu-manization, and contemporary consequences." *Journal of Personality and Social Psychology* 94, no. 2: 292.

Gökarıksel, Banu, and Sara Smith. 2017. "Intersectional feminism beyond US flag hijab and pussy hats in Trump's America." *Gender, Place and Culture* 24, no. 5: 628–644.

Goldberg, Jesse A. 2020. "Scenes of resurrection: Black Lives Matter, die-ins, and the here and now of queer futurity." *Women and Performance: A Journal of Feminist Theory* 30, no. 2: 127–139.

Gorman, Michael R. 2014. *The Empress Is a Man: Stories from the Life of Jose Sarria*. Routledge.

Grant, Jaime M., Lisa A. Mottet, Justin Tanis, Jack Harrison, Jody L. Herman, and Mara Keisling. 2011. *Injustice at Every Turn: A Report of the National Transgender*

Discrimination Survey. Washington: National Center for Transgender Equality and National Gay and Lesbian Task Force. Available at: https://transequality.org/sites/default/files/docs/resources/NTDS_Report.pdf

Greer, Elizabeth Diane. 2018."'There was something grotesque': The application and limits of respectability in the daughters of Bilitis." *Master's Theses.* 345.

Grosfoguel, Ramán. 2004. "Race and ethnicity or racialized ethnicities? Identities within global coloniality." *Ethnicities* 4, no. 3: 315–336.

Gumbs, Alexis Pauline. 2020. *Beyond Survival: Strategies and Stories from the Transformative Justice Movement.* Ejeris Dixon and Leah Lakshmi Piepzna-Samarasinha (Eds.). Chico, CA: AK Press.

Haag, Ann Murray. 2007. "The Indian Boarding School era and its continuing impact on tribal families and the provision of government services." *Tulsa Law Review* 43: 149.

Hall, Edith. 1989. *Inventing the Barbarian: Greek Self-definition Through Tragedy, The Theatrical Cast of Athens: Interactions between Greek Drama and Society,* pp. 184–224. Oxford.

Hall, Stuart. 1989. "Cultural identity and cinematic representation." *Framework: The Journal of Cinema and Media* 36: 68–81.

Halpern, Jodi. 2001. *From Detached Concern to Empathy: Humanizing Medical Practice.* Oxford University Press.

Hamamoto, Darrell Y. 1994. *Monitored Peril: Asian Americans and the Politics of TV Representation.* University of Minnesota Press.

Hamilton, Christopher J., and James R. Mahalik. 2009. "Minority stress, masculinity, and social norms predicting gay men's health risk behaviors." *Journal of Counseling Psychology* 56, no. 1: 132.

Hammonds, E. 2004. "Black (w)holes and the geometry of black female sexuality." In *The Black Studies Reader* 6, no. 2, edited by Jaqueline Bobo, Cynthia Hudley, and Claudine Michel. New York: Routledge. 313–326.

Han, Chong-suk. 2006. "Being an Oriental, I could never be completely a man: Gay Asian men and the intersection of race, gender, sexuality, and class." *Race, Gender and Class* 13, no. 3: 82–97.

Han, Chong-suk, Kristopher Proctor, and Kyung-Hee Choi. 2014. "I know a lot of gay Asian men who are actually tops: Managing and negotiating gay racial stigma." *Sexuality and Culture* 18, no. 2: 219–234.

Han, Chong-suk, and Kyung-Hee Choi. 2018. "Very few people say "No Whites": Gay men of color and the racial politics of desire." *Sociological Spectrum* 38, no. 3: 145–161.

Hancock, Ange-Marie. 2003. "Contemporary welfare reform and the public identity of the 'welfare queen.'" *Race, Gender and Class* 10, no. 1: 31–59.

Hancock, Ange-Marie. 2016. *Intersectionality: An Intellectual History.* Oxford University Press.

Hankin, Kelly. 2002. *The Girls in the Back Room: Looking at the Lesbian Bar.* University of Minnesota Press.

Hankivsky, Olena, Colleen Reid, Renee Cormier, Colleen Varcoe, Natalie Clark, Cecilia Benoit, and Shari Brotman. 2010. "Exploring the promises of intersectionality for advancing women's health research." *International Journal for Equity in Health* 9, no. 1: 1–15.

Hanson, Kenneth R. 2021. "Collective exclusion: How white heterosexual dating app norms reproduce status quo hookup culture." *Sociological Inquiry* 1, no. 1.

Haq, Husna. 2014. "Notre Dame's 'White Privilege Seminar': Racist indoctrination or education?" *Christian Science Monitor.* December 8, 2014. Retrieved from: https://www.csmonitor.com/USA/Society/2014/1208/Notre-Dame-s-White -Privilege-Seminar-Racist-indoctrination-or-education.

Haque, Afshana, Carolyn Y. Tubbs, Emily P. Kahumoku-Fessler, and Matthew D. Brown. 2019. "Microaggressions and Islamophobia: Experiences of Muslims across the United States and clinical implications." *Journal of Marital and Family Therapy* 45: 76–91.

Haque, Amber. 2004. "Psychology from Islamic perspective: Contributions of early Muslim scholars and challenges to contemporary Muslim psychologists." *Journal of Religion and Health* 43, no. 4: 357–377.

Hardiman, Rita. 1982. "White identity development: A process oriented model for describing the racial consciousness of White Americans." PhD diss., University of Massachusetts Amherst.

Harris, Laura. 2008. "On teaching a black queer Harlem renaissance." In *Teaching the Harlem Renaissance: Course design and classroom strategies*, edited by Michael Soto. New York: Peter Lang Publishing. 75–82.

Harris, Leonard. 2001. "Outing Alain L. Locke: empowering the silenced." In *Sexual Identities, Queer Politics*, edited by Mark Blasius. Princeton: Princeton University Press. 321–341.

Haslam, Nick. 2006. "Dehumanization: An integrative review." *Personality and Social Psychology Review* 10, no. 3: 252–264.

Haslam, Nick, and Steve Loughnan. 2014. "Dehumanization and infrahumanization." *Annual Review of Psychology* 65: 399–423.

Hatzenbuehler, Mark L., Jo C. Phelan, and Bruce G. Link. 2013. "Stigma as a fundamental cause of population health inequalities." *American Journal of Public Health* 103, no. 5: 813–821.

Haynes, Anna. 2006. "Frida Kahlo: An Artist' in between'." *Identity and Marginality, eSharp* 6: 2.

Heap, Chad C. 2000. *Homosexuality in the City: A Century of Research at the University of Chicago.* Vol. 87. University of Chicago Library.

Helms, Janet E., and Donelda Ann Cook. 1999. *Using Race and Culture in Counseling and Psychotherapy: Theory and Process.* Allyn & Bacon.

Henkel, Kristin E., Krysten Brown, and Seth C. Kalichman. 2008. "AIDS-related stigma in individuals with other stigmatized identities in the USA: A review of layered stigmas." *Social and Personality Psychology Compass* 2, no. 4: 1586–1599.

Henrich, Joseph, Steven J. Heine, and Ara Norenzayan. 2010. "The weirdest people in the world?." *Behavioral and Brain Sciences* 33, no. 2–3: 61–83.

Herek, Gregory M. 1999 "AIDS and stigma." *American Behavioral Scientist* 42, no. 7: 1106–1116.

Herek, G. M., and Aaron Belkin. 2006. "Sexual Orientation and Military Service: Prospects for Organizational and Individual Change in the United States." In

Military life: The psychology of serving in peace and combat: Military culture, edited by T. W. Britt, A. B. Adler, & C. A. Castro. Praeger Security International. 119–142.

Herek, Gregory M., and Linda D. Garnets. 2007. "Sexual orientation and mental health." *Annual Review of Clinical Psychology* 3: 353–375.

Herek, Gregory M., J. Roy Gillis, and Jeanine C. Cogan. 1999. "Psychological sequelae of hate-crime victimization among lesbian, gay, and bisexual adults." *Journal of Consulting and Clinical Psychology* 67, no. 6: 945.

Herrera, Hayden. 2002. *Frida: A Biography of Frida Kahlo*. Harper Perennial.

Heyes, Cressida. 2009. "All cosmetic surgery is "ethnic": Asian eyelids, feminist indignation, and the politics of whiteness." In *Cosmetic Surgery: A Feminist Primer*, edited by Cressida Haynes and Meredith Jones. Farnham, UK: Ashgate Publishing Company. 191–205.

Heynen, Nik. 2009. "Bending the bars of empire from every ghetto for survival: the Black Panther Party's radical antihunger politics of social reproduction and scale." *Annals of the Association of American Geographers* 99, no. 2: 406–422.

History Matters. 2017. ""Kill the Indian, and Save the Man": Capt. Richard H. Pratt on the Education of Native Americans". *Official Report of the Nineteenth Annual Conference of Charities and Correction* 1892: 46–59. Reprinted in Richard H. Pratt. 1973. "The Advantages of Mingling Indians with Whites," *Americanizing the American Indians: Writings by the "Friends of the Indian" 1880–1900*. Cambridge: Mass. Harvard University Press. 260–271. American Social History Productions.

Hirobe, Izumi. 2001. *Japanese Pride, American Prejudice: Modifying the Exclusion Clause of the 1924 Immigration Act*. Stanford University Press.

Hodson, Gordon, Nour Kteily, and Mark Hoffarth. 2014. "Of filthy pigs and subhuman mongrels: Dehumanization, disgust, and intergroup prejudice." *TPM: Testing, Psychometrics, Methodology in Applied Psychology* 21, no. 3: 267–284.

Hogan, Steve and Lee Hudson. 1998. *Completely Queer: The Gay and Lesbian Encyclopedia*. New York: Henry Holt and Company.

hooks, bell. 1986. "Sisterhood: Political solidarity between women." *Feminist Review* 23, no. 1: 125–138.

hooks, bell. 1989. "Choosing the margin as a space of radical openness." *Framework: The Journal of Cinema and Media* 36: 15–23.

hooks, bell. 2006. *Outlaw Culture: Resisting Representations*. Routledge.

Hoshall, Leora. 2012. "Afraid of who you are: No promo homo laws in public school sex education." *Texas Journal of Women and the Law* 22: 219.

House of Commons Debates, 39th Parliament, 1st sess., No. 46. June 22, 2006.http://www.parl.gc.ca/HousePublications/Publication.aspx?Pub=Hansard&Mee=46&Language=E&Parl=39&Ses=1. Accessed September 1, 2021.

Howard, John. 1997. *Carryin'on in the Lesbian and Gay South*. NYU Press.

Howard, John. 1999. *Men Like That: A Southern Queer History*. University of Chicago Press.

Howard, John. 2009. *Concentration Camps on the Home Front: Japanese Americans in the House of Jim Crow*. University of Chicago Press.

Howard, Susanna D., Kevin L. Lee, Aviva G. Nathan, Hannah C. Wenger, Marshall H. Chin, and Scott C. Cook. 2019. "Healthcare experiences of transgender people of color." *Journal of general internal medicine* 34, no. 10: 2068–2074.

Human Rights Commission [HRC] Foundation. 2020. "LGBTQ youth are living in crisis: Key findings." *Project Thrive.* https://hrc-prod-requests.s3-us-west -2.amazonaws.com/ProjectThrive_YRBSData_Statement_122120.pdf?mtime =20210104125112&focal=none. Accessed August 3, 2021.

Hughes, Tonda L., Timothy P. Johnson, and Alicia K. Matthews. 2008. "Sexual orientation and smoking: Results from a multisite women's health study." *Substance Use and Misuse* 43, no. 8–9: 1218–1239.

Human Rights Campaign [HRC]. 2021. "Violence Against the Transgender and Gender Non- Conforming Community in 2020." *HRC Website.* Retrieved from: https://www.hrc.org/resources/violence-against-the-trans-and-gender -non- conforming-community-in-2020.

Hunziker, Alyssa A. 2020. "Playing Indian, playing Filipino: Native American and Filipino interactions at the Carlisle Indian Industrial School." *American Quarterly* 72, no. 2: 423–448.

Hutchinson, George. 2007. *The Cambridge Companion to the Harlem Renaissance.* New York: Cambridge University Press.

Hwang, David Henry. 1988. *M. butterfly.* Dramatists Play Service Inc.

IBM Institute for Business Value. 2021. *Striving for Authenticity: LGBT+ Views on Enduring Discrimination and Expanding Inclusion.* New York: IBM. 1–15.

Irwin, Marc H., and Samuel Roll. 1995. "The psychological impact of sexual abuse of Native American boarding-school children." *Journal of the American Academy of Psychoanalysis* 23, no. 3: 461–473.

Iyer, Aarti, Colin Wayne Leach, and Faye J. Crosby. 2003. "White guilt and racial compensation: The benefits and limits of self-focus." *Personality and Social Psychology Bulletin* 29, no. 1: 117–129.

Jackson, Andrew, Sam B. Smith, Harriet Chappell Owsley, and Harold D. Moser. 1980. *The Papers of Andrew Jackson: 1821-1824.* Vol. 5. University of Tennessee Press.

Jackson, John P., and Nadine M. Weidman. 2004. *Race, Racism, and Science: Social Impact and Interaction.* Abc-Clio.

Jacobson, Matthew Frye. 1999. *Whiteness of a Different Color.* Harvard University Press.

Jansen, Wiebren S., Menno W. Vos, Sabine Otten, Astrid Podsiadlowski, and Karen I. van der Zee. 2016. "Colorblind or colorful? How diversity approaches affect cultural majority and minority employees." *Journal of Applied Social Psychology* 46, no. 2: 81–93.

Jay, Karla, and Allen Young, eds. 1992. *Out of the Closets: Voices of Gay Liberation.* NYU Press.

Jean, Tyra. 2020. "Black lives matter: police brutality in the era of COVID-19." *North Carolina Medical Journal* 81: 137–140.

Jean-Phillippe, Mackenzie. 2020. "Bridgerton doesn't need to elaborate on its inclusion of black characters." *Oprah Magazine*, December 29, 2020. Retrieved from:

https://www.oprahmag.com/entertainment/tv-movies/a35083112/bridgerton-race
-historical-accuracy/.

Jessica, H. "Queer histories at the crossroads of America." *Communities and Place: A Thematic Approach to the Histories of LGBTQ Communities in the United States*: 231.

Jeung, Russell. 2021. "Stop AAPI Hate National Report." *Stop AAPI Hate Website.* February 28, 2021. Retrieved from: https://secureservercdn.net/104.238.69.231/a1w.90d.myftpupload.com/wp-content/uploads/2021/03/210312-Stop-AAPI-Hate-National-Report-.pdf.

Jewish Women's Archive, n.d. "Jewish Women and LGBTQ Pride." April 26, 2021. Retrieved from: https://jwa.org/discover/throughtheyear/june/glbt.

Jim Chuchu. 2014. *All Oppression is Connection*. Nairobi. Retrieved from: https://www.jimchuchu.com/oppression. Accessed on September 14, 2021.

Johnson, A., and R. Johnson. 1979. *Propaganda and Aesthetics: The Literary Politics of Afro-American Magazines in the Twentieth Century*, pp. 80–81. Amherst: The University of Massachusetts Press.

Johnson, David K. 2004. *The Lavender Scare*. Chicago, IL: The University of Chicago Press. 114.

Johnson, E. Patrick. 2001. "'Quare' studies, or (almost) everything I know about queer studies I learned from my grandmother." *Text and Performance Quarterly* 21, no. 1: 1–25.

Johnson, Joy L., Joan L. Bottorff, Annette J. Browne, Sukhdev Grewal, B. Ann Hilton, and Heather Clarke. 2004. "Othering and being othered in the context of health care services." *Health Communication* 16, no. 2: 255–271.

Johnston, Douglas M. 2016. "Combating islamophobia." *Journal of Ecumenical Studies* 51, no. 2: 165–173.

Jones, Robert Jr. "Thank You for Everything, Victoria Cruz." *BC/Stories.* June 17, 2019. https://www.brooklyn.cuny.edu/web/news/bcstories/thank-you-for-every-thing-victoria-cruz.php. Accessed September 5, 2021.

Jones, Stacy Holman, and Tony E. Adams. 2016. "Autoethnography is a queer method." In *Queer Methods and Methodologies*, edited by Kath Browne and Catherine Nash. New York: Routledge. 195–214.

Jones, Susan R., and Marylu K. McEwen. 2000. "A conceptual model of multiple dimensions of identity." *Journal of College Student Development* 41, no. 4: 405–414.

Kahn, Ellen, Ashland Johnson, Mark Lee, and Liam Miranda. 2018. *LGBTQ Youth Report 2018*. Human Rights Campaign.

Kamiya, Gary. "Chinatown school was at the center of anti-Japanese crusade in S.F." *SF Gate.* August 22, 2014. https://www.sfgate.com/bayarea/article/Chinatown-school-was-at-center-of-anti-Japanese-5706859.php.

Karpinski, Stephanie, and Jennifer Collins. 2020. "The LGBT Fight for Marriage Equality in the United States." *COLS Undergraduate Research Symposium.*

Katoa-Taholo, Leilani AH. 2019. "Kaimana: An integrative study of reclaiming our cultural power for Pacific Islander well-being and collective care." PhD diss., The University of Utah.

Kauanui, J. Kēhaulani. 2008. "Native Hawaiian decolonization and the politics of gender." *American Quarterly* 60, no. 2: 281–287.

Kaufman, Gil. "'The Show Must Be Paused': What to know about the music indus-try's response to George Floyd's death." *billboard*. June 1, 2020. https://www.bill-board.com/articles/business/record-labels/9394552/show-must-be-paused-george -floyd-death-atlantic-execs. Accessed September 2, 2021.

Kayal, Philip M. 2018. *Bearing Witness: Gay Men's Health Crisis and the Politics of AIDS*. Routledge.

Kelly, Jeffrey A., Janet S. St. Lawrence, Yuri A. Amirkhanian, Wayne J. DiFranceisco, Michelle Anderson-Lamb, Luis I. Garcia, and Manh T. Nguyen. 2013. "Levels and predictors of HIV risk behavior among Black men who have sex with men." *AIDS Education and Prevention* 25: 49–61.

Kennedy, Elizabeth Lapovsky and Madeline D. Davis. 1993. *Boots of Leather, Slippers of Gold: The History of a Lesbian Community*. New York: Routledge.

Kepner, Jim, Stephen Murray, and V. Bullough. 2002. "Henry Gerber (1895-1972): Grandfather of the American gay movement." In *Before Stonewall: Activists for Gay and Lesbian Rights in Historical Context*, edited by Vern Bullough. New Tork: Harrington Park Press. 24–34.

Khan, Coco. 2020. "'I thought I was a lost cause': How therapy is failing people of colour." *The Guardian*. February 10, 2020. Retrieved from: https://www.the-guardian.com/lifeandstyle/2020/feb/10/therapy-failing-bme-patients-mental-health -counselling.

Kim, Elaine H. 1982. *Asian American Literature, an Introduction to the Writings and Their Social Context*. Temple University Press.

Kimmel, Michael S. 1994. *Older Men's Lives*. Vol. 6. Sage Publishers.

Kinderman, Peter. 2017. "Don't curse the darkness, light a candle." *British Psychological Society*. January 4, 2017. Retrieved from: https://www.bps.org.uk/ blogs/presidential-blog/don%E2%80%99t-curse-darkness-light-candle.

Kissack, Terence. 1995. "Freaking fag revolutionaries: New York's gay liberation front, 1969-1971." *Radical History Review* 62: 104–134.

Kline, Wendy. 2010. "Eugenics in the United States." In *The Oxford Handbook of the History of Eugenics*, edited by Alison Bashford and Philippa Levine. Oxford: Oxford University Press.

Krauthamer, Barbara. 2013. *Black Slaves, Indian Masters: Slavery, Emancipation, and Citizenship in the Native American South*. UNC Press Books.

Kteily, Nour, Gordon Hodson, and Emile Bruneau. 2016. "They see us as less than human: Metadehumanization predicts intergroup conflict via reciprocal dehuman-ization." *Journal of Personality and Social Psychology* 110, no. 3: 343.

Kteily, Nour S., and Emile Bruneau. 2017. "Darker demons of our nature: The need to (re) focus attention on blatant forms of dehumanization." *Current Directions in Psychological Science* 26, no. 6: 487–494.

Kumashiro, Kevin K. 1999. "Supplementing normalcy and otherness: Queer Asian American men reflect on stereotypes, identity, and oppression." *International Journal of Qualitative Studies in Education* 12, no. 5: 491–508.

Kumashiro, Kevin. 2001. "Queer students of color and antiracist, antiheterosexist education: Paradoxes of identity and activism." In *Troubling Intersections of Race and Sexuality: Queer Students of Color and Anti-Oppressive Education*, edited by Kevin Kumashiro. Rowman & Littlefield. 1–25.

Ladder, The. "The Purpose of the Daughters of Bilitis." *The Ladder*. May 1957. Vol 1. No 8. https://documents.alexanderstreet.com/d/1003347887. Accessed September 13, 2021.

Lamont, Michèle, Bo Yun Park, and Elena Ayala-Hurtado. 2017 "Trump's electoral speeches and his appeal to the American white working class." *The British Journal of Sociology* 68: 153–180.

Lavoie, Denise. "Daunte Wright: Doting dad, ballplayer, slain by police." *Associated Press*. April 14, 2021. https://apnews.com/article/daunte-wright-shooting-minnesota-f70fb7fc4c205740507b7ec53d7315f0. Accessed September 1, 2021.

Lawrence, Shammara. "Kylie Jenner and Khloe Kardashian Accused of Stealing Ideas From Indie Black Designers." *Teen Vogue*. July 16, 2017. https://www.teenvogue.com/story/kylie-jenner-khloe-kardashian-stealing-black-designers. Accessed September 1, 2021.

Lawrence, Tim. 1989. "A history of drag balls, houses and the culture of voguing." *Voguing and the House Ballroom Scene of New York City* 92: 3–10.

Laws, Mike. "Why we capitalize 'Black' (and not 'white')." *Columbia Journalism Review*. June 16, 2020. https://www.cjr.org/analysis/capital-b-black-styleguide.php.

Lawson, Kenneth. 2015. "Police shooting of black men and implicit racial bias: Can't we all just get along." *University of Hawai'i Law Review* 37: 339.

Lawson, Philip. 2014. *The East India Company: A History*. Routledge.

Lee, Erika. 2003. *At America's Gates: Chinese Immigration During the Exclusion Era, 1882-1943*. University of North Carolina Press.

Lee, Eunjung, A. Ka Tat Tsang, Marion Bogo, Marjorie Johnstone, and Jessica Herschman. 2018. "Enactments of racial microaggression in everyday therapeutic encounters." *Smith College Studies in Social Work* 88, no. 3: 211–236.

Lee, Jennifer, and Frank D. Bean. 2007. "Reinventing the color line immigration and America's new racial/ethnic divide." *Social Forces* 86, no. 2: 561–586.

Lee, Robert G. 1999. *Orientals: Asian Americans in Popular Culture*. Philadelphia, PA: Temple University Press.

Lee, Wallace. 2003. *Sexual Encounters: Pacific Texts, Modern Sexualities*. Ithaca, NY: Cornell University Press.

Legal, Lambda. 2014. "Protected and served? Survey of LGBT/HIV contact with police, courts, prisons, and security." New York: Lambda Legal. Retrieved at: https://www.lambdalegal.org/protected-and-served

Leong, Russell. 2014. *Asian American Sexualities: Dimensions of the Gay and Lesbian Experience*. Routledge.

Leung, Hay Ding Adrian. 2016. "Being gay and Asian: The journey to finding a voice in New York City." PhD diss., The New School.

Leung, Wing Fai. 2014. "Perceptions of the East—Yellow peril: An archive of anti-Asian fear." *The Irish Times*.

Levin, Sam. 2019. "Compton's Cafeteria riot: a historic act of trans resistance, three years before Stonewall." *The Guardian*. June 21, 2019. Retrieved from: https://www.theguardian.com/lifeandstyle/2019/jun/21/stonewall-san-francisco-riot-tenderloin-neighborhood-trans-women.

Levine, Martin P. 1979. "Gay ghetto." *Journal of Homosexuality* 4, no. 4: 363–377.

LeVine, Robert A., and Donald T. Campbell. 1973. "Ethnocentrism: Theories of conflict, ethnic attitudes, and group behavior." *The Journal of Politics* 35, no. 4: 1022–1028.

Lewis, Christian. "M. Butterfly" Surprisingly Relevant". *HuffPost.* October 26, 2017.

Lin, Luona, Karen Stamm, and Peggy Christidis. 2018. "Demographics of the US psychology workforce." *Washington, DC.*

Lindsay, P. 2018. ""Coming Out": From assimilation to visibility handouts." *Los Angeles LGBT Center.* https://lalgbtcenter.org/images/OutForSafeSchools/Los-Angeles-LGBT-Center-October-Coming-Out-Handouts.pdf. Accessed September 1, 2021.

Lipsitz, George. 1995. "The possessive investment in whiteness: Racialized social democracy and the 'white' problem in American studies." *American Quarterly* 47, no. 3: 369–387.

Lipsitz Bem, Sandra. 1993. "The lenses of gender." *Transforming the Debate on Sexual Inequality.* New Haven–London.

Little, Becky. 2017. "How Boarding Schools Tried to 'Kill the Indian' Through Assimilation." *History.com.*

Lockhart, John, 2002. *The Gay Man's Guide to Growing Older.* Alyson Publishing.

Loeser, Lewis H. 1945. "The sexual psychopath in the military service: (A study of 270 cases)." *American Journal of Psychiatry* 102, no. 1: 92–101.

Loofburrow, Lili. "The moment that should have changed everything." *Slate.* October 7, 2020. https://slate.com/news-and-politics/2020/10/trump-access-hollywood-tape-revisited.html. Accessed September 1, 2021.

Lorde, Audre. 1980. "When will the ignorance end?" *Gay Insurgent*, summer: 12–14.

Lorde, Audre. 1982. *Zami, a New Spelling of My Name.* Freedom, CA: Crossing.

Lorde, Audre. 1993. "The uses of the erotic: The erotic as power." In *The Lesbian and Gay Studies Reader*, edited by Henry Abelove, Michele Aina Barale, & David M. Halperin. New York: Routledge. 339–343.

Lorde, Audre. 2003. "The master's tools will never dismantle the master's house." *Feminist Postcolonial Theory: A Reader* 25: 27.

Lorde, Audre. 2012. Learning from the 60s. *Sister Outsider: Essays and Speeches.* Berkeley, CA: Crossing Press.

Lorde, Audre. 2017. *A Burst of Light: And Other Essays.* Courier Dover Publications.

Louis, Winnifred R., Emma Thomas, Cassandra M. Chapman, Tulsi Achia, Susilo Wibisono, Zahra Mirnajafi, and Lisa Droogendyk. 2019. "Emerging research on intergroup prosociality: Group members' charitable giving, positive contact, allyship, and solidarity with others." *Social and Personality Psychology Compass* 13, no. 3: 5–16.

Lyon, Cherstin. 2011. *Prisons and Patriots: Japanese American Wartime Citizenship, Civil Disobedience, and Historical Memory.* Philadelphia, PA: Temple University Press.

Lyons, Kim. "Facebook says its AI mislabeling a video of Black men as "primates" was "unacceptable." *The Verge.* September 4, 2021. https://www.theverge.com

/2021/9/4/22657026/facebook-mislabeling-video-black-men-primates-algorithm. Accessed September 1, 2021.

Ma, Sheng-mei. 2000. *The Deathly Embrace: Orientalism and Asian American Identity*. University of Minnesota Press.

Malebranche, David J., Errol L. Fields, Lawrence O. Bryant, and Shaun R. Harper. 2009. "Masculine socialization and sexual risk behaviors among Black men who have sex with men: A qualitative exploration." *Men and Masculinities* 12, no. 1: 90–112.

Maltry, Melanie, and Kristin Tucker. 2002. "Female fem (me) ininities: New articulations in queer gender identities and subversion." *Journal of Lesbian Studies* 6, no. 2: 89–102.

Manalansan IV, Martin F. 2003. *Global Divas*. Duke University Press.

Mandler, C. "Please stop wearing those pussy hats to women's marches." *Seventeen*. January 18, 2019. https://www.seventeen.com/life/a15854506/stop-wearing-pussy -hats-womens-marches/. Accessed September 14, 2021.

Mangaoang, G. 1994. "From the 1970s to the 1990s: Perspective of a gay Filipino American activist." *Amerasia Journal* 20, no. 1: 33–44.

Mannes, Marc. 1996. "Factors and events leading to the passage of the Indian Child Welfare Act." In *A History of Child Welfare*, edited by Eve P. Smith, Lisa A. Merkel-HolguÃn. New Brunswick: Transaction Publishers. 257–275.

Marcuse, Herbert. 1969. *An Essay on Liberation*. Beacon Press, Vol. 319.

Mariposa Film Group. 1977. *Word Is Out: Stories of Some of Our Lives* (Theatrical film). New York: Mariposa Film Group.

Marshall, James P. 2013. *Student Activism and Civil Rights in Mississippi: Protest Politics and the Struggle for Racial Justice, 1960-1965*. Baton Rouge: Louisiana State University, 165.

Martin, Debra L., and Alan H. Goodman. 2002 "Health conditions before Columbus: paleopathology of native North Americans." *Western Journal of Medicine* 176, no. 1: 65.

Martín-Baró, Ignacio. 1994. "Toward a liberation psychology." In *Writings for a Liberation Psychology*, edited by Adrianne Aron Shawn Corne. Harvard: Harvard University Press. 17–32.

Martis, Eternity. "A capital idea: Reflections on the politics of capitalization." *Ryerson Review of Journalism*. April 19, 2016. https://rrj.ca/a-capital-idea/.

Matias, Cheryl E., and Janiece Mackey. 2016. "Breakin' down whiteness in antiracist teaching: Introducing critical whiteness pedagogy." *The Urban Review* 48, no. 1: 32–50.

Matsukawa, Yuko. 2002. "Representing the Oriental in nineteenth-century trade cards." In *Re-Collecting Early Asian America: Essays in Cultural History*, edited by Josephine Lee, Imogene Lim, and Yuko Matsukawa. Philadelphia: Temple University Press. 200–217.

Mays, Vickie M., and Susan D. Cochran. 2001. "Mental health correlates of perceived discrimination among lesbian, gay, and bisexual adults in the United States." *American Journal of Public Health* 91, no. 11: 1869–1876.

McAlear, Rob. 2019. "Hate, narrative, and propaganda in the Turner diaries." *The Journal of American Culture* 32, no. 3: 192.

McCall, L. 2008. "The complexity of intersectionality." In *Intersectionality and Beyond*, edited by Emily Grabham, Davina Cooper, Jane Krishnadas, and Didi Herman. Routledge-Cavendish. 65–92.

McClellan, Robert. 1971. *The Heathen Chinese: A Study of American Attitudes Toward China, 1890-1905*. The Ohio State University Press.

McKee, Mionnay. 2016. "Uncloseting the Harlem renaissance: A look at the movement through a queer lens." *CUNY Academic Works*.

McMahon, Katherine. 2010. "Pride is a protest, stonewall was a riot." *Reclaiming the Political in Manchester's Queer Activism*.

Meeker, Martin. 2012. "The queerly disadvantaged and the making of San Francisco's war on poverty, 1964–1967." *Pacific Historical Review* 81, no. 1: 21–59.

Memmi, Albert. 2013. *The Colonizer and the Colonized*. Routledge.

Menchaca, Martha. 1997. "Early racist discourses: The roots of deficit thinking." In *The Evolution of Deficit Thinking: Educational Thought and Practice*, edited by R. Valencia. Oxen: RoutledgeFalmer. 13–40.

Menchavez, Andre. "It's time to talk about the mental health impacts of being asian and queer." *GLAAD*. August 30, 2019. https://www.glaad.org/amp/asian-queer-mental-health. Accessed September 11, 2021.

Mencia, Alexa. "10 miles apart: George Floyd's girlfriend was Daunte Wright's former teacher, relative says." *Kare*. April 14, 2021. https://www.kare11.com/article/news/local/george-floyd/george-floyd-girlfriend-courteney-ross-teacher-daunte-wright/89-fec5af81-4891-47e2-8d92-4468287400d6. Accessed August 1, 2021.

Meyer, Ilan H. 1995. "Minority stress and mental health in gay men." *Journal of Health and Social Behavior* 36, no. 1: 38–56.

Meyer, Ilan H. 2003. "Prejudice, social stress, and mental health in lesbian, gay, and bisexual populations: Conceptual issues and research evidence." *Psychological Bulletin* 129, no. 5: 674.

Meyer, Leisa D. 1992. "Creating GI Jane: the regulation of sexuality and sexual behavior in the Women's Army Corps during World War II." *Feminist Studies* 18, no. 3: 581–601.

Meyer, Michaela DE. 2020. "Black Panther, queer erasure, and intersectional representation in popular culture." *Review of Communication* 20, no. 3: 236–243.

Meyer, Oanh, Nolan Zane, and Young Il Cho. 2011. "Understanding the psychological processes of the racial match effect in Asian Americans." *Journal of Counseling Psychology* 58, no. 3: 335.

Mignolo, Walter D. 2002. "The geopolitics of knowledge and the colonial difference." *South Atlantic Quarterly* 101, no. 1: 57–96.

Minh-ha, Trinh T. "There is no such thing as a documentary" *Frieze*. November 1, 2018.

Miranda, Mariana, Maria Gouveia-Pereira, and Jeroen Vaes. 2014. "When in Rome… Identification and acculturation strategies among minority members moderate the dehumanisation of the majority outgroup." *European Journal of Social Psychology* 44, no. 4: 327–336.

Mitchell Jr, Donald, and Darris R. Means. 2014. ""Quadruple consciousness": A literature review and new theoretical consideration for understanding the experiences of Black gay and bisexual college men at predominantly white institutions." *Journal of African American Males in Education* 5, no. 1: 23–35.

Miu, Adriana S., and Jessica R. Moore. 2021. "Behind the masks: Experiences of mental health practitioners of color during the COVID-19 pandemic." *Academic Psychiatry* 45, no. 5: 1–6.

Mondaire Jones joins Ritchie Torres as first gay Black men elected to Congress." *NBC News.* November 5, 2020. https://www.nbcnews.com/feature/nbc-out/mondaire-jones-joins-ritchie-torres-first-gay-black-men-elected-n1246693. Accessed September 1, 2021.

Moraga, Cherríe, and Gloria Anzaldúa, eds. 2015. *This Bridge Called My Back: Writings by Radical Women of Color.* Suny Press.

Morgensen, Scott Lauria. 2010. "Settler homonationalism: Theorizing settler colonialism within queer modernities." *GLQ: A Journal of Lesbian and Gay Studies* 16, no. 1–2: 105–131.

Morgensen, Scott Lauria. 2011. *Spaces Between Us: Queer Settler Colonialism and Indigenous Decolonization.* University of Minnesota Press.

Movement Advancement Project and Center for American Progress. 2015. "Paying an unfair price: The financial penalty for LGBT people of color in America." https://www.lgbtmap.org/unfair-price-lgbt-people-of-color. Accessed September 2, 2021.

Mullen, Brian, Rupert Brown, and Colleen Smith. 1992. "Ingroup bias as a function of salience, relevance, and status: An integration." *European Journal of Social Psychology* 22, no. 2: 103–122.

Mumford, Kevin. 2008. *Newark: A History of Race, Rights, and Riots in America.* Vol. 10. NYU Press.

Mumford, Kevin. 2016. *Not Straight, Not White: Black Gay Men from the March on Washington to the AIDS Crisis.* UNC Press Books.

Muñoz, José Esteban. 1999. *Disidentifications: Queers of Color and the Performance of Politics.* Vol. 2. University of Minnesota Press.

Muñoz, José Esteban. 2009. *Cruising Utopia.* New York University Press.

Nadal, Kevin L., Tanya Erazo, Julia Schulman, Heather Han, Tamara Deutsch, R. Ruth, and E. Santacruz. 2017. "Caught at the intersections: Microaggressions toward lesbian, gay, bisexual, transgender, and queer people of color." In *LGBT Psychology and Mental Health: Emerging Research and Advances*, edited by R. Ruth & E. Santacruz. Praeger/ABC-CLIO. 133–152.

Nakanishi, Don T. 2009. "Surviving democracy's "mistake": Japanese Americans & the enduring legacy of Executive Order 9066." *Amerasia Journal* 35, no. 3: 52–84.

Nawyn, Stephanie J., Judith A. Richman, Kathleen M. Rospenda, and Tonda L. Hughes. 2000. "Sexual identity and alcohol-related outcomes: Contributions of workplace harassment." *Journal of Substance Abuse* 11, no. 3: 289–304.

Nestle, Joan. 2008. *Women's House of Detention, 1931-1974.* Outhistory.org. para 4–5.

Neuman, Gerald L. 1994. "Justifying US naturalization policies." *Immigration and Nationality Law Review* 16: 83.

New York City Civilian Complaint Review Board. 2016. "Pride, prejudice and policing: An evaluation of LGBTQ-related complaints from January 2010 through December 2015."

Newman, Benjamin, Jennifer L. Merolla, Sono Shah, Danielle Casarez Lemi, Loren Collingwood, and S. Karthick Ramakrishnan. 2021. "The trump effect: an experimental investigation of the emboldening effect of racially inflammatory elite communication." *British Journal of Political Science* 51, no. 3: 1138–1159.

Nichols, Jack. "African-American probably first U.S. gay movement president." *Gay Today. 2002*. http://gaytoday.com/events/081202ev.asp. Accessed March 2, 2021.

Nickeas, Peter. "Chicago police say bodycam footage shows less than a second passes from when 13-year-old is seen holding a handgun and is shot by officer." *CNN News*. April 16, 2021. https://www.cnn.com/2021/04/15/us/adam-toledo-police-shooting-body-camera/index.html. Accessed September 1, 2021.

Nietzsche, Friedrich. 1967. *The Will to Power*, translated by Walter Kaufmann and R. J. Hollingdale. New York: Random House.

Nixon, Angelique V. 2020. "Intentional BlackLove: Space making, visionary solidarity, and black feminisms movement building." *Development* 63, no. 1: 79–82.

Nunez, Theron A. 1958. "Creek Nativism and the Creek War of 1813-1814." *Ethnohistory* 5, no. 1: 1–47.

Oh, Reginald. 2020. "Dehumanization, immigrants, and equal protection." *California Western Law Review* 56, no. 1: 5.

Olson, Lester C. 1998 "Liabilities of language: Audre Lorde reclaiming difference." *Quarterly Journal of Speech* 84, no. 4: 448–470.

Ong, Anthony D., Thomas Fuller-Rowell, and Anthony L. Burrow. 2009. "Racial discrimination and the stress process." *Journal of Personality and Social Psychology* 96, no. 6: 1259.

Ordover, Nancy. 2003. *American Eugenics: Race, Queer Anatomy, and the Science of Nationalism*. University of Minnesota Press.

Ott, Brian L., and Greg Dickinson. 2019. *The Twitter Presidency: Donald J. Trump and the Politics of White Rage*. Routledge.

Pascoe, E. A., and L. S. Richman. 2009. "Perceived discrimination and health: a meta-analytic review." *Psychological Bulletin* 135: 531–554.

Pascoe, Peggy. 2009. *What Comes Naturally: Miscegenation Law and the Making of Race in America*. Oxford University Press on Demand.

Paulet, Anne. 2007. "To change the world: The use of American Indian education in the Philippines." *History of Education Quarterly* 47, no. 2: 173–202.

Pavetich, Melissa, and Sofia Stathi. 2021. "Investigating antecedents of Islamophobia: The role of perceived control over terrorism, threat, meta-dehumanization, and dehumanization." *Journal of Community and Applied Social Psychology* 31, no. 4: 5–10.

Peacock, Kent W. 2016. "Race, the homosexual, and the Mattachine Society of Washington, 1961–1970." *Journal of the History of Sexuality* 25, no. 2: 267–296.

Peck, Raoul, and Alexandra Strauss, eds. 2017. *I Am Not Your Negro*. Magnolia Home Entertainment.

Persch, Jasmin Allen. "School that barred 7-year-old's dreadlocks changes dress-code policy." *Today*. September 10, 2013. https://www.today.com/parents/school-barred-7-year-olds-dreadlocks-changes-dress-code-policy-8c11122821. Accessed September 1, 2021.

Petermon, Jade D., and Leland G. Spencer. 2019. "Black queer womanhood matters: searching for the queer herstory of Black Lives Matter in television dramas." *Critical Studies in Media Communication* 36, no. 4: 339–356.

Philipson, Robert. 2011. *T'Ain't Nobody's Bizness: Queer Blues Divas of the 1920s*, directed by Robert Philipson. Shoga Films.

Poon, Maurice Kwong-Lai. 2000. "Inter-racial same-sex abuse: The vulnerability of gay men of Asian descent in relationships with Caucasian men." *Journal of Gay and Lesbian Social Services* 11, no. 4: 39–67.

Potter, Sharyn J., Kim Fountain, and Jane G. Stapleton. 2012. "Addressing sexual and relationship violence in the LGBT community using a bystander framework." *Harvard Review of Psychiatry* 20, no. 4: 201–208.

Prasad, Ajnesh. 2007. "Cultural relativism in human rights discourse." *Peace Review* 19, no. 4: 589–596.

Prichep, Deena. "a campus more colorful than reality: Beware that college brochure." *NPR News.* December 29, 2013. https://www.npr.org/2013/12/29/257765543/a-campus-more-colorful-than-reality-beware-that-college-brochure. Accessed September 14, 2021.

Prichep, Deena. "For LGBTQ people of color, discrimination compounds." *NPR News.* November 25, 2017.

Prilleltensky, Isaac. 2003. "Understanding, resisting, and overcoming oppression: Toward psychopolitical validity." *American Journal of Community Psychology* 31, no. 1–2: 195–201.

Pritchard, Eric Darnell. 2013. "For colored kids who committed suicide, our outrage isn't enough: Queer youth of color, bullying, and the discursive limits of identity and safety." *Harvard Educational Review* 83, no. 2: 320–345.

Prucha, Francis Paul. 2000. "Documents of United States Indian Policy". Library of Congress Cataloging-in-Publication Data, United States of America: 33.

Puar, Jasbir K. 2007. "Introduction: Homonationalism and biopolitics." In *Terrorist Assemblages*, pp. 1–36. Duke University Press.

Quesada, Uriel, Letitia Gomez, and Salvador Vidal-Ortiz. 2015. *Queer Brown Voices: Personal Narratives of Latina/o LGBT Activism.* University of Texas Press.

Quijano, Anibal. 2000. "Coloniality of power and Eurocentrism in Latin America." *International Sociology* 15, no. 2: 215–232.

Rahman, Momin. 2010. "Queer as intersectionality: Theorizing gay Muslim identities." *Sociology* 44, no. 5: 944–961.

Ramirez, Rachel. "The history of fetishizing Asian women." *Vox.* March 19, 2021. https://www.vox.com/22338807/asian-fetish-racism-atlanta-shooting. Accessed August 2, 2021.

Rand, Erin. 2014. *Reclaiming Queer: Activist and Academic Rhetorics of Resistance.* University of Alabama Press.

Ransby, Barbara. 2003. *Ella Baker and the Black Freedom Movement: A Radical Democratic vision.* University of North Carolina Press.

Rasmussen, Birgit Brander, Eric Klinenberg, Irene J. Nexica, and Matt Wray, eds. 2001. *The Making and Unmaking of Whiteness.* Duke University Press.

Ratts, Manivong J., Anneliese A. Singh, Sylvia Nassar-McMillan, S. Kent Butler, and Julian Rafferty McCullough. 2016."Multicultural and social justice counseling competencies: Guidelines for the counseling profession." *Journal of Multicultural Counseling and Development* 44, no. 1: 28–48.

Ray-Belcourt, Billy. 2016. "Can the other of native studies speak?" *Decolonization: Indigineity, Education and Society.* February 1, 2016. https://decolonization.wordpress.com/2016/02/01/can-the-other-of-native-studies-speak/. Accessed on August 2, 2021.

Reilly, Philip R. 2015. "Eugenics and involuntary sterilization: 1907–2015." *Annual Review of Genomics and Human Genetics* 16: 351–368.

Reus-Smit, Christian. 2013. *Individual Rights and the Making of the International System.* Cambridge University Press.

Riemer, Matthew, and Leighton Brown.2019. *We Are Everywhere: Protest, Power, and Pride in the History of Queer Liberation.* Ten Speed Press.

Rivera, Alexandra M. and Dale D. Maglalang. 2017. "Recentering Asianness in the discourse on homonationalism." In *The Psychic Life of Racism in Gay Men's Communities*, edited by Damien Riggs. Lexington Books. 123.

Rizal, Jose. 1912. *The Philippines a Century Hence.* Philippine Education Company.

Robinson, Greg. 2016. *The Great Unknown: Japanese American Sketches.* University Press of Colorado.

Roediger, David. 1995. *Wages of Whiteness: Race and the Making of the American Working Class.* New York: Verso.

Roediger, David. 2005. "What's wrong with these pictures-race, narratives of admission, and the liberal self-representations of historically white colleges and universities." *Washington University Journal of Law and Policy* 18: 203.

Rohrer, Judy. 2014. "Prop 8 and lesbian and gay citizenship." In *Queering the Biopolitics of Citizenship in the Age of Obama*, edited by Judy Rohrer. New York: Palgrave Macmillan. 41–55.

Rosenberg, Noah A., Jonathan K. Pritchard, James L. Weber, Howard M. Cann, Kenneth K. Kidd, Lev A. Zhivotovsky, and Marcus W. Feldman. 2002. "Genetic structure of human populations." *Science* 298, no. 5602: 2381–2385.

Rosenberg, Stanley. 2017. *Accessing the Healing Power of the Vagus Nerve: Self-help Exercises for Anxiety, Depression, Trauma, and Autism.* North Atlantic Books.

Rothbaum, Barbara Olasov, Elizabeth A. Meadows, Patricia Resick, and David W. Foy. 2000. "Cognitive-behavioral therapy." In E. B. Foa, T. M. Keane, and M. J. Friedman (Eds.), *Effective Treatments for PTSD: Practice Guidelines from the International Society for Traumatic Stress Studies*, pp. 320–325. The Guilford Press.

Rothman, Joshua D. 2016. "The contours of cotton capitalism." In *Slavery's Capitalism*, edited by Sven Beckert and Seth Rockman. University of Pennsylvania Press. 122–145.

Rowden, Terry. 2007. "Harlem undercover: Difference and desire in African American popular music, 1920–1940." *English Language Notes* 45, no. 2: 23–31.

Royles, Dan. 2017. "Race, homosexuality, and the AIDS epidemic." *Black Perspectives.* July 6, 2017. Retrieved from: https://www.aaihs.org/race-homosexuality-and-the-aids-epidemic/.

Rucker, Phillip and Andy Phillip. 2017. "Trump campaigned against Muslims but will preach tolerance in Saudi speech." *The Washington Post.* May 19, 2017.

https://www.washingtonpost.com/politics/trump-campaigned-against-muslims-but-will-preach-tolerance-in-saudi-speech/2017/05/19/6357c60c-3ca7-11e7-9e48-c4f199710b69_story.html. Accessed September 2, 2021.

Rutledge, Leigh. 1992. *The Gay Decades: From Stonewall to the Present — The People and Events that Shaped Gay Lives.* New York: Penguin.

Ryan, Caitlin, Stephen T. Russell, David Huebner, Rafael Diaz, and Jorge Sanchez. 2010. "Family acceptance in adolescence and the health of LGBT young adults." *Journal of child and adolescent psychiatric nursing* 23, no. 4: 205–213.

Said, Edward. 1993. "The politics of knowledge." In *Race, Identity and Representation in Education*, edited by Cameron McCarthy, Warren Crichlow, Greg Dimitriadis, and Nadine Dolby. New York: Routledge. 306–314.

Salahieh, Nouran, Erin Myers, Kareen Wynter, and Carlos Saucedo. "Thousands march through Hollywood for 'All Black Lives Matter' solidarity protest." *KTLA News.* June 14, 2020. https://ktla.com/news/local-news/all-black-lives-matter-protest-set-to-begin-in-hollywood-sunday-morning/. Accessed September 1, 2021.

Samuels, W. 2000. "From the wild, wild west to Harlem's literary salons." *Black Issues Book Review* 2, no. 5: 14.

Sanchez, James Chase. 2018. "Trump, the KKK, and the versatility of white supremacy rhetoric." *Journal of Contemporary Rhetoric* 8: 44–56.

Sangalang, Cindy C., and Cindy Vang. 2017. "Intergenerational trauma in refugee families: A systematic review." *Journal of Immigrant and Minority Health* 19, no. 3: 745–754.

Sarno, E. L., J. J. Mohr, S. D. Jackson, and R. E. Fassinger. 2015. When identities collide: Conflicts in allegiances among LGB people of color. *Cultural Diversity and Ethnic Minority Psychology* 21, no. 4: 550.

Sashkevich, Alex. 2019. "The power of language: How words shape people, culture." *Stanford News,* August 22, 2019. Retrieved from: https://news.stanford.edu/2019/08/22/the-power-of-language-how-words-shape-people-culture/.

Saul, Jennifer M. 2017. "Racial figleaves, the shifting boundaries of the permissible, and the rise of Donald Trump." *Philosophical Topics* 45, no. 2: 97–116.

Scaer, Robert C. 2001. "The neurophysiology of dissociation and chronic disease." *Applied Psychophysiology and Biofeedback* 26, no. 1: 73–91.

Schwartz, Matthew. 2020. "Trump tells agencies to end trainings on 'white privilege' and 'critical race theory'" *National Public Radio.* September 5, 2020. Retrieved from: https://www.npr.org/2020/09/05/910053496/trump-tells-agencies-to-end-trainings-on-white-privilege-and-critical-race-theory.

Schwarz, A. B. Christa. 2003. *Gay Voices of the Harlem Renaissance.* Indiana University Press.

Sears, Brad, Kerith J. Conron, and Andrew R. Flores. 2021. "The impact of the fall 2020 COVID-19 surge on LGBT adults in the US." February 2021. *UCLA Williams Institute.* Retrieved from: https://williamsinstitute.law.ucla.edu/publications/covid-surge-lgbt/.

Segal, Elizabeth A. 2011. "Social empathy: A model built on empathy, contextual understanding, and social responsibility that promotes social justice." *Journal of Social Service Research* 37, no. 3: 266–277.

Semega, Jessica L., Kayla R. Fontenot, and Melissa A. Kollar. 2020. "Income and poverty in the United States: 2019." *Current Population Reports* 60–259.

Serwer, Adam. "The myth of the kindly General Lee." *The Atlantic.* June 4, 2017. https://www.theatlantic.com/politics/archive/2017/06/the-myth-of-the-kindly-general-lee/529038/. Accessed September 1, 2021.

Shah, Nayan. 2005 "Between 'oriental depravity' and 'natural degenerates': Spatial borderlands and the making of ordinary Americans." *American Quarterly* 57, no. 3: 703–725.

Shek, Yen Ling. 2007. "Asian American masculinity: A review of the literature." *The Journal of Men's Studies* 14, no. 3: 379–391.

Shelton, Kimber and Edward A. Delgado-Romero. 2013. "Sexual orientation microaggressions: The experience of lesbian, gay, bisexual, and queer clients in psychotherapy." *Psychology of Sexual Orientation and Gender Diversity* 1: 59.

Shepard, Benjamin. 2013. "From community organization to direct services: The Street Trans Action Revolutionaries to Sylvia Rivera law project." *Journal of Social Service Research* 39, no. 1: 95–114.

Sherif, Muzafer. 1966. *In Common Predicament: Social Psychology of Intergroup Conflict and Cooperation.* Houghton Mifflin.

Shilcutt, Katharine. "Eddie Glaude Jr. talks racial justice in America in Special Lecture." *Rice University News and Media Relations.* January 25, 2021. https://news.rice.edu/2021/01/25/eddie-glaude-jr-talks-racial-justice-in-america-in-special-campbell-lecture/. Accessed March 3, 2021.

Shilts, Randy. 1982. *The Mayor of Castro Street.* New York: St. Martin's Press.

Silverman, Victor, and Susan Stryker. 2005. "Screaming queens: The riot at Compton's Cafeteria." USA, *Frameline.*

Simpson, Leanne. 2008. Our elder brothers: The lifeblood of resurgence. In L. Simpson (ed.), *Lighting the Eighth Fire*, pp. 73–88. Winnipeg: Arbeiter Ring Publishing.

Singh, Anneliese A., Brandee Appling, and Heather Trepal. 2020. "Using the multicultural and social justice counseling competencies to decolonize counseling practice: The important roles of theory, power, and action." *Journal of Counseling and Development* 98, no. 3: 261–271.

Singh, Anneliese A., Brean Parker, Anushka R. Aqil, and Falon Thacker. 2020. "Liberation psychology and LGBTQ+ communities: Naming colonization, uplifting resilience, and reclaiming ancient his-stories, her-stories, and t-stories." In L. Comas-Díaz and E. Torres Rivera (eds.), *Liberation Psychology: Theory, Method, Practice, and Social Justice*, pp. 207–224. American Psychological Association.

Smith, Andrea. 2016. "Heteropatriarchy and the three pillars of white supremacy." In *Color of Violence*, edited by INCITE! Women of Color Against Violence. Duke University Press. 66–73.

Smith, David 2017. Counting the Dead: Estimating the Loss of Life in the Indigenous Holocaust, 1492-Present. 2017, Nov 3. Native American Symposium.

Smith, Laura, Debbie-Ann Chambers, and Lucinda Bratini. 2009. "When oppression is the pathogen: The participatory development of socially just mental health practice." *American Journal of Orthopsychiatry* 79, no. 2: 159–168.

Sollenberger, Roger. "Two GOP congressmen sought pardons for their connection to Capitol attack: report." *Salon.* January 20, 2021. https://www.salon.com/2021/01/20/two-gop-congressmen-sought-pardons-for-their-connection-to-capitol-attack-report/. Accessed September 1, 2021.

Sorisio, Carolyn. 1997. "A tale of two feminisms: Power and victimization in contemporary feminist debate". In *Third Wave Agenda*, 143.

Sosin, Kate. "Rep. Sharice Davids new children's book aims to reflect Native, LGBTQ+ kids." *The 19th.* June 2, 2021. https://19thnews.org/2021/06/rep-sharice-davids-new-childrens-book-aims-to-reflect-native-lgbtq-kids/?fbclid=IwAR1Y0-9mPaZvIwX0mmI202YfDrWoRuNP9-AUIxqmU1yCbXJFNBB9swHR1UE. Accessed September 14, 2021.

Stanley, Jason. 2020 *How Fascism Works: The Politics of Us and Them.* Random House Trade Paperbacks.

Stannard, David E. 1992. *American Holocaust: The Conquest of the New World.* New York: Oxford University Press. 146, ix–x.

Steele, Claude M. and Joshua Aronson 1995. Stereotype threat and the intellectual test performance of African Americans. *Journal of Personality and Social Psychology* 69, no. 5: 797.

Stephan, Walter G., C. Lausanne Renfro, Victoria M. Esses, Cookie White Stephan, and Tim Martin. 2005. "The effects of feeling threatened on attitudes toward immigrants." *International Journal of Intercultural Relations* 29, no. 1: 1–19.

Stephan, Walter G., and Cookie White Stephan. 2000. "An integrated threat theory of prejudice." In *Reducing Prejudice and Discrimination*, edited by S. Oskamp. New Jersey: Lawrence Erlbaum Associates Publishers. 23–45.

Stern, Jessica. 2003. *Terror in the Name of God.* New York: Ecco.

Stewart, Jeffrey C. 2018. *The New Negro: The Life of Alain Locke.* Oxford University Press.

Stillwell, Devon. 2012. "Eugenics visualized: The exhibit of the third International Congress of Eugenics, 1932." *Bulletin of the History of Medicine* 86, no. 2: 206–236.

Stokes, Mason. 2003. *Gay Rebel of the Harlem Renaissance: Selections from the Work of Richard Bruce Nugent.* Duke University Press, pp. 908–913.

Stop AAPI Hate. 2020."The return of the Yellow Peril." *Stop AAPI Report 2020.* October 20, 2020. Retrieved from: https://stopaapihate.org/wp-content/uploads/2021/04/Stop-AAPI-Hate-Report-2020-Candidates-and-Anti-Asian-Rhetoric-201021.pdf.

Stryker, Susan. 2002. "Anatomy of a Riot: The Role of the 1966 Compton's Cafeteria Disturbance in the Politicization of San Francisco's Transgender Community." Presented at the *American Historical Society Association Annual Meeting*, San Francisco, CA, 5 January 2002.

Sturken, Marita. 2015. "The 9/11 memorial museum and the remaking of ground zero." *American Quarterly* 67, no. 2: 471–490.

Sue, Derald Wing. 2010. "Microaggressions, marginality, and oppression." In *Microaggressions and Marginality, Manifestation, Dynamics, and Impact*, edited by Derald Wing Sue. Hoboken, NJ: Wiley & Sons.

Sue, Derald Wing, Christina M. Capodilupo, Gina C. Torino, Jennifer M. Bucceri, Aisha Holder, Kevin L. Nadal, and Marta Esquilin. 2007 "Racial microaggressions in everyday life: Implications for clinical practice." *American Psychologist* 62, no. 4: 271.

Sue, Derald Wing, Patricia Arredondo, and Roderick J. McDavis. 1992. "Multicultural counseling competencies and standards: A call to the profession." *Journal of Counseling and Development* 70, no. 4: 477–486.

Sueyoshi, Amy. 2012. *Queer Compulsions: Race, Nation, and Sexuality in the Affairs of Yone Noguchi.* Honolulu: University of Hawai'i Press.

Sueyoshi, Amy. 2013. "Making whites from the dark side: Teaching whiteness studies at San Francisco State University." *The History Teacher* 46, no. 3: 373–396.

Sueyoshi, Amy. 2016. "Queer Asian American historiography." In *The Oxford Handbook of Asian American History*, pp. 267–276.

Sueyoshi, Amy. 2018. *Discriminating Sex: White Leisure and the Making of the American "Oriental."* University of Illinois Press.

Sueyoshi, Amy. 2019. "Remembering Asian Pacific American activism in Queer history." In *Identities and Place: Changing Labels and Intersectional Communities of LGBTQ and Two-Spirit People in the United States*, edited by Katherine Crawford-Lackey and Megan E. Springate. New York: Berghahn Books. 130.

Summers, Anthony. 2012. *Official and Confidential: The Secret Life of J. Edgar Hoover.* Open Road Media.

Sun, C., R. Liberman, A. Butler, S. Y. Lee, and R. Webb. 2015. Shifting receptions: Asian American stereotypes and the exploration of comprehensive media literacy. *The Communication Review* 18, no. 4: 294–314.

Sutherland, Edwin H. 1949. "The sexual psychopath laws." *Journal of Criminal Law and Criminology* 40: 543.

Syed, Moin, and Jillian Fish. 2018. "Revisiting Erik Erikson's legacy on culture, race, and ethnicity." *Identity* 18, no. 4: 274–283.

Szymanski, Dawn M. 2005. "Heterosexism and sexism as correlates of psychological distress in lesbians." *Journal of Counseling and Development* 83, no. 3: 355–360.

Tajfel, Henri, Michael G. Billig, Robert P. Bundy, and Claude Flament. 1971. "Social categorization and intergroup behaviour." *European Journal of Social Psychology* 1, no. 2: 149–178.

Takemoto, Tina. 2014. "Looking for Jiro Onuma: A queer meditation on the incarceration of Japanese Americans during World War II." *GLQ: A Journal of Lesbian and Gay Studies* 20, no. 3: 241–275.

Taney, Roger B. 1857. "Dred Scott v. Sandford." In *The African American Experience: Black History and Culture Through Speeches, Letters, Editorials, Poems, Songs and Stories*, pp. 267–270.

Taylor, Keeanga-Yamahtta. 2016. *From #BlackLivesMatter to Black Liberation.* Haymarket Books.

Tedeschi, James T., and Thomas V. Bonoma. 2017. "Power and influence: An introduction." In *The Social Influence Processes*, pp. 1–49. Routledge.

Tehranian, John. 2000. "Performing whiteness: Naturalization litigation and the construction of racial identity in America." *The Yale Law Journal* 109, no. 4: 817–848.

Tervalon, Melanie, and Jann Murray-Garcia. 1998. "Cultural humility versus cultural competence: A critical distinction in defining physician training outcomes in multicultural education." *Journal of Health Care for the Poor and Underserved* 9, no. 2: 117–125.

Teves, Stephanie Nohelani. 2018. *Defiant Indigeneity: The Politics of Hawaiian Performance.* UNC Press Books.

"Text of International Covenant on Economic, Social and Cultural Rights" ohchr.org. Archived from the original on March 3, 2012. Accessed September 1, 2021.

Thelin, John R. 2019. "An embarrassment of riches: Admission and ambition in American Higher Education." *Society* 56, no. 4: 329–334.

Theodore, Allen. 1994. *The Invention of the White Race.* New York: Verso.

Thevenin, Rose Carine. 2004. "The greatest single threat': A study of the Black Panther Party, 1966—1971." *Michigan State University Library.*

Thistlethwaite, Polly. 2019. *Where Were the Lesbians in the Stonewall Riots?: The Women's House of Detention & Lesbian Resistance.* CUNY Academic Works.

Thomas, A. 2019. "Who is a settler, according to Indigenous and black scholars: Descendants of slaves in Canada don't fit into our common definition." *Vice Canada.*

Thompson, Vetta L. Sanders, and Hyter Alexander. 2006. "Therapists' race and African American clients' reactions to therapy." *Psychotherapy: Theory, Research, Practice, Training* 43, no. 1: 99.

Thornton, Russell. 1987. *American Indian Holocaust and Survival: A Population History Since 1492* (Vol. 186). University of Oklahoma Press.

Tiong, Annabel. "Say their names: How students are responding to the BLM movement". *Los Angeles Times.* June 1, 2020.

Toribio, Helen C. 1998. "We are revolution: A reflective history of the Union of Democratic Filipinos (KDP)." *Amerasia Journal* 24, no. 2: 155–178.

Tsang, Daniel. 1980. "Third World lesbians and gays meet." *Gay Insurgent* 6, no. 11: 84–85.

Tsang, Daniel C. 2001. Slicing silence: Asian progressives come out. In *Asian Americans: The Movement and the Moment.* UCLA Asian American Studies Center Press.

Tsui, Kitty. 1992. *Who Says We Don't Talk About Sex?* Boston: Alyson Publications.

Tuck, Eve, and K. Wayne Yang. 2012. "Decolonization is not a metaphor." *Decolonization: Indigeneity, Education and Society* 1, no. 1: 1–14.

University of Southern California [USC] Annenberg Initiative. 2020. "Inequality in 1,300 popular films: Examining portrayals of gender, race/ethnicity, LGBTQ & Disability from 2007 to 2019." Los Angeles: USC Press. Retrieved at: https://assets.uscannenberg.org/docs/aii-inequality_1300_popular_films_09-08-2020.pdf.

U.S. Census Bureau. 2000. *LGBT (Lesbian, Gay, Bisexual, & Transgender) Fact Sheet.* Retrieved from http://2010.census.gov/partners/pdffactsheet_General_LGBT.pdf.

Vaid-Menon, Alok. "Alok Vaid-Menon: 'It's time for a new beauty paradigm.' *CNN News.* March 3, 2020. https://www.cnn.com/style/article/alok-vaid-menon-beauty-thinkpiece/index.html. Accessed August 4, 2021.

Valocchi, Steve. 2001. "Individual identities, collective identities, and organizational structure: The relationship of the political left and gay liberation in the United States." *Sociological Perspectives* 44, no. 4: 445–467.

van Mens-Verhulst, Janneke, and H. Lorraine Radtke. 2006. "Intersectionality and health care: Support for the diversity turn in research and practice." Unpublished paper.

Vance, Carole S. 1984. "Pleasure and danger: Toward a politics of sexuality." *Pleasure and Danger: Exploring Female Sexuality* 1, no. 3.

Varanasi, Anuradha. "Decolonizing therapy: Why an apolitical mental health system doesn't work." *Rewire.* April 19, 2021. https://www.rewire.org/decolonizing -therapy-mental-health/?fbclid=IwAR0JC-9BmWCp5SHKbIdLgLYf28X86rfiv cjQXNo1KtQvuA9vmDJ0bnd2Puw. Accessed September 1, 2021.

Villarosa, Linda. 2019 "America's hidden HIV epidemic." In *The Social Medicine Reader, Volume II, Third Edition*, pp. 235–253. Duke University Press.

Villarosa, Linda. 2021. "Gay Harlem renaissance." *The Root.* July 23, 2011. https:// www.theroot.com/the-gay-harlem-renaissance-1790864926. Accessed September 1, 2021.

Vizenor, Gerald. 1999. *Manifest Manners: Narratives on Postindian Survivance.* University of Nebraska Press.

Vu, Milkie, Jingjing Li, Regine Haardörfer, Michael Windle, and Carla J. Berg. 2019. "Mental health and substance use among women and men at the intersections of identities and experiences of discrimination: Insights from the intersectionality framework." *BMC Public Health* 19, no. 1: 1–13.

Ward, Jane. 2008. "White normativity: The cultural dimensions of whiteness in a racially diverse LGBT organization." *Sociological Perspectives* 51, no. 3: 563–586.

Wareham, Jamie. 2020. "Why many LGBT people have started using a New Pride Flag." *Forbes.* July 12, 2020. https://www.forbes.com/sites/jamiewareham/2020 /07/12/why-lgbt-people-have-started-using-a-new-pride-flag-nhs-black-lives-mat- ters/?sh=6e70a4cb125a. Accessed August 2, 2021.

Warnock, Amanda. 2019. "The dehumanization of immigrants and refugees: A com- parison of dehumanizing rhetoric by all candidates in three US Presidential elec- tions." *The Journal of Purdue Undergraduate Research* 9, no. 1: 7.

Weatherby, Meagan Lynn. 2005. "Becoming the Bridge: Border-crossing, Intersectionality, and Wave Theory in Contemporary Feminist Movement." *Syracuse University.*

Whalen, Garry M., and Richard S. Rubin. 1977. "Labor relations and affirmative action: A tug-of-war." *Public Personnel Management* 6, no. 3: 149-155.

Whidden, Michael J. 2000. "Unequal justice: Arabs in America and United States antiterrorism legislation." *Fordham Law Review* 69: 2825.

White, Patricia. 1999. *Uninvited: Classical Hollywood Cinema and Lesbian Representability.* Indiana University Press.

Whitfield, Stephen J. 2010. "Franz Boas: The anthropologist as public intellectual." *Society* 47, no. 5: 430–438.

Wijeyesinghe, Charmaine L. 2012. "The intersectional model of multiracial identity: Integrating multiracial identity theories and intersectional perspectives on social identity." *New Perspectives on Racial Identity Development: Integrating Emerging Frameworks* 2: 81–107.

Wiley, Michelle. 2021. "700 Anti-Asian hate incidents reported in Bay area during pandemic - true figures might be even worse." *KQED News.* February 12, 2020.

Retrieved from: https://www.kqed.org/news/11859965/700-anti-asian-hate-inci-dents-reported-in-bay-area-during-pandemic-true-figures-might-be-even-worse.

Will Roscoe. 1998., *Changing Ones: Third and Fourth Genders in Native North America*, p. 31. New York: St. Martin's.

Williams, David C. 2006. "Like a loaded weapon: The Rehnquist court, Indian rights, and the legal history of racism in America." *Perspectives on Politics* 4, no. 3: 604–605.

Williams, David R., Harold W. Neighbors, and James S. Jackson. 2003. "Racial/ethnic discrimination and health: Findings from community studies." *American Journal of Public Health* 93, no. 2: 200–208.

Williams, Michael Paul. 2020. "Virginia-born Ella Baker organized civil rights activists in the 20th Century. Her influence is still felt today." *Associated Press.* August 14. https://apnews.com/article/race-and-ethnicity-virginia-racial-injustice-archive-martin-luther-king-jr-e50f0d42d4ef4e63801dbc65cf371982. Accessed on August 1, 2021.

Williams, Michael Vinson. 2013. *Medgar Evers: Mississippi Martyr.* University of Arkansas Press.

Williams, Sara M., Laura M. Frey, Dese'Rae L. Stage, and Julie Cerel. 2018. "Exploring lived experience in gender and sexual minority suicide attempt survivors." *American Journal of Orthopsychiatry* 88, no. 6: 691.

Williams, Walter. 1986. *The Spirit and the Flesh: Sexual Diversity in American Indian Culture*, 2nd edition. Boston: Beacon, 179.

Wilson, James F. 2010. *Bulldaggers, Pansies, and Chocolate Babies: Performance, Race, and Sexuality in the Harlem Renaissance.* University of Michigan Press.

Wilson, Patrick A., Pamela Valera, Ana Ventuneac, Ivan Balan, Matt Rowe, and Alex Carballo-Diéguez. 2009. "Race-based sexual stereotyping and sexual partnering among men who use the internet to identify other men for bareback sex." *Journal of Sex Research* 46, no. 5: 399–413.

Wilton, Leo. 2009. "Men who have sex with men of color in the age of AIDS: The sociocultural contexts of stigma, marginalization, and structural inequalities." In *HIV/AIDS in US Communities of Color*, pp. 179–211. New York: Springer.

Wolfe, Jade. 2021. "The Imposter Phenomenon and Its Relationship Between Anxiety and Students." *PhD diss., Dublin, National College of Ireland.*

Wong, Angie. 2019. "A Sorry State of affairs: Chinese arrivants, indigenous hosts, and settler colonial apologies." *University of Windsor.*

Wong, Kevin Scott. 1997. "Rethinking the center from the margins." *American Quarterly* 49, no. 2: 415–422.

Woolford, Andrew. 2015. *This Benevolent Experiment: Indigenous Boarding Schools, Genocide, and Redress in Canada and the United States.* University of Nebraska Press.

World Heritage Encyclopedia. 2021. "Homosexuality and Roman Catholicism." *Project Gutenberg Self-Publishing Press.* Retrieved from: http://self.gutenberg.org/articles/Homosexuality_and_Roman_Catholicism.

Xavier, Jessica M., Marilyn Bobbin, Ben Singer, and Earline Budd. 2005. "A needs assessment of transgendered people of color living in Washington, DC." *International Journal of Transgenderism* 8, no. 2–3: 31–47.

Yardley, William. 2014. "Storme DeLarverie, early leader in the gay rights movement, dies at 93." *The New York Times* 29.

Yellow Horse, Aggie, Russell Jeung, Richard Lim, Boaz Tang, Megan Im, Lauryn Higashayima et al. 2021. "Stop AAPI Hate National Report." June 30, 2021. https://stopaapihate.org/wp-content/uploads/2021/08/Stop-AAPI-Hate-Report-National-v2-210830.pdf. Accessed September 11, 2021.

Yi, Jacqueline, and Nathan R. Todd. 2021. "Internalized model minority myth among Asian Americans: Links to anti-Black attitudes and opposition to affirmative action." *Cultural Diversity and Ethnic Minority Psychology* 27, no. 4: 569–578.

Yoshihara, Mari. 2002. *Embracing the East: White Women and American Orientalism.* Oxford University Press.

Young, Harvey. 2016. "An interview with David Henry Hwang." *Theatre Survey* 57, no. 2: 232–237.

Zamboni, Brian D., and Isiaah Crawford. 2007. "Minority stress and sexual problems among African-American gay and bisexual men." *Archives of Sexual Behavior* 36, no. 4: 569–578.

Zimman, Lal. 2019. "Trans self-identification and the language of neoliberal selfhood: Agency, power, and the limits of monologic discourse." *International Journal of the Sociology of Language* 256: 147–175.

Index

About the Author

Dr. Alex Rivera is a psychologist and researcher whose work is centered on intersectionality, trauma, and power for multiply marginalized people, particularly queer and trans Black, Indigenous and People of Color (QTBIPOC). She is clinical director of the Bay Area mental health organization, Lotus Mental Health, and is on the editorial board of *The Counseling Psychologist*. Prior to her directorship, Rivera was program manager for Stanford University's Weiland Health Initiative, which focused on improving policy and mental health access for queer and trans students. She received her doctorate at the PGSP-Stanford PsyD Consortium and has published numerous articles and book chapters on identity and mental health, including chapters in the upcoming book *Psychology of Inequity: Social Actions and Movements* (2022) and *The Psychic Life of Racism in Gay Men's Communities* (2017).

www.ingramcontent.com/pod-product-compliance
Lightning Source LLC
Chambersburg PA
CBHW050638280326
41932CB00015B/2700